The Easy
Instant Pot
Cookbook

for Beginners

2000+

Days of Simple and Wholesome Instant Pot Recipes for Busy
Families and deliciousness-Conscious Cooks. Incl. Tips & Tricks

Francis S. Davis

Table of Contents

Chapter 3   Beef, Pork, and Lamb   22

Chapter 4   Fish and Seafood   32

Chapter 8   Stews and Soups   67

Appendix   Instant Pot Cooking Timetable   79

INTRODUCTION

Welcome to the world of Instant Pot cooking! This revolutionary kitchen appliance is here for you!

As a foodie and home cook, I've always been passionate about creating delicious meals for my family and friends. But as much as I love spending time in the kitchen, I also know how busy life can get. Between work, family, and other commitments, there's often little time left over for cooking.

That's why I fell in love with the Instant Pot. This amazing kitchen appliance allows me to create healthy, flavorful meals in a fraction of the time it would take with traditional cooking methods. And as I experimented with different recipes and ingredients, I discovered a whole new world of possibilities for my Instant Pot.

Inspired by my love for the Instant Pot and my passion for cooking, I decided to write this cookbook. I wanted to share my knowledge and experience with others who are looking for a faster, easier way to cook delicious meals at home.

But this cookbook is more than just a collection of recipes. It's a celebration of the Instant Pot and all the amazing things it can do. From pressure cooking to slow cooking, sautéing to steaming, the Instant Pot is a versatile and powerful tool that can help you create a wide range of dishes.

And with easy-to-follow recipes and step-by-step instructions, even novice cooks can create delicious meals that will impress their friends and family.

So why wait? Start exploring the endless possibilities of Instant Pot cooking today and take your culinary skills to the next level with the help of this cookbook. Whether you're a seasoned chef or a beginner in the kitchen, the Instant Pot Cookbook has everything you need to create healthy, delicious meals that your whole family will love.

Benefits of the Instant Pot

The Instant Pot is a versatile and powerful kitchen appliance that offers many benefits, including:

1. Faster cooking time: The Instant Pot can cook food up to 70% faster than traditional cooking methods, saving you time in the kitchen.

2. Energy efficient: The Instant Pot uses less energy than traditional ovens or stovetops, making it an eco-friendly option.

3. Versatility: The Instant Pot can pressure cook, slow cook, sauté, steam, and even make yogurt, allowing you to create a wide range of dishes.

4. Consistent results: The Instant Pot produces consistent results every time, ensuring your food is cooked evenly and thoroughly.

5. Healthier meals: The Instant Pot allows you to cook with less oil and fat, resulting in healthier meals with fewer calories.

6. Easy to use: The Instant Pot is easy to use, with simple controls and pre-programmed settings for different types of food.

7. Safe and convenient: The Instant Pot comes with features like automatic shut-off and pressure release, making it safe and convenient to use.

8. Saves space: The Instant Pot can replace several appliances in your kitchen, such as a rice cooker, slow cooker, and pressure cooker, saving you valuable counter and storage space.

9. Great for meal prep: The Instant Pot allows you to cook large batches of food at once, making it perfect for meal prep and batch cooking.

10. Delicious taste: Despite its speed and efficiency, the Instant Pot still produces deliciously flavorful food that is sure to satisfy your taste buds.

Chapter 1 Breakfasts

Blueberry Almond Cereal

Prep time: 5 minutes | Cook time: 2 minutes | Serves 4

- ⅓ cup crushed roasted almonds
- ¼ cup almond flour
- ¼ cup unsalted butter, softened
- ¼ cup vanilla-flavored egg white protein powder
- 2 tablespoons Swerve
- 1 teaspoon blueberry extract
- 1 teaspoon ground cinnamon

1. Add all the ingredients to the Instant Pot and stir to combine. 2. Lock the lid, select the Manual mode and set the cooking time for 2 minutes on High Pressure. When the timer goes off, do a natural pressure release for 10 minutes, then release any remaining pressure. Open the lid. 3. Stir well and pour the mixture onto a sheet lined with parchment paper to cool. It will be crispy when completely cool. 4. Serve the cereal in bowls.

Coddled Huevos Rancheros

Prep time: 5 minutes | Cook time: 10 minutes | Serves 2

- 2 teaspoons unsalted butter
- 4 large eggs
- 1 cup drained cooked black beans, or two-thirds 15-ounce can black beans, rinsed and drained
- Two 7-inch corn or whole-wheat tortillas, warmed
- ½ cup chunky tomato salsa (such as Pace brand)
- 2 cups shredded romaine lettuce
- 1 tablespoon chopped fresh cilantro
- 2 tablespoons grated Cotija cheese

1. Pour 1 cup water into the Instant Pot and place a long-handled silicone steam rack into the pot. (If you don't have the long-handled rack, use the wire metal steam rack and a homemade sling) 2. Coat each of four 4-ounce ramekins with ½ teaspoon butter. Crack an egg into each ramekin. Place the ramekins on the steam rack in the pot. 3. Secure the lid and set the Pressure Release to Sealing. Select the Steam setting and set the cooking time for 3 minutes at low pressure. (The pot will take about 5 minutes to come up to pressure before the cooking program begins.) 4. While the eggs are cooking, in a small saucepan over low heat, warm the beans for about 5 minutes, stirring occasionally. Cover the saucepan and remove from the heat. (Alternatively, warm the beans in a covered bowl in a microwave for 1 minute. Leave the beans covered until ready to serve.) 5. When the cooking program ends, let the pressure release naturally for 5 minutes, then move the Pressure Release to Venting

to release any remaining steam. Open the pot and, wearing heat-resistant mitts, grasp the handles of the steam rack and carefully lift it out of the pot. 6. Place a warmed tortilla on each plate and spoon ½ cup of the beans onto each tortilla. Run a knife around the inside edge of each ramekin to loosen the egg and unmold two eggs onto the beans on each tortilla. Spoon the salsa over the eggs and top with the lettuce, cilantro, and cheese. Serve right away.

Cheesy Vegetable Frittata

Prep time: 10 minutes | Cook time: 10 minutes | Serves 4

- 4 eggs, beaten
- 2 ounces (57 g) Pecorino cheese, grated
- 3 ounces (85 g) okra, chopped
- 2 ounces (57 g) radish, chopped
- 1 tablespoon cream cheese
- 1 teaspoon sesame oil

1. Heat up sesame oil in the instant pot on Sauté mode. 2. Add chopped okra and radish and sauté the vegetables for 4 minutes. 3. Then stir them well and add cream cheese and beaten eggs. 4. Stir the mixture well and top with cheese. 5. Close the lid and cook the frittata on Sauté mode for 6 minutes more.

Bacon Spaghetti Squash Fritters

Prep time: 20 minutes | Cook time: 15 minutes | Serves 4

- ½ cooked spaghetti squash
- 2 tablespoons cream cheese
- ½ cup shredded whole-milk Mozzarella cheese
- 1 egg
- ½ teaspoon salt
- ¼ teaspoon pepper
- 1 stalk green onion, sliced
- 4 slices cooked bacon, crumbled
- 2 tablespoons coconut oil

1. Remove seeds from cooked squash and use fork to scrape strands out of shell. Place strands into cheesecloth or kitchen towel and squeeze to remove as much excess moisture as possible. 2. Place cream cheese and Mozzarella in small bowl and microwave for 45 seconds to melt together. Mix with spoon and place in large bowl. Add all ingredients except coconut oil to bowl. Mixture will be wet like batter. 3. Press the Sauté button and then press the Adjust button to set heat to Less. Add coconut oil to Instant Pot. When fully preheated, add 2 to 3 tablespoons of batter to pot to make a fritter. Let fry until firm and completely cooked through.

Cynthia's Yogurt

Prep time: 10 minutes | Cook time: 8 hours | Serves 16

- 1 gallon low-fat milk
- ¼ cup low-fat plain yogurt

with active cultures

1. Pour milk into the inner pot of the Instant Pot. 2. Lock lid, move vent to sealing, and press the yogurt button. Press Adjust till it reads "boil." 3. When boil cycle is complete (about 1 hour), check the temperature. It should be at 185°F. If it's not, use the Sauté function to warm to 185. 4. After it reaches 185°F, unplug Instant Pot, remove inner pot, and cool. You can place on cooling rack and let it slowly cool. If in a hurry, submerge the base of the pot in cool water. Cool milk to 110°F. 5. When mixture reaches 110, stir in the ¼ cup of yogurt. Lock the lid in place and move vent to sealing. 6. Press Yogurt. Use the Adjust button until the screen says 8:00. This will now incubate for 8 hours. 7. After 8 hours (when the cycle is finished), chill yogurt, or go immediately to straining in step 8. 8. After chilling, or following the 8 hours, strain the yogurt using a nut milk bag. This will give it the consistency of Greek yogurt.

Pork and Quill Egg Cups

Prep time: 15 minutes | Cook time: 15 minutes | Serves 4

- 10 ounces (283 g) ground pork
- 1 jalapeño pepper, chopped
- 1 tablespoon butter, softened
- 1 teaspoon dried dill
- ½ teaspoon salt
- 1 cup water
- 4 quill eggs

1. In a bowl, stir together all the ingredients, except for the quill eggs and water. Transfer the meat mixture to the silicone muffin molds and press the surface gently. 2. Pour the water and insert the trivet in the Instant Pot. Put the meat cups on the trivet. 3. Crack the eggs over the meat mixture. 4. Set the lid in place. Select the Manual mode and set the cooking time for 15 minutes on High Pressure. When the timer goes off, do a quick pressure release. Carefully open the lid. 5. Serve warm.

Pulled Pork Hash

Prep time: 10 minutes | Cook time: 15 minutes | Serves 4

- 4 eggs
- 10 ounces (283 g) pulled pork, shredded
- 1 teaspoon coconut oil
- 1 teaspoon red pepper
- 1 teaspoon chopped fresh cilantro
- 1 tomato, chopped
- ¼ cup water

1. Melt the coconut oil in the instant pot on Sauté mode. 2. Then add pulled pork, red pepper, cilantro, water, and chopped tomato. 3. Cook the ingredients for 5 minutes. 4. Then stir it well with the help of the spatula and crack the eggs over it. 5. Close the lid. 6. Cook the meal on Manual mode (High Pressure) for 7 minutes. Then make a quick pressure release.

Avocado Green Power Bowl

Prep time: 10 minutes | Cook time: 10 minutes | Serves 1

- 1 cup water
- 2 eggs
- 1 tablespoon coconut oil
- 1 tablespoon butter
- 1 ounce (28 g) sliced almonds
- 1 cup fresh spinach, sliced
- into strips
- ½ cup kale, sliced into strips
- ½ clove garlic, minced
- ½ teaspoon salt
- ⅛ teaspoon pepper
- ½ avocado, sliced
- ⅛ teaspoon red pepper flakes

1. Pour water into Instant Pot and place steam rack on bottom. Place eggs on steam rack. Click lid closed. Press the Manual button and adjust time for 6 minutes. When timer beeps, quick-release the pressure. Set eggs aside. 2. Pour water out, clean pot, and replace. Press the Sauté button and add coconut oil, butter, and almonds. Sauté for 2 to 3 minutes until butter begins to turn golden and almonds soften. Add spinach, kale, garlic, salt, and pepper to Instant Pot. Sauté for 4 to 6 minutes until greens begin to wilt. Press the Cancel button. Place greens in bowl for serving. Peel eggs, cut in half, and add to bowl. Slice avocado and place in bowl. Sprinkle red pepper flakes over all. Serve warm.

Shredded Potato Omelet

Prep time: 15 minutes | Cook time: 20 minutes | Serves 6

- 3 slices bacon, cooked and crumbled
- 2 cups shredded cooked potatoes
- ¼ cup minced onion
- ¼ cup minced green bell pepper
- 1 cup egg substitute
- ¼ cup fat-free milk
- ¼ teaspoon salt
- ⅛ teaspoon black pepper
- 1 cup 75%-less-fat shredded cheddar cheese
- 1 cup water

1. With nonstick cooking spray, spray the inside of a round baking dish that will fit in your Instant Pot inner pot. 2. Sprinkle the bacon, potatoes, onion, and bell pepper around the bottom of the baking dish. 3. Mix together the egg substitute, milk, salt, and pepper in mixing bowl. Pour over potato mixture. 4. Top with cheese. 5. Add water, place the steaming rack into the bottom of the inner pot and then place the round baking dish on top. 6. Close the lid and secure to the locking position. Be sure the vent is turned to sealing. Set for 20 minutes on Manual at high pressure. 7. Let the pressure release naturally. 8. Carefully remove the baking dish with the handles of the steaming rack and allow to stand 10 minutes before cutting and serving.

Bell Peppers Stuffed with Eggs

Prep time: 5 minutes | Cook time: 14 minutes | Serves 2

- 2 eggs, beaten
- 1 tablespoon coconut cream
- ¼ teaspoon dried oregano
- ¼ teaspoon salt
- 1 large bell pepper, cut into halves and deseeded
- 1 cup water

1. In a bowl, stir together the eggs, coconut cream, oregano and salt. 2. Pour the egg mixture in the pepper halves. 3. Pour the water and insert the trivet in the Instant Pot. Put the stuffed pepper halves on the trivet. 4. Set the lid in place. Select the Manual mode and set the cooking time for 14 minutes on High Pressure. When the timer goes off, do a quick pressure release. Carefully open the lid. 5. Serve warm.

Cheddar Chicken Casserole

Prep time: 10 minutes | Cook time: 20 minutes | Serves 6

- 1 cup ground chicken
- 1 teaspoon olive oil
- 1 teaspoon chili flakes
- 1 teaspoon salt
- 1 cup shredded Cheddar cheese
- ½ cup coconut cream

1. Press the Sauté button on the Instant Pot and heat the oil. Add the ground chicken, chili flakes and salt to the pot and sauté for 10 minutes. Stir in the remaining ingredients. 2. Set the lid in place. Select the Manual mode and set the cooking time for 10 minutes on High Pressure. When the timer goes off, do a quick pressure release. Carefully open the lid. 3. Let the dish cool for 10 minutes before serving.

Baked Eggs

Prep time: 15 minutes | Cook time: 20 minutes | Serves 8

- 1 cup water
- 2 tablespoons no-trans-fat tub margarine, melted
- 1 cup reduced-fat buttermilk baking mix
- 1½ cups fat-free cottage cheese
- 2 teaspoons chopped onion
- 1 teaspoon dried parsley
- ½ cup grated reduced-fat cheddar cheese
- 1 egg, slightly beaten
- 1¼ cups egg substitute
- 1 cup fat-free milk

1. Place the steaming rack into the bottom of the inner pot and pour in 1 cup of water. 2. Grease a round springform pan that will fit into the inner pot of the Instant Pot. 3. Pour melted margarine into springform pan. 4. Mix together buttermilk baking mix, cottage cheese, onion, parsley, cheese, egg, egg substitute, and milk in large mixing bowl. 5. Pour mixture over melted margarine. Stir slightly to distribute margarine. 6. Place the springform pan onto the steaming rack, close the lid, and secure to the locking position. Be sure the vent is turned to sealing. Set for 20 minutes on Manual at high pressure. 7. Let the pressure release naturally. 8. Carefully remove the springform pan with the handles of the steaming rack and allow to stand 10 minutes before cutting and serving.

Pumpkin Mug Muffin

Prep time: 5 minutes | Cook time: 9 minutes | Serves 1

- ½ cup Swerve
- ½ cup blanched almond flour
- 2 tablespoons organic pumpkin purée
- 1 teaspoon sugar-free chocolate chips
- 1 tablespoon organic coconut flour
- 1 egg
- 1 tablespoon coconut oil
- ½ teaspoon pumpkin pie spice
- ½ teaspoon ground nutmeg
- ½ teaspoon ground cinnamon
- ⅛ teaspoon baking soda

1. Mix the Swerve, almond flour, pumpkin purée, chocolate chips, coconut flour, egg, coconut oil, pumpkin pie spice, nutmeg, cinnamon, and baking soda in a large bowl. Transfer this mixture into a well-greased, Instant Pot-friendly mug. 2. Pour 1 cup of filtered water into the inner pot of the Instant Pot, and insert the trivet. Cover the mug in foil and place on top of the trivet. 3. Close the lid, set the pressure release to Sealing, and select Manual. Set the Instant Pot to 9 minutes on High Pressure. 4. Once cooked, release the pressure immediately by switching the valve to Venting. Be sure your muffin is done by inserting a toothpick into the cake and making sure it comes out clean, as cook times may vary. 5. Remove mug and enjoy!

Herbed Buttery Breakfast Steak

Prep time: 5 minutes | Cook time: 1 minute | Serves 2

- ½ cup water
- 1 pound (454 g) boneless beef sirloin steak
- ½ teaspoon salt
- ½ teaspoon black pepper
- 1 clove garlic, minced
- 2 tablespoons butter, softened
- ¼ teaspoon dried rosemary
- ¼ teaspoon dried parsley
- Pinch of dried thyme

1. Pour the water into the Instant Pot and put the trivet in the pot. 2. Rub the steak all over with salt and black pepper. Place the steak on the trivet. 3. In a small bowl, stir together the remaining ingredients. Spread half of the butter mixture over the steak. 4. Set the lid in place. Select the Manual mode and set the cooking time for 1 minute on Low Pressure. When the timer goes off, perform a quick pressure release. Carefully open the lid. 5. Remove the steak from the pot. Top with the remaining half of the butter mixture. Serve hot.

Soft-Scrambled Eggs

Prep time: 5 minutes | Cook time: 7 minutes | Serves 4

- 6 eggs
- 2 tablespoons heavy cream
- 1 teaspoon salt
- ¼ teaspoon pepper
- 2 tablespoons butter
- 2 ounces (57 g) cream cheese, softened

1. In large bowl, whisk eggs, heavy cream, salt, and pepper. Press the Sauté button and then press the Adjust button to set heat to Less. 2. Gently push eggs around pot with rubber spatula. When they begin to firm up, add butter and softened cream cheese. Continue stirring slowly in a figure-8 pattern until eggs are fully cooked, approximately 7 minutes total.

Mexican Breakfast Beef Chili

Prep time: 5 minutes | Cook time: 45 minutes | Serves 4

- 2 tablespoons coconut oil
- 1 pound (454 g) ground grass-fed beef
- 1 (14-ounce / 397-g) can sugar-free or low-sugar diced tomatoes
- ½ cup shredded full-fat Cheddar cheese (optional)
- 1 teaspoon hot sauce
- ½ teaspoon chili powder
- ½ teaspoon crushed red pepper
- ½ teaspoon ground cumin
- ½ teaspoon kosher salt
- ½ teaspoon freshly ground black pepper

1. Set the Instant Pot to Sauté and melt the oil. 2. Pour in ½ cup of filtered water, then add the beef, tomatoes, cheese, hot sauce, chili powder, red pepper, cumin, salt, and black pepper to the Instant Pot, stirring thoroughly. 3. Close the lid, set the pressure release to Sealing, and hit Cancel to stop the current program. Select Manual, set the Instant Pot to 45 minutes on High Pressure and let cook. 4. Once cooked, let the pressure naturally disperse from the Instant Pot for about 10 minutes, then carefully switch the pressure release to Venting. 5. Open the Instant Pot, serve, and enjoy!

Slow-Cooked Granola with Nuts

Prep time: 5 minutes | Cook time: 2 hours 30 minutes | Serves 10

- 1 cup raw almonds
- 1 cup pumpkin seeds
- 1 cup raw walnuts
- 1 cup raw cashews
- 1 tablespoon coconut oil
- ¼ cup unsweetened coconut chips
- 1 teaspoon sea salt
- 1 teaspoon cinnamon

1. In a large bowl, stir together the almonds, pumpkin seeds, walnuts, cashews and coconut oil. Make sure all the nuts are coated with the coconut oil. Place the nut mixture in the Instant Pot and cover the pot with a paper towel. 2. Lock the lid. Select the Slow Cook mode and set the cooking time for 1 hour on More. When the timer goes off, stir the nuts. Set the timer for another hour. 3. Again, when the timer goes off, stir the nut mixture and add the coconut chips. Set the timer for another 30 minutes. The cashews should become a nice golden color. 4. When the timer goes off, transfer the nut mixture to a baking pan to cool and sprinkle with the sea salt and cinnamon. Serve.

Spinach and Cheese Frittata

Prep time: 5 minutes | Cook time: 20 minutes | Serves 4 to 5

- 6 eggs
- 1 cup chopped spinach
- 1 cup shredded full-fat Cheddar cheese
- 1 cup shredded full-fat Monterey Jack cheese (optional)
- 2 tablespoons coconut oil
- 1 cup chopped bell peppers
- ½ teaspoon dried parsley
- ½ teaspoon dried basil
- ½ teaspoon ground turmeric
- ½ teaspoon freshly ground black pepper
- ½ teaspoon kosher salt

1. Pour 1 cup of filtered water into the inner pot of the Instant Pot, then insert the trivet. 2. In a large bowl, combine the eggs, spinach, Cheddar cheese, Monterey Jack cheese, coconut oil, bell peppers, parsley, basil, turmeric, black pepper, and salt, and stir thoroughly. Transfer this mixture into a well-greased Instant Pot-friendly dish. 3. Using a sling if desired, place the dish onto the trivet, and cover loosely with aluminum foil. Close the lid, set the pressure release to Sealing, and select Manual. Set the Instant Pot to 20 minutes on High Pressure, and let cook. 4. Once cooked, let the pressure naturally disperse from the Instant Pot for about 10 minutes, then carefully switch the pressure release to Venting. 5. Open the Instant Pot, serve, and enjoy!

Pecan and Walnut Granola

Prep time: 10 minutes | Cook time: 2 minutes | Serves 12

- 2 cups chopped raw pecans
- 1¾ cups vanilla-flavored egg white protein powder
- 1¼ cups unsalted butter, softened
- 1 cup sunflower seeds
- ½ cup chopped raw walnuts
- ½ cup slivered almonds
- ½ cup sesame seeds
- ½ cup Swerve
- 1 teaspoon ground cinnamon
- ½ teaspoon sea salt

1. Add all the ingredients to the Instant Pot and stir to combine. 2. Lock the lid, select the Manual mode and set the cooking time for 2 minutes on High Pressure. When the timer goes off, do a natural pressure release for 10 minutes, then release any remaining pressure. Open the lid. 3. Stir well and pour the granola onto a sheet of parchment paper to cool. It will become crispy when completely cool. Serve the granola in bowls.

Bacon and Spinach Eggs

Prep time: 5 minutes | Cook time: 9 minutes | Serves 4

- 2 tablespoons unsalted butter, divided
- ½ cup diced bacon
- ⅓ cup finely diced shallots
- ⅓ cup chopped spinach, leaves only
- Pinch of sea salt
- Pinch of black pepper
- ½ cup water
- ¼ cup heavy whipping cream
- 8 large eggs
- 1 tablespoon chopped fresh chives, for garnish

1. Set the Instant Pot on the Sauté mode and melt 1 tablespoon of the butter. Add the bacon to the pot and sauté for about 4 minutes, or until crispy. Using a slotted spoon, transfer the bacon bits to a bowl and set aside. 2. Add the remaining 1 tablespoon of the butter and shallots to the pot and sauté for about 2 minutes, or until tender. Add the spinach leaves and sauté for 1 minute, or until wilted. Season with sea salt and black pepper and stir. Transfer the spinach to a separate bowl and set aside. 3. Drain the oil from the pot into a bowl. Pour in the water and put the trivet inside. 4. With a paper towel, coat four ramekins with the bacon grease. In each ramekin, place 1 tablespoon of the heavy whipping cream, reserved bacon bits and sautéed spinach. Crack two eggs without breaking the yolks in each ramekin. Cover the ramekins with aluminum foil. Place two ramekins on the trivet and stack the other two on top. 5. Lock the lid. Select the Manual mode and set the cooking time for 2 minutes at Low Pressure. When the timer goes off, use a natural pressure release for 5 minutes, then release any remaining pressure. Carefully open the lid. 6. Carefully take out the ramekins and serve garnished with the chives.

Coddled Eggs and Smoked Salmon Toasts

Prep time: 5 minutes | Cook time: 10 minutes | Serves 4

- 2 teaspoons unsalted butter
- 4 large eggs
- 4 slices gluten-free or whole-grain rye bread
- ½ cup plain 2 percent Greek yogurt
- 4 ounces cold-smoked salmon, or 1 medium avocado, pitted, peeled, and
- sliced
- 2 radishes, thinly sliced
- 1 Persian cucumber, thinly sliced
- 1 tablespoon chopped fresh chives
- ¼ teaspoon freshly ground black pepper

1. Pour 1 cup water into the Instant Pot and place a long-handled silicone steam rack into the pot. (If you don't have the long-handled rack, use the wire metal steam rack and a homemade sling) 2. Coat each of four 4-ounce ramekins with ½ teaspoon butter. Crack an egg into each ramekin. Place the ramekins on the steam rack in the pot. 3. Secure the lid and set the Pressure Release to Sealing. Select the Steam setting and set the cooking time for 3 minutes at low pressure. (The pot will take about 5 minutes to come up to pressure before the cooking program begins.) 4. While eggs are cooking, toast the bread in a toaster until golden brown. Spread the yogurt onto the toasted slices, put the toasts onto plates, and then top each toast with the smoked salmon, radishes, and cucumber. 5. When the cooking program ends, let the pressure release naturally for 5 minutes, then move the Pressure Release to Venting to release any remaining steam. Open the pot and, wearing heat-resistant mitts, grasp the handles of the steam rack and lift it out of the pot. 6. Run a knife around the inside edge of each ramekin to loosen the egg and unmold one egg onto each toast. Sprinkle the chives and pepper on top and serve right away. 7. Note 8. The yolks of these eggs are fully cooked through. If you prefer the yolks slightly less solid, perform a quick pressure release rather than letting the pressure release naturally for 5 minutes.

Cranberry Almond Grits

Prep time: 10 minutes | Cook time: 10 minutes | Serves 5

- ¾ cup stone-ground grits or polenta (not instant)
- ½ cup unsweetened dried cranberries
- Pinch kosher salt
- 1 tablespoon unsalted butter or ghee (optional)
- 1 tablespoon half-and-half
- ¼ cup sliced almonds, toasted

1. In the electric pressure cooker, stir together the grits, cranberries, salt, and 3 cups of water. 2. Close and lock the lid. Set the valve to sealing. 3. Cook on high pressure for 10 minutes. 4. When the cooking is complete, hit Cancel and quick release the pressure. 5. Once the pin drops, unlock and remove the lid. 6. Add the butter (if using) and half-and-half. Stir until the mixture is creamy, adding more half-and-half if necessary. 7. Spoon into serving bowls and sprinkle with almonds.

Avocado Breakfast Sandwich

Prep time: 5 minutes | Cook time: 15 minutes | Serves 1

- 2 slices bacon
- 2 eggs
- 1 avocado

1. Press the Sauté button. Press the Adjust button to set heat to Low. Add bacon to Instant Pot and cook until crispy. Remove and set aside. 2. Crack egg over Instant Pot slowly, into bacon grease. Repeat with second egg. When edges become golden, after 2 to 3 minutes, flip. Press the Cancel button. 3. Cut avocado in half and scoop out half without seed. Place in small bowl and mash with fork. Spread on one egg. Place bacon on top and top with second egg. Let cool 5 minutes before eating.

Cauliflower and Cheese Quiche

Prep time: 10 minutes | Cook time: 10 minutes | Serves 2

- 1 cup chopped cauliflower
- ¼ cup shredded Cheddar cheese
- 5 eggs, beaten
- 1 teaspoon butter
- 1 teaspoon dried oregano
- 1 cup water

1. Grease the instant pot baking pan with butter from inside. 2. Pour water in the instant pot. 3. Sprinkle the cauliflower with dried oregano and put it in the prepared baking pan. Flatten the vegetables gently. 4. After this, add eggs and stir the vegetables. 5. Top the quiche with shredded cheese and transfer it in the instant pot. Close and seal the lid. Cook the quiche on Manual mode (High Pressure) for 10 minutes. Make a quick pressure release.

Egg Bites with Sausage and Peppers

Prep time: 5 minutes | Cook time: 15 minutes | Serves 7

- 4 large eggs
- ¼ cup vegan cream cheese (such as Tofutti brand) or cream cheese
- ¼ teaspoon fine sea salt
- ¼ teaspoon freshly ground black pepper
- 3 ounces lean turkey sausage, cooked and crumbled, or 1 vegetarian sausage (such
- as Beyond Meat brand), cooked and diced
- ½ red bell pepper, seeded and chopped
- 2 green onions, white and green parts, minced, plus more for garnish (optional)
- ¼ cup vegan cheese shreds or shredded sharp Cheddar cheese

1. In a blender, combine the eggs, cream cheese, salt, and pepper. Blend on medium speed for about 20 seconds, just until combined. Add the sausage, bell pepper, and green onions and pulse for 1 second once or twice. You want to mix in the solid ingredients without grinding them up very much. 2. Pour 1 cup water into the Instant Pot. Generously grease a 7-cup egg-bite mold or seven 2-ounce silicone baking cups with butter or coconut oil, making sure to coat each cup well. Place the prepared mold or cups on a long-handled silicone steam rack. (If you don't have the long-handled rack, use the wire metal steam rack and a homemade sling) 3. Pour ¼ cup of the egg mixture into each prepared mold or cup. Holding the handles of the steam rack, carefully lower the egg bites into the pot. 4. Secure the lid and set the Pressure Release to Sealing. Select the Steam setting and set the cooking time for 8 minutes at low pressure. (The pot will take about 5 minutes to come up to pressure before the cooking program begins.) 5. When the cooking program ends, let the pressure release naturally for 5 minutes, then move the Pressure Release to Venting to release any remaining steam. Open the pot. The egg muffins will have puffed up quite a bit during cooking, but they will deflate and settle as they

cool. Wearing heat-resistant mitts, grasp the handles of the steam rack and carefully lift the egg bites out of the pot. Sprinkle the egg bites with the cheese, then let them cool for about 5 minutes, until the cheese has fully melted and you are able to handle the mold or cups comfortably. 6. Pull the sides of the egg mold or cups away from the egg bites, running a butter knife around the edge of each bite to loosen if necessary. Transfer the egg bites to plates, garnish with more green onions (if desired), and serve warm. To store, let cool to room temperature, transfer to an airtight container, and refrigerate for up to 3 days; reheat gently in the microwave for about 1 minute before serving.

Eggs Benedict

Prep time: 5 minutes | Cook time: 1 minute | Serves 3

- 1 teaspoon butter
- 3 eggs
- ¼ teaspoon salt
- ½ teaspoon ground black
- pepper
- 1 cup water
- 3 turkey bacon slices, fried

1. Grease the eggs molds with the butter and crack the eggs inside. Sprinkle with salt and ground black pepper. 2. Pour the water and insert the trivet in the Instant Pot. Put the eggs molds on the trivet. 3. Set the lid in place. Select the Manual mode and set the cooking time for 1 minute on High Pressure. When the timer goes off, do a quick pressure release. Carefully open the lid. 4. Transfer the eggs onto the plate. Top the eggs with the fried bacon slices.

Mini Chocolate Chip Muffins

Prep time: 5 minutes | Cook time: 20 minutes | Serves 7

- 1 cup blanched almond flour
- 2 eggs
- ¾ cup sugar-free chocolate chips
- 1 tablespoon vanilla extract
- ½ cup Swerve, or more to
- taste
- 2 tablespoons salted grass-fed butter, softened
- ½ teaspoon salt
- ¼ teaspoon baking soda

1. Pour 1 cup of filtered water into the inner pot of the Instant Pot, then insert the trivet. Using an electric mixer, combine flour, eggs, chocolate chips, vanilla, Swerve, butter, salt, and baking soda. Mix thoroughly. Transfer this mixture into a well-greased Instant Pot-friendly muffin (or egg bites) mold. 2. Using a sling if desired, place the pan onto the trivet and cover loosely with aluminum foil. Close the lid, set the pressure release to Sealing, and select Manual. Set the Instant Pot to 20 minutes on High Pressure and let cook. 3. Once cooked, let the pressure naturally disperse from the Instant Pot for about 10 minutes, then carefully switch the pressure release to Venting. 4. Open the Instant Pot and remove the pan. Let cool, serve, and enjoy!

Three-Cheese Quiche

Prep time: 10 minutes | Cook time: 6 minutes | Serves 6

- 6 eggs, beaten
- 2 tablespoon cream cheese
- 1 teaspoon Italian seasoning
- ¼ cup shredded Cheddar cheese
- 3 ounces (85 g) Monterey Jack cheese, shredded
- 2 ounces (57 g) Mozzarella, shredded
- 1 cup water, for cooking

1. Pour water in the instant pot. 2. In the mixing bowl, mix up eggs cream cheese, Italian seasoning, and all types of cheese. 3. Pour the mixture in the baking cups (molds) and place them in the instant pot. 4. Close and seal the lid. 5. Cook the quiche cups for 6 minutes on Manual mode (High Pressure). 6. Make a quick pressure release.

Parmesan Baked Eggs

Prep time: 5 minutes | Cook time: 10 minutes | Serves 1

- 1 tablespoon butter, cut into small pieces
- 2 tablespoons keto-friendly low-carb Marinara sauce
- 3 eggs
- 2 tablespoons grated Parmesan cheese
- ¼ teaspoon Italian seasoning
- 1 cup water

1. Place the butter pieces on the bottom of the oven-safe bowl. Spread the marinara sauce over the butter. Crack the eggs on top of the marinara sauce and top with the cheese and Italian seasoning. 2. Cover the bowl with aluminum foil. Pour the water and insert the trivet in the Instant Pot. Put the bowl on the trivet. 3. Set the lid in place. Select the Manual mode and set the cooking time for 10 minutes on Low Pressure. When the timer goes off, do a quick pressure release. Carefully open the lid. 4. Let the eggs cool for 5 minutes before serving.

Breakfast Farro with Berries and Walnuts

Prep time: 8 minutes | Cook time: 10 minutes | Serves 6

- 1 cup farro, rinsed and drained
- 1 cup unsweetened almond milk
- ¼ teaspoon kosher salt
- ½ teaspoon pure vanilla extract
- 1 teaspoon ground cinnamon
- 1 tablespoon pure maple syrup
- 1½ cups fresh blueberries, raspberries, or strawberries (or a combination)
- 6 tablespoons chopped walnuts

1. In the electric pressure cooker, combine the farro, almond milk, 1 cup of water, salt, vanilla, cinnamon, and maple syrup. 2. Close and lock the lid. Set the valve to sealing. 3. Cook on high pressure for 10 minutes. 4. When the cooking is complete, allow the pressure to release naturally for 10 minutes, then quick release any remaining pressure. Hit Cancel. 5. Once the pin drops, unlock and remove the lid. 6. Stir the farro. Spoon into bowls and top each serving with ¼ cup of berries and 1 tablespoon of walnuts.

Vegetable and Cheese Bake

Prep time: 7 minutes | Cook time: 9 minutes | Serves 3

- 3 eggs, beaten
- ¼ cup coconut cream
- ¼ teaspoon salt
- 3 ounces (85 g) Brussel sprouts, chopped
- 2 ounces (57 g) tomato, chopped
- 3 ounces (85 g) provolone cheese, shredded
- 1 teaspoon butter
- 1 teaspoon smoked paprika

1. Grease the instant pot pan with the butter. 2. Put eggs in the bowl, add salt, and smoked paprika. Whisk the eggs well. 3. After this, add chopped Brussel sprouts and tomato. 4. Pour the mixture into the instant pot pan and sprinkle over with the shredded cheese. 5. Pour 1 cup of the water in the instant pot. Then place the pan with the egg mixture and close the lid. 6. Cook the meal on Manual (High Pressure) for 4 minutes. Then make naturally release for 5 minutes.

Chocolate Chip Pancake

Prep time: 5 minutes | Cook time: 37 minutes | Serves 5 to 6

- 4 tablespoons salted grass-fed butter, softened
- 2 cups blanched almond flour
- ½ cup Swerve, or more to taste
- 1 ¼ cups full-fat coconut milk
- ¼ cup sugar-free chocolate chips
- ¼ cup organic coconut flour
- 2 eggs
- 1 tablespoon chopped walnuts
- ¼ teaspoon baking soda
- ½ teaspoon salt
- ½ cup dark berries, for serving (optional)

1. Grease the bottom and sides of your Instant Pot with the butter. Make sure you coat it very liberally. 2. In a large bowl, mix together the almond flour, Swerve, milk, chocolate chips, coconut flour, eggs, walnuts, baking soda, and salt. Add this mixture to the Instant Pot. Close the lid, set the pressure release to Sealing, and select Multigrain. Set the Instant Pot to 37 minutes on Low Pressure, and let cook. 3. Switch the pressure release to Venting and open the Instant Pot. Confirm your pancake is cooked, then carefully remove it using a spatula. Serve with the berries (if desired), and enjoy!

Blueberry Oat Mini Muffins

- ½ cup rolled oats
- ¼ cup whole wheat pastry flour or white whole wheat flour
- ½ tablespoon baking powder
- ½ teaspoon ground cardamom or ground cinnamon
- ⅛ teaspoon kosher salt
- 2 large eggs
- ½ cup plain Greek yogurt
- 2 tablespoons pure maple syrup
- 2 teaspoons extra-virgin olive oil
- ½ teaspoon vanilla extract
- ½ cup frozen blueberries (preferably small wild blueberries)

1. In a large bowl, stir together the oats, flour, baking powder, cardamom, and salt. 2. In a medium bowl, whisk together the eggs, yogurt, maple syrup, oil, and vanilla. 3. Add the egg mixture to oat mixture and stir just until combined. Gently fold in the blueberries. 4. Scoop the batter into each cup of the egg bite mold. 5. Pour 1 cup of water into the electric pressure cooker. Place the egg bite mold on the wire rack and carefully lower it into the pot. 6. Close and lock the lid of the pressure cooker. Set the valve to sealing. 7. Cook on high pressure for 10 minutes. 8. When the cooking is complete, allow the pressure to release naturally for 10 minutes, then quick release any remaining pressure. Hit Cancel. 9. Lift the wire rack out of the pot and place on a cooling rack for 5 minutes. Invert the mold onto the cooling rack to release the muffins. 10. Serve the muffins warm or refrigerate or freeze.

Southwestern Frittata with Avocados

- 2 tablespoons coconut oil
- ¼ cup diced onion
- ¼ cup diced green chilies
- ½ green bell pepper, diced
- 8 eggs
- 1 teaspoon salt
- ½ teaspoon chili powder
- ¼ teaspoon garlic powder
- ¼ teaspoon pepper
- ¼ cup heavy cream
- 4 tablespoons melted butter
- ½ cup shredded Cheddar cheese
- 1 cup water
- 2 avocados
- ¼ cup sour cream

1. Press the Sauté button and add coconut oil to Instant Pot. Add onion, chilies, and bell pepper. Sauté until onion is translucent and peppers begin to soften, approximately 3 minutes. While sautéing, whisk eggs, seasoning, heavy cream, and butter in large bowl. Pour into 7-inch round baking pan. 2. Press the Cancel button. Add onion and pepper mixture to egg mixture. Mix in Cheddar. Cover pan with aluminum foil. 3. Pour water into Instant Pot, and scrape bottom of pot if necessary to remove any stuck-on food. Place steam rack into pot and put in baking dish with eggs on top. Click lid closed. 4. Press the Manual button and set time for 25 minutes. 5. While food

is cooking, cut avocados in half, remove pit, scoop out of shell and slice thinly. When timer beeps, quick-release the pressure. Serve with avocado slices and a spoonful of sour cream.

Hard-boiled Eggs

- 9 large eggs

1. Pour 1 cup of water into the electric pressure cooker and insert an egg rack. Gently stand the eggs in the rack, fat ends down. If you don't have an egg rack, place the eggs in a steamer basket or on a wire rack. 2. Close and lock the lid of the pressure cooker. Set the valve to sealing. 3. Cook on high pressure for 2 minutes. 4. When the cooking is complete, hit Cancel and allow the pressure to release naturally. 5. Once the pin drops, unlock and remove the lid. 6. Using tongs, carefully remove the eggs from the pressure cooker. Peel or refrigerate the eggs when they are cool enough to handle.

Classic Coffee Cake

Base:
- 2 eggs
- 2 tablespoons salted grass-fed butter, softened
- 1 cup blanched almond flour
- 1 cup chopped pecans
- ¼ cup sour cream, at room temperature

Topping:
- 1 cup sugar-free chocolate chips
- 1 cup chopped pecans
- ½ cup Swerve, or more to

- ¼ cup full-fat cream cheese, softened
- ½ teaspoon salt
- ½ teaspoon ground cinnamon
- ½ teaspoon ground nutmeg
- ¼ teaspoon baking soda

taste
- ½ cup heavy whipping cream

1. Pour 1 cup of filtered water into the inner pot of the Instant Pot, then insert the trivet. Using an electric mixer, combine the eggs, butter, flour, pecans, sour cream, cream cheese, salt, cinnamon, nutmeg, and baking soda. Mix thoroughly. Transfer this mixture into a well-greased, Instant Pot-friendly pan (or dish). 2. Using a sling if desired, place the pan onto the trivet, and cover loosely with aluminum foil. Close the lid, set the pressure release to Sealing, and select Manual. Set the Instant Pot to 40 minutes on High Pressure and let cook. 3. While cooking, in a large bowl, mix the chocolate chips, pecans, Swerve, and whipping cream thoroughly. Set aside. 4. Once cooked, let the pressure naturally disperse from the Instant Pot for about 10 minutes, then carefully switch the pressure release to Venting. 5. Open the Instant Pot and remove the pan. Evenly sprinkle the topping mixture over the cake. Let cool, serve, and enjoy!

Cheddar Broccoli Egg Bites

Prep time: 10 minutes | Cook time: 10 minutes | Serves 7

- 5 eggs, beaten
- 3 tablespoons heavy cream
- ⅛ teaspoon salt
- ⅛ teaspoon black pepper
- 1 ounce (28 g) finely
- chopped broccoli
- 1 ounce (28 g) shredded Cheddar cheese
- ½ cup water

1. In a blender, combine the eggs, heavy cream, salt and pepper and pulse until smooth. 2. Divide the chopped broccoli among the egg cups equally. Pour the egg mixture on top of the broccoli, filling the cups about three-fourths of the way full. Sprinkle the Cheddar cheese on top of each cup. 3. Cover the egg cups tightly with aluminum foil. 4. Pour the water and insert the trivet in the Instant Pot. Put the egg cups on the trivet. 5. Lock the lid. Select the Manual mode and set the cooking time for 10 minutes on High Pressure. Once the timer goes off, perform a natural pressure release for 5 minutes, then release any remaining pressure. Carefully open the lid. 6. Serve immediately.

Kale and Egg Bake

Prep time: 10 minutes | Cook time: 10 minutes | Serves 2

- ½ cup chopped kale
- 3 eggs, beaten
- 1 tablespoon organic almond milk
- 1 teaspoon coconut oil,
- melted
- ¼ teaspoon ground black pepper
- 1 cup water, for cooking

1. In the mixing bowl, mix up chopped kale, eggs, almond milk, and ground black pepper. 2. Grease the ramekins with coconut oil. 3. Pour the kale-egg mixture in the ramekins and flatten it with the help of the spatula, if needed. 4. Pour water and insert the trivet in the instant pot. 5. Put the ramekins with egg mixture on the trivet and close the lid. 6. Cook the breakfast on Manual mode (High Pressure) for 10 minutes. Make a quick pressure release.

Breakfast Burrito Bowls

Prep time: 10 minutes | Cook time: 15 minutes | Serves 4

- 6 eggs
- 3 tablespoons melted butter
- 1 teaspoon salt
- ¼ teaspoon pepper
- ½ pound (227 g) cooked breakfast sausage
- ½ cup shredded sharp Cheddar cheese
- ½ cup salsa
- ½ cup sour cream
- 1 avocado, cubed
- ¼ cup diced green onion

1. In large bowl, mix eggs, melted butter, salt, and pepper. Press the Sauté button and then press the Adjust button to set the heat to Less. 2. Add eggs to Instant Pot and cook for 5 to 7 minutes while gently moving with rubber spatula. When eggs begin to firm up, add cooked breakfast sausage and cheese and continue to cook until eggs are fully cooked. Press the Cancel button. 3. Divide eggs into four bowls and top with salsa, sour cream, avocado, and green onion.

Cheese Egg Muffins

Prep time: 5 minutes | Cook time: 10 minutes | Serves 6

- 4 eggs
- 2 tablespoons heavy cream
- ¼ teaspoon salt
- ⅛ teaspoon pepper
- ⅓ cup shredded Cheddar cheese
- 1 cup water

1. In a large bowl, whisk eggs and heavy cream. Add salt and pepper. 2. Pour mixture into 6 silicone cupcake baking molds. Sprinkle cheese into each cup. 3. Pour water into Instant Pot and place steam rack in bottom of pot. Carefully set filled silicone molds steadily on steam rack. If all do not fit, separate into two batches. 4. Click lid closed. Press the Manual button and adjust time for 10 minutes. When timer beeps, allow a quick release and remove lid. Egg bites will look puffy at first, but will become smaller once they begin to cool. Serve warm.

Chapter 2 Poultry

Creamy Nutmeg Chicken

Prep time: 20 minutes | Cook time: 10 minutes | Serves 6

- 1 tablespoon canola oil
- 6 boneless chicken breast halves, skin and visible fat removed
- ¼ cup chopped onion
- ¼ cup minced parsley
- 2 (10¾-ounce) cans 98% fat-free, reduced-sodium cream
- of mushroom soup
- ½ cup fat-free sour cream
- ½ cup fat-free milk
- 1 tablespoon ground nutmeg
- ¼ teaspoon sage
- ¼ teaspoon dried thyme
- ¼ teaspoon crushed rosemary

1. Press the Sauté button on the Instant Pot and then add the canola oil. Place the chicken in the oil and brown chicken on both sides. Remove the chicken to a plate. 2. Sauté the onion and parsley in the remaining oil in the Instant Pot until the onions are tender. Press Cancel on the Instant Pot, then place the chicken back inside. 3. Mix together the remaining ingredients in a bowl then pour over the chicken. 4. Secure the lid and set the vent to sealing. Set on Manual mode for 10 minutes. 5. When cooking time is up, let the pressure release naturally.

Tangy Meatballs

Prep time: 10 minutes | Cook time: 10 minutes | Makes 20 meatballs

- 1 pound (454 g) ground chicken
- 1 egg, lightly beaten
- ½ medium onion, diced
- 1 teaspoon garlic powder
- 1 teaspoon pepper
- 1 teaspoon salt
- 1 cup water
- Sauce:
- 2 teaspoons erythritol
- 1 teaspoon rice vinegar
- ½ teaspoon sriracha

1. Stir together the ground chicken, beaten egg, onion, garlic powder, salt, and pepper in a large bowl. Shape into bite-sized balls with your hands. 2. Pour the water into Instant Pot and insert a steamer basket. Put the meatballs in the basket. 3. Secure the lid. Select the Manual mode and set the cooking time for 10 minutes at High Pressure. 4. Meanwhile, whisk together all ingredients for the sauce in a separate bowl. 5. Once cooking is complete, do a quick pressure release. Carefully open the lid. 6. Toss the meatballs in the prepared sauce and serve.

Chicken Curry with Eggplant

Prep time: 15 minutes | Cook time: 12 minutes | Serves 4

- 1 eggplant, chopped
- ¼ cup chopped fresh cilantro
- 1 teaspoon curry powder
- 1 cup coconut cream
- 1 teaspoon coconut oil
- 1 pound (454 g) chicken breast, skinless, boneless, cubed

1. Put the coconut oil and chicken breast in the instant pot. 2. Sauté the ingredients on Sauté mode for 5 minutes. 3. Then stir well and add cilantro, eggplant, coconut cream, and curry powder. 4. Close and seal the lid. 5. Cook the meal on Manual mode (High Pressure) for 7 minutes. 6. Make a quick pressure release and transfer the cooked chicken in the serving bowls.

Baked Cheesy Mushroom Chicken

Prep time: 5 minutes | Cook time: 15 minutes | Serves 4

- 1 tablespoon butter
- 2 cloves garlic, smashed
- ½ cup chopped yellow onion
- 1 pound (454 g) chicken breasts, cubed
- 10 ounces (283 g) button mushrooms, thinly sliced
- 1 cup chicken broth
- ½ teaspoon shallot powder
- ½ teaspoon turmeric powder
- ½ teaspoon dried basil
- ½ teaspoon dried sage
- ½ teaspoon cayenne pepper
- ⅓ teaspoon ground black pepper
- Kosher salt, to taste
- ½ cup heavy cream
- 1 cup shredded Colby cheese

1. Set your Instant Pot to Sauté and melt the butter. 2. Add the garlic, onion, chicken, and mushrooms and sauté for about 4 minutes, or until the vegetables are softened. 3. Add the remaining ingredients except the heavy cream and cheese to the Instant Pot and stir to incorporate. 4. Lock the lid. Select the Meat/Stew mode and set the cooking time for 6 minutes at High Pressure. 5. When the timer beeps, perform a natural pressure release for 10 minutes, then release any remaining pressure. Carefully remove the lid. 6. Stir in the heavy cream until heated through. Pour the mixture into a baking dish and scatter the cheese on top. 7. Bake in the preheated oven at 400ºF (205ºC) until the cheese bubbles. 8. Allow to cool for 5 minutes and serve.

Dijon Turkey

Prep time: 15 minutes | Cook time: 14 minutes | Serves 4

- 14 ounces (397 g) ground turkey
- 1 tablespoon Dijon mustard
- ½ cup coconut flour
- 1 teaspoon onion powder
- 1 teaspoon salt
- ½ cup chicken broth
- 1 tablespoon avocado oil

1. In the mixing bowl, mix up ground turkey, Dijon mustard, coconut flour, onion powder, and salt. 2. Make the meatballs with the help of the fingertips. 3. Then pour avocado oil in the instant pot and heat it up for1 minute. 4. Add the meatballs and cook them for 2 minutes from each side. 5. Then add chicken broth. Close and seal the lid. 6. Cook the meatballs for 10 minutes. Make a quick pressure release.

Broccoli Chicken Divan

Prep time: 15 minutes | Cook time: 10 minutes | Serves 4

- 1 cup chopped broccoli
- 2 tablespoons cream cheese
- ½ cup heavy cream
- 1 tablespoon curry powder
- ¼ cup chicken broth
- ½ cup grated Cheddar cheese
- 6 ounces (170 g) chicken fillet, cooked and chopped

1. Mix up broccoli and curry powder and put the mixture in the instant pot. 2. Add heavy cream and cream cheese. 3. Then add chicken and mix up the ingredients. 4. Then add chicken broth and heavy cream. 5. Top the mixture with Cheddar cheese. Close and seal the lid. 6. Cook the meal on Manual mode (High Pressure) for 10 minutes. Allow the natural pressure release for 5 minutes, open the lid and cool the meal for 10 minutes.

Pecorino Chicken

Prep time: 10 minutes | Cook time: 15 minutes | Serves 3

- 2 ounces (57 g) Pecorino cheese, grated
- 10 ounces (283 g) chicken breast, skinless, boneless
- 1 tablespoon butter
- ¾ cup heavy cream
- ½ teaspoon salt
- ½ teaspoon red hot pepper

1. Chop the chicken breast into the cubes. 2. Toss butter in the instant pot and preheat it on the Sauté mode. 3. Add the chicken cubes. 4. Sprinkle the poultry with the salt and red hot pepper. 5. Add cream and mix up together all the ingredients. 6. Close the lid of the instant pot and seal it. 7. Set Poultry mode and put a timer on 15 minutes. 8. When the time is over, let the chicken rest for 5 minutes more. 9. Transfer the meal on the plates and sprinkle with the grated cheese. The cheese shouldn't melt immediately.

Chicken and Kale Sandwiches

Prep time: 10 minutes | Cook time: 10 minutes | Serves 2

- 4 ounces (113 g) kale leaves
- 8 ounces (227 g) chicken fillet
- 1 tablespoon butter
- 1 ounce (28 g) lemon
- ¼ cup water

1. Dice the chicken fillet. 2. Squeeze the lemon juice over the poultry. 3. Transfer the poultry into the instant pot; add water and butter. 4. Close the lid and cook the chicken on the Poultry mode for 10 minutes. 5. When the chicken is cooked, place it on the kale leaves to make the medium sandwiches.

Buttered Chicken

Prep time: 15 minutes | Cook time: 15 minutes | Serves 4

- 1 (14½-ounce / 411-g) can diced tomatoes, undrained
- 5 or 6 garlic cloves, minced
- 1 tablespoon minced fresh ginger
- 1 teaspoon ground turmeric
- 1 teaspoon cayenne
- 1 teaspoon smoked paprika
- 2 teaspoons garam masala, divided
- 1 teaspoon ground cumin
- 1 teaspoon salt
- 1 pound (454 g) boneless,
- skinless chicken breasts or thighs
- ½ cup unsalted butter, cut into cubes, or ½ cup coconut oil
- ½ cup heavy (whipping) cream or full-fat coconut milk
- ¼ to ½ cup chopped fresh cilantro
- 4 cups cauliflower rice or cucumber noodles

1. Put the tomatoes, garlic, ginger, turmeric, cayenne, paprika, 1 teaspoon of garam masala, cumin, and salt in the inner cooking pot of the Instant Pot. Mix thoroughly, then place the chicken pieces on top of the sauce. 2. Lock the lid into place. Select Manual and adjust the pressure to High. Cook for 10 minutes. When the cooking is complete, let the pressure release naturally. Unlock the lid. Carefully remove the chicken and set aside. 3. Using an immersion blender in the pot, blend together all the ingredients into a smooth sauce. (Or use a stand blender, but be careful with the hot sauce and be sure to leave the inside lid open to vent.) After blending, let the sauce cool before adding the remaining ingredients or it will be thinner than is ideal. 4. Add the butter cubes, cream, remaining 1 teaspoon of garam masala, and cilantro. Stir until well incorporated. The sauce should be thick enough to coat the back of a spoon when you're done. 5. Remove half the sauce and freeze it for later or refrigerate for up to 2 to 3 days. 6. Cut the chicken into bite-size pieces. Add it back to the sauce. 7. Preheat the Instant Pot by selecting Sauté and adjust to Less for low heat. Let the chicken heat through. Break it up into smaller pieces if you like, but don't shred it. 8. Serve over cauliflower rice or raw cucumber noodles.

Cheesy Stuffed Cabbage

Prep time: 30 minutes | Cook time: 18 minutes | Serves 6 to 8

- 1 to 2 heads savoy cabbage
- 1 pound ground turkey
- 1 egg
- 1 cup reduced-fat shredded cheddar cheese
- 2 tablespoons evaporated skim milk
- ¼ cup reduced-fat shredded Parmesan cheese
- ¼ cup reduced-fat shredded mozzarella cheese
- ¼ cup finely diced onion
- ¼ cup finely diced bell
- pepper
- ¼ cup finely diced mushrooms
- 1 teaspoon salt
- ½ teaspoon black pepper
- 1 teaspoon garlic powder
- 6 basil leaves, fresh and cut chiffonade
- 1 tablespoon fresh parsley, chopped
- 1 quart of your favorite pasta sauce

1. Remove the core from the cabbages. 2. Boil pot of water and place 1 head at a time into the water for approximately 10 minutes. 3. Allow cabbage to cool slightly. Once cooled, remove the leaves carefully and set aside. You'll need about 15 or 16. 4. Mix together the meat and all remaining ingredients except the pasta sauce. 5. One leaf at a time, put a heaping tablespoon of meat mixture in the center. 6. Tuck the sides in and then roll tightly. 7. Add ½ cup sauce to the bottom of the inner pot of the Instant Pot. 8. Place the rolls, fold-side down, into the pot and layer them, putting a touch of sauce between each layer and finally on top. (You may want to cook the rolls in two batches.) 9. Lock lid and make sure vent is at sealing. Set timer on 18 minutes on Manual at high pressure, then manually release the pressure when cook time is over.

Mexican Chicken with Red Salsa

Prep time: 10 minutes | Cook time: 20 minutes | Serves 8

- 2 pounds (907 g) boneless, skinless chicken thighs, cut into bite-size pieces
- 1½ tablespoons ground cumin
- 1½ tablespoons chili powder
- 1 tablespoon salt
- 2 tablespoons vegetable oil
- 1 (14½-ounce / 411-g) can
- diced tomatoes, undrained
- 1 (5-ounce / 142-g) can sugar-free tomato paste
- 1 small onion, chopped
- 3 garlic cloves, minced
- 2 ounces (57 g) pickled jalapeños from a can, with juice
- ½ cup sour cream

1. Preheat the Instant Pot by selecting Sauté and adjusting to high heat. 2. In a medium bowl, coat the chicken with the cumin, chili powder, and salt. 3. Put the oil in the inner cooking pot. When it is shimmering, add the coated chicken pieces. (This step lets the spices bloom a bit to get their full flavor.) Cook the chicken for 4 to 5 minutes. 4. Add the tomatoes, tomato paste, onion, garlic, and jalapeños. 5. Lock the lid into place. Select Manual and adjust the pressure to High. Cook for 15 minutes. When the cooking is

complete, let the pressure release naturally for 10 minutes, then quick-release any remaining pressure. Unlock and remove the lid. 6. Use two forks to shred the chicken. Serve topped with the sour cream. This dish is good with mashed cauliflower, steamed vegetables, or a salad.

Smoky Whole Chicken

Prep time: 20 minutes | Cook time: 21 minutes | Serves 6

- 2 tablespoons extra-virgin olive oil
- 1 tablespoon kosher salt
- 1½ teaspoons smoked paprika
- 1 teaspoon freshly ground black pepper
- ½ teaspoon herbes de Provence
- ¼ teaspoon cayenne pepper
- 1 (3½ pounds) whole chicken, rinsed and patted dry, giblets removed
- 1 large lemon, halved
- 6 garlic cloves, peeled and crushed with the flat side of a knife
- 1 large onion, cut into 8 wedges, divided
- 1 cup Chicken Bone Broth, low-sodium store-bought chicken broth, or water
- 2 large carrots, each cut into 4 pieces
- 2 celery stalks, each cut into 4 pieces

1. In a small bowl, combine the olive oil, salt, paprika, pepper, herbes de Provence, and cayenne. 2. Place the chicken on a cutting board and rub the olive oil mixture under the skin and all over the outside. Stuff the cavity with the lemon halves, garlic cloves, and 3 to 4 wedges of onion. 3. Pour the broth into the electric pressure cooker. Add the remaining onion wedges, carrots, and celery. Insert a wire rack or trivet on top of the vegetables. 4. Place the chicken, breast-side up, on the rack. 5. Close and lock the lid of the pressure cooker. Set the valve to sealing. 6. Cook on high pressure for 21 minutes. 7. When the cooking is complete, hit Cancel and allow the pressure to release naturally for 15 minutes, then quick release any remaining pressure. 8. Once the pin drops, unlock and remove the lid. 9. Carefully remove the chicken to a clean cutting board. Remove the skin and cut the chicken into pieces or shred/chop the meat, and serve.

Sage Chicken Thighs

Prep time: 10 minutes | Cook time: 16 minutes | Serves 4

- 1 teaspoon dried sage
- 1 teaspoon ground turmeric
- 2 teaspoons avocado oil
- 4 skinless chicken thighs
- 1 cup water
- 1 teaspoon sesame oil

1. Rub the chicken thighs with dried sage, ground turmeric, sesame oil, and avocado oil. 2. Then pour water in the instant pot and insert the steamer rack. 3. Place the chicken thighs on the rack and close the lid. 4. Cook the meal on Manual (High Pressure) for 16 minutes. 5. Then make a quick pressure release and open the lid. 6. Let the cooked chicken thighs cool for 10 minutes before serving.

Classic Chicken Salad

Prep time: 5 minutes | Cook time: 12 minutes | Serves 8

- 2 pounds (907 g) chicken breasts
- 1 cup vegetable broth
- 2 sprigs fresh thyme
- 1 teaspoon granulated garlic
- 1 teaspoon onion powder
- 1 bay leaf
- ½ teaspoon ground black
- pepper
- 1 cup mayonnaise
- 2 stalks celery, chopped
- 2 tablespoons chopped fresh chives
- 1 teaspoon fresh lemon juice
- 1 teaspoon Dijon mustard
- ½ teaspoon coarse sea salt

1. Combine the chicken, broth, thyme, garlic, onion powder, bay leaf, and black pepper in the Instant Pot. 2. Lock the lid. Select the Poultry mode and set the cooking time for 12 minutes at High Pressure. 3. When the timer beeps, perform a natural pressure release for 10 minutes, then release any remaining pressure. Carefully remove the lid. 4. Remove the chicken from the Instant Pot and let rest for a few minutes until cooled slightly. 5. Slice the chicken breasts into strips and place in a salad bowl. Add the remaining ingredients and gently stir until well combined. Serve immediately.

Unstuffed Peppers with Ground Turkey and Quinoa

Prep time: 0 minutes | Cook time: 35 minutes | Serves 8

- 2 tablespoons extra-virgin olive oil
- 1 yellow onion, diced
- 2 celery stalks, diced
- 2 garlic cloves, chopped
- 2 pounds 93 percent lean ground turkey
- 2 teaspoons Cajun seasoning blend (plus 1 teaspoon fine sea salt if using a salt-free blend)
- ½ teaspoon freshly ground black pepper
- ¼ teaspoon cayenne pepper
- 1 cup quinoa, rinsed
- 1 cup low-sodium chicken broth
- One 14½-ounce can fire-roasted diced tomatoes and their liquid
- 3 red, orange, and/or yellow bell peppers, seeded and cut into 1-inch squares
- 1 green onion, white and green parts, thinly sliced
- 1½ tablespoons chopped fresh flat-leaf parsley
- Hot sauce (such as Crystal or Frank's RedHot) for serving

1. Select the Sauté setting on the Instant Pot and heat the oil for 2 minutes. Add the onion, celery, and garlic and sauté for about 4 minutes, until the onion begins to soften. Add the turkey, Cajun seasoning, black pepper, and cayenne and sauté, using a wooden spoon or spatula to break up the meat as it cooks, for about 6 minutes, until cooked through and no streaks of pink remain. 2. Sprinkle the quinoa over the turkey in an even layer. Pour the broth and the diced tomatoes and their liquid over the quinoa, spreading the tomatoes on top. Sprinkle the bell peppers over the top in an even layer. 3. Secure the lid and set the Pressure Release to Sealing. Press the Cancel button to reset the cooking program, then select the Pressure Cook or Manual setting and set the cooking time for 8 minutes at high pressure. (The pot will take about 15 minutes to come up to pressure before the cooking program begins.) 4. When the cooking program ends, let the pressure release naturally for at least 15 minutes, then move the Pressure Release to Venting to release any remaining steam. Open the pot and sprinkle the green onion and parsley over the top in an even layer. 5. Spoon the unstuffed peppers into bowls, making sure to dig down to the bottom of the pot so each person gets an equal amount of peppers, quinoa, and meat. Serve hot, with hot sauce on the side.

Simple Chicken Masala

Prep time: 10 minutes | Cook time: 17 minutes | Serves 3

- 12 ounces (340 g) chicken fillet
- 1 tablespoon masala spices
- 1 tablespoon avocado oil
- 3 tablespoons organic almond milk

1. Heat up avocado oil in the instant pot on Sauté mode for 2 minutes. 2. Meanwhile, chop the chicken fillet roughly and mix it up with masala spices. 3. Add almond milk and transfer the chicken in the instant pot. 4. Cook the chicken bites on Sauté mode for 15 minutes. Stir the meal occasionally.

Stuffed Chicken with Spinach and Feta

Prep time: 10 minutes | Cook time: 25 minutes | Serves 4

- ½ cup frozen spinach
- ⅓ cup crumbled feta cheese
- 1¼ teaspoons salt, divided
- 4 (6-ounce / 170-g) boneless, skinless chicken breasts, butterflied
- ¼ teaspoon pepper
- ¼ teaspoon dried oregano
- ¼ teaspoon dried parsley
- ¼ teaspoon garlic powder
- 2 tablespoons coconut oil
- 1 cup water

1. Combine the spinach, feta cheese, and ¼ teaspoon of salt in a medium bowl. Divide the mixture evenly and spoon onto the chicken breasts. 2. Close the chicken breasts and secure with toothpicks or butcher's string. Sprinkle the chicken with the remaining 1 teaspoon of salt, pepper, oregano, parsley, and garlic powder. 3. Set your Instant Pot to Sauté and heat the coconut oil. 4. Sear each chicken breast until golden brown, about 4 to 5 minutes per side. 5. Remove the chicken breasts and set aside. 6. Pour the water into the Instant Pot and scrape the bottom to remove any chicken or seasoning that is stuck on. Add the trivet to the Instant Pot and place the chicken on the trivet. 7. Secure the lid. Select the Manual mode and set the cooking time for 15 minutes at High Pressure. 8. Once cooking is complete, do a natural pressure release for 15 minutes, then release any remaining pressure. Carefully open the lid. Serve warm.

Rubbed Whole Chicken

Prep time: 20 minutes | Cook time: 25 minutes | Serves 4

- 1½ pound (680 g) whole chicken
- 1 tablespoon poultry seasoning
- 2 tablespoons avocado oil
- 2 cups water

1. Pour water in the instant pot. 2. Then rub the chicken with poultry seasoning and avocado oil. 3. Put the chicken in the instant pot. Close and seal the lid. 4. Cook the meal in Manual mode for 25 minutes. When the time is finished, allow the natural pressure release for 10 minutes.

Pulled BBQ Chicken and Texas-Style Cabbage Slaw

Prep time: 5 minutes | Cook time: 20 minutes | Serves 6

Chicken
- 1 cup water
- ¼ teaspoon fine sea salt
- 3 garlic cloves, peeled

Cabbage Slaw
- ½ head red or green cabbage, thinly sliced
- 1 red bell pepper, seeded and thinly sliced
- 2 jalapeño chiles, seeded and cut into narrow strips
- 2 carrots, julienned
- 1 large Fuji or Gala apple, julienned
- ½ cup chopped fresh cilantro
- 2 bay leaves
- 2 pounds boneless, skinless chicken thighs (see Note)
- 3 tablespoons fresh lime juice
- 3 tablespoons extra-virgin olive oil
- ½ teaspoon ground cumin
- ¼ teaspoon fine sea salt
- ¾ cup low-sugar or unsweetened barbecue sauce
- Cornbread, for serving

1. To make the chicken: Combine the water, salt, garlic, bay leaves, and chicken thighs in the Instant Pot, arranging the chicken in a single layer. 2. Secure the lid and set the Pressure Release to Sealing. Select the Poultry, Pressure Cook, or Manual setting and set the cooking time for 10 minutes at high pressure. (The pot will take about 10 minutes to come up to pressure before the cooking program begins.) 3. To make the slaw: While the chicken is cooking, in a large bowl, combine the cabbage, bell pepper, jalapeños, carrots, apple, cilantro, lime juice, oil, cumin, and salt and toss together until the vegetables and apples are evenly coated. 4. When the cooking program ends, perform a quick pressure release by moving the Pressure Release to Venting, or let the pressure release naturally. Open the pot and, using tongs, transfer the chicken to a cutting board. Using two forks, shred the chicken into bite-size pieces. Wearing heat-resistant mitts, lift out the inner pot and discard the cooking liquid. Return the inner pot to the housing. 5. Return the chicken to the pot and stir in the barbecue sauce. You can serve it right away or heat it for a minute or two on the Sauté setting, then return the pot to its Keep Warm setting until

ready to serve. 6. Divide the chicken and slaw evenly among six plates. Serve with wedges of cornbread on the side.

Mexican Turkey Tenderloin

Prep time: 5 minutes | Cook time: 8 minutes | Serves 6

- 1 cup Low-Sodium Salsa or bottled salsa
- 1 teaspoon chili powder
- ½ teaspoon ground cumin
- ¼ teaspoon dried oregano
- 1½ pounds unseasoned turkey tenderloin or
- boneless turkey breast, cut into 6 pieces
- Freshly ground black pepper
- ½ cup shredded Monterey Jack cheese or Mexican cheese blend

1. In a small bowl or measuring cup, combine the salsa, chili powder, cumin, and oregano. Pour half of the mixture into the electric pressure cooker. 2. Nestle the turkey into the sauce. Grind some pepper onto each piece of turkey. Pour the remaining salsa mixture on top. 3. Close and lock the lid of the pressure cooker. Set the valve to sealing. 4. Cook on high pressure for 8 minutes. 5. When the cooking is complete, hit Cancel. Allow the pressure to release naturally for 10 minutes, then quick release any remaining pressure. 6. Once the pin drops, unlock and remove the lid. 7. Sprinkle the cheese on top, and put the lid back on for a few minutes to let the cheese melt. 8. Serve immediately.

Chicken Enchilada Bowl

Prep time: 10 minutes | Cook time: 35 minutes | Serves 4

- 2 (6-ounce / 170-g) boneless, skinless chicken breasts
- 2 teaspoons chili powder
- ½ teaspoon garlic powder
- ½ teaspoon salt
- ¼ teaspoon pepper
- 2 tablespoons coconut oil
- ¾ cup red enchilada sauce
- ¼ cup chicken broth
- 1 (4-ounce / 113-g) can green chilies
- ¼ cup diced onion
- 2 cups cooked cauliflower rice
- 1 avocado, diced
- ½ cup sour cream
- 1 cup shredded Cheddar cheese

1. Sprinkle the chili powder, garlic powder, salt, and pepper on chicken breasts. 2. Set your Instant Pot to Sauté and melt the coconut oil. Add the chicken breasts and sear each side for about 5 minutes until golden brown. 3. Pour the enchilada sauce and broth over the chicken. Using a wooden spoon or rubber spatula, scrape the bottom of pot to make sure nothing is sticking. Stir in the chilies and onion. 4. Secure the lid. Select the Manual mode and set the cooking time for 25 minutes at High Pressure. 5. Once cooking is complete, do a quick pressure release. Carefully open the lid. 6. Remove the chicken and shred with two forks. Serve the chicken over the cauliflower rice and place the avocado, sour cream, and Cheddar cheese on top.

Turmeric Chicken Nuggets

Prep time: 10 minutes | Cook time: 9 minutes | Serves 5

- 8 ounces (227 g) chicken fillet
- 1 teaspoon ground turmeric
- ½ teaspoon ground coriander
- ½ cup almond flour
- 2 eggs, beaten
- ½ cup butter

1. Chop the chicken fillet roughly into the medium size pieces. 2. In the mixing bowl, mix up ground turmeric, ground coriander, and almond flour. 3. Then dip the chicken pieces in the beaten egg and coat in the almond flour mixture. 4. Toss the butter in the instant pot and melt it on Sauté mode for 4 minutes. 5. Then put the coated chicken in the hot butter and cook for 5 minutes or until the nuggets are golden brown.

Paprika Chicken Wings

Prep time: 10 minutes | Cook time: 13 minutes | Serves 4

- 1 pound (454 g) boneless chicken wings
- 1 teaspoon ground paprika
- 1 teaspoon avocado oil
- ¼ teaspoon minced garlic
- ¾ cup beef broth

1. Pour the avocado oil in the instant pot. 2. Rub the chicken wings with ground paprika and minced garlic and put them in the instant pot. 3. Cook the chicken on Sauté mode for 4 minutes from each side. 4. Then add beef broth and close the lid. 5. Sauté the meal for 5 minutes more.

Chicken Piccata

Prep time: 5 minutes | Cook time: 25 minutes | Serves 4

- 4 (6-ounce / 170-g) boneless, skinless chicken breasts
- ½ teaspoon salt
- ½ teaspoon garlic powder
- ¼ teaspoon pepper
- 2 tablespoons coconut oil
- 1 cup water
- 2 cloves garlic, minced
- 4 tablespoons butter
- Juice of 1 lemon
- ¼ teaspoon xanthan gum

1. Sprinkle the chicken with salt, garlic powder, and pepper. 2. Set your Instant Pot to Sauté and melt the coconut oil. 3. Add the chicken and sear each side for about 5 to 7 minutes until golden brown. 4. Remove the chicken and set aside on a plate. 5. Pour the water into the Instant Pot. Using a wooden spoon, scrape the bottom if necessary to remove any stuck-on seasoning or meat. Insert the trivet and place the chicken on the trivet. 6. Secure the lid. Select the Manual mode and set the cooking time for 10 minutes at High Pressure. 7. Once cooking is complete, do a natural pressure release for 10 minutes, then release any remaining pressure. Carefully

open the lid. 8. Remove the chicken and set aside. Strain the broth from the Instant Pot into a large bowl and return to the pot. 9. Set your Instant Pot to Sauté again and add the remaining ingredients. Cook for at least 5 minutes, stirring frequently, or until the sauce is cooked to your desired thickness. 10. Pour the sauce over the chicken and serve warm.

Barbecue Shredded Chicken

Prep time: 5 minutes | Cook time: 25 minutes | Serves 4

- 1 (5-pound / 2.2-kg) whole chicken
- 3 teaspoons salt
- 1 teaspoon pepper
- 1 teaspoon dried parsley
- 1 teaspoon garlic powder
- ½ medium onion, cut into 3 to 4 large pieces
- 1 cup water
- ½ cup sugar-free barbecue sauce, divided

1. Scatter the chicken with salt, pepper, parsley, and garlic powder. Put the onion pieces inside the chicken cavity. 2. Pour the water into the Instant Pot and insert the trivet. Place seasoned chicken on the trivet. Brush with half of the barbecue sauce. 3. Lock the lid. Select the Manual mode and set the cooking time for 25 minutes at High Pressure. 4. When the timer beeps, perform a natural pressure release for 10 minutes, then release any remaining pressure. Carefully remove the lid. 5. Using a clean brush, add the remaining half of the sauce to chicken. For crispy skin or thicker sauce, you can broil in the oven for 5 minutes until lightly browned. 6. Slice or shred the chicken and serve warm.

Chicken Casserole

Prep time: 15 minutes | Cook time: 15 minutes | Serves 4

- 1 cup broccoli florets
- 1½ cups Alfredo sauce
- ½ cup chopped fresh spinach
- ¼ cup whole-milk ricotta cheese
- ½ teaspoon salt
- ¼ teaspoon pepper
- 1 pound (454 g) thin-sliced deli chicken
- 1 cup shredded whole-milk Mozzarella cheese
- 1 cup water

1. Put the broccoli florets in a large bowl. Add the Alfredo sauce, spinach, ricotta, salt, and pepper to the bowl and stir to mix well. Using a spoon, separate the veggie mix into three sections. 2. Layer the chicken into the bottom of a 7-cup glass bowl. Place one section of the veggie mix on top in an even layer and top with a layer of shredded Mozzarella cheese. Repeat until all veggie mix has been used and finish with a layer of Mozzarella cheese. Cover the dish with aluminum foil. 3. Pour the water into the Instant Pot and insert the trivet. Place the dish on the trivet. 4. Secure the lid. Select the Manual mode and set the cooking time for 15 minutes at High Pressure. 5. Once cooking is complete, do a quick pressure release. Carefully open the lid. 6. If desired, broil in oven for 3 to 5 minutes until golden. Serve warm.

Chicken Fajitas with Bell Peppers

Prep time: 10 minutes | Cook time: 5 minutes | Serves 4

- 1½ pounds (680 g) boneless, skinless chicken breasts
- ¼ cup avocado oil
- 2 tablespoons water
- 1 tablespoon Mexican hot sauce
- 2 cloves garlic, minced
- 1 teaspoon lime juice
- 1 teaspoon ground cumin
- 1 teaspoon salt
- 1 teaspoon erythritol
- ¼ teaspoon chili powder
- ¼ teaspoon smoked paprika
- 5 ounces (142 g) sliced yellow bell pepper strips
- 5 ounces (142 g) sliced red bell pepper strips
- 5 ounces (142 g) sliced green bell pepper strips

1. Slice the chicken into very thin strips lengthwise. Cut each strip in half again. Imagine the thickness of restaurant fajitas when cutting. 2. In a measuring cup, whisk together the avocado oil, water, hot sauce, garlic, lime juice, cumin, salt, erythritol, chili powder, and paprika to form a marinade. Add to the pot, along with the chicken and peppers. 3. Close the lid and seal the vent. Cook on High Pressure for 5 minutes. Quick release the steam.

Speedy Chicken Cacciatore

Prep time: 5 minutes | Cook time: 30 minutes | Serves 6

- 2 pounds boneless, skinless chicken thighs
- 1½ teaspoons fine sea salt
- ½ teaspoon freshly ground black pepper
- 2 tablespoons extra-virgin olive oil
- 3 garlic cloves, chopped
- 2 large red bell peppers, seeded and cut into ¼ by 2-inch strips
- 2 large yellow onions, sliced
- ½ cup dry red wine
- 1½ teaspoons Italian seasoning
- ½ teaspoon red pepper flakes (optional)
- One 14½ ounces can diced tomatoes and their liquid
- 2 tablespoons tomato paste
- Cooked brown rice or whole-grain pasta for serving

1. Season the chicken thighs on both sides with 1 teaspoon of the salt and the black pepper. 2. Select the Sauté setting on the Instant Pot and heat the oil and garlic for 2 minutes, until the garlic is bubbling but not browned. Add the bell peppers, onions, and remaining ½ teaspoon salt and sauté for 3 minutes, until the onions begin to soften. Stir in the wine, Italian seasoning, and pepper flakes (if using). Using tongs, add the chicken to the pot, turning each piece to coat it in the wine and spices and nestling them in a single layer in the liquid. Pour the tomatoes and their liquid on top of the chicken and dollop the tomato paste on top. Do not stir them in. 3. Secure the lid and set the Pressure Release to Sealing. Press the Cancel button to reset the cooking program, then select the Poultry, Pressure Cook, or Manual setting and set the cooking time for 12

minutes at high pressure. (The pot will take about 15 minutes to come up to pressure before the cooking program begins.) 4. When the cooking program ends, perform a quick pressure release by moving the Pressure Release to Venting, or let the pressure release naturally. Open the pot and, using tongs, transfer the chicken and vegetables to a serving dish. 5. Spoon some of the sauce over the chicken and serve hot, with the rice on the side.

Kung Pao Chicken

Prep time: 5 minutes | Cook time: 17 minutes | Serves 5

- 2 tablespoons coconut oil
- 1 pound (454 g) boneless, skinless chicken breasts, cubed
- 1 cup cashews, chopped
- 6 tablespoons hot sauce
- ½ teaspoon chili powder
- ½ teaspoon finely grated ginger
- ½ teaspoon kosher salt
- ½ teaspoon freshly ground black pepper

1. Set the Instant Pot to Sauté and melt the coconut oil. 2. Add the remaining ingredients to the Instant Pot and mix well. 3. Secure the lid. Select the Manual mode and set the cooking time for 17 minutes at High Pressure. 4. Once cooking is complete, do a quick pressure release. Carefully open the lid. 5. Serve warm.

Chicken Casablanca

Prep time: 20 minutes | Cook time: 12 minutes | Serves 8

- 2 large onions, sliced
- 1 teaspoon ground ginger
- 3 garlic cloves, minced
- 2 tablespoons canola oil, divided
- 3 pounds skinless chicken pieces
- 3 large carrots, diced
- 2 large potatoes, unpeeled, diced
- ½ teaspoon ground cumin
- ½ teaspoon salt
- ½ teaspoon pepper
- ¼ teaspoon cinnamon
- 2 tablespoons raisins
- 14½-ounce can chopped tomatoes
- 3 small zucchini, sliced
- 15-ounce can garbanzo beans, drained
- 2 tablespoons chopped parsley

1. Using the Sauté function of the Instant Pot, cook the onions, ginger, and garlic in 1 tablespoon of the oil for 5 minutes, stirring constantly. Remove onions, ginger, and garlic from pot and set aside. 2. Brown the chicken pieces with the remaining oil, then add the cooked onions, ginger and garlic back in as well as all of the remaining ingredients, except the parsley. 3. Secure the lid and make sure vent is in the sealing position. Cook on Manual mode for 12 minutes. 4. When cook time is up, let the pressure release naturally for 5 minutes and then release the rest of the pressure manually.

Cheese Stuffed Chicken

Prep time: 15 minutes | Cook time: 20 minutes | Serves 4

- 12 ounces (340 g) chicken fillet
- 4 ounces (113 g) provolone cheese, sliced
- 1 tablespoon cream cheese
- ½ teaspoon dried cilantro
- ½ teaspoon smoked paprika
- 1 cup water, for cooking

1. Beat the chicken fillet well and rub it with dried cilantro and smoked paprika. 2. Then spread it with cream cheese and top with Provolone cheese. 3. Roll the chicken fillet into the roll and wrap in the foil. 4. Pour water and insert the rack in the instant pot. 5. Place the chicken roll on the rack. Close and seal the lid. 6. Cook it on Manual mode (High Pressure) for 20 minutes. 7. Make a quick pressure release and slice the chicken roll into the servings.

Paprika Chicken with Tomato

Prep time: 10 minutes | Cook time: 20 minutes | Serves 2

- 8 ounces (227 g) chicken fillet, sliced
- 1 tomato, chopped
- 2 tablespoons mascarpone
- 1 teaspoon coconut oil
- 1 teaspoon ground paprika
- ½ teaspoon ground turmeric
- 1 tablespoon butter

1. Rub the chicken fillet with ground paprika, ground turmeric, and paprika. 2. Put the sliced chicken in the instant pot. 3. Add tomato, mascarpone, coconut oil, and butter. 4. Close the lid and cook the meal on Sauté mode for 20 minutes. 5. Stir it every 5 minutes to avoid burning.

Marjoram Chicken Wings with Cream Cheese

Prep time: 7 minutes | Cook time: 10 minutes | Serves 2

- 1 teaspoon marjoram
- 1 teaspoon cream cheese
- ½ green pepper
- ½ teaspoon salt
- ½ teaspoon ground black pepper
- 14 ounces (397 g) chicken wings
- ¾ cup water
- 1 teaspoon coconut oil

1. Rub the chicken wings with the marjoram, salt, and ground black pepper. 2. Blend the green pepper until you get a purée. 3. Rub the chicken wings in the green pepper purée. 4. Then toss the coconut oil in the instant pot bowl and preheat it on the Sauté mode. 5. Add the chicken wings and cook them for 3 minutes from each side or until light brown. 6. Then add cream cheese and water. 7. Cook the meal on Manual mode for 4 minutes at High Pressure. 8. When the time is over, make a quick pressure release. 9. Let the cooked chicken wings chill for 1 to 2 minutes and serve them!

Chicken Tagine

Prep time: 15 minutes | Cook time: 11 minutes | Serves 4

- 2 (15-ounce / 425-g) cans chickpeas, rinsed, divided
- 1 tablespoon extra-virgin olive oil
- 5 garlic cloves, minced
- 1½ teaspoons paprika
- ½ teaspoon ground turmeric
- ½ teaspoon ground cumin
- ¼ teaspoon ground ginger
- ¼ teaspoon cayenne pepper
- 1 fennel bulb, 1 tablespoon fronds minced, stalks discarded, bulb halved and cut lengthwise into ½-inch-thick wedges
- 1 cup chicken broth
- 3 (2-inch) strips lemon zest, plus lemon wedges for serving
- 4 (5- to 7-ounce / 142- to 198-g) bone-in chicken thighs, skin removed, trimmed
- ½ teaspoon table salt
- ½ cup pitted large brine-cured green or black olives, halved
- ⅓ cup raisins
- 2 tablespoons chopped fresh parsley

1. Using potato masher, mash ½ cup chickpeas in bowl to paste. Using highest sauté function, cook oil, garlic, paprika, turmeric, cumin, ginger, and cayenne in Instant Pot until fragrant, about 1 minute. Turn off Instant Pot, then stir in remaining whole chickpeas, mashed chickpeas, fennel wedges, broth, and zest. 2. Sprinkle chicken with salt. Nestle chicken skinned side up into pot and spoon some of cooking liquid over top. Lock lid in place and close pressure release valve. Select high pressure cook function and cook for 10 minutes. 3. Turn off Instant Pot and quick-release pressure. Carefully remove lid, allowing steam to escape away from you. Discard lemon zest. Stir in olives, raisins, parsley, and fennel fronds. Season with salt and pepper to taste. Serve with lemon wedges.

Chicken in Mushroom Gravy

Prep time: 10 minutes | Cook time: 10 minutes | Serves 6

- 6 (5 ounces each) boneless, skinless chicken-breast halves
- Salt and pepper to taste
- ¼ cup dry white wine or
- low-sodium chicken broth
- 10¾-ounce can 98% fat-free, reduced-sodium cream of mushroom soup
- 4 ounces sliced mushrooms

1. Place chicken in the inner pot of the Instant Pot. Season with salt and pepper. 2. Combine wine and soup in a bowl, then pour over the chicken. Top with the mushrooms. 3. Secure the lid and make sure the vent is set to sealing. Set on Manual mode for 10 minutes. 4. When cooking time is up, let the pressure release naturally.

Thai Coconut Chicken

Prep time: 10 minutes | Cook time: 15 minutes | Serves 4

- 1 tablespoon coconut oil
- 1 pound (454 g) chicken, cubed
- 2 cloves garlic, minced
- 1 shallot, peeled and chopped
- 1 teaspoon Thai chili, minced
- 1 teaspoon fresh ginger root, julienned
- ⅓ teaspoon cumin powder
- 1 tomato, peeled and chopped
- 1 cup vegetable broth
- ⅓ cup unsweetened coconut milk
- 2 tablespoons coconut aminos
- 1 teaspoon Thai curry paste
- Salt and freshly ground black pepper, to taste

1. Set your Instant Pot to Sauté and heat the coconut oil. 2. Brown the chicken cubes for 2 to 3 minutes, stirring frequently. Reserve the chicken in a bowl. 3. Add the garlic and shallot and sauté for 2 minutes until tender. Add a splash of vegetable broth to the pot, if needed. 4. Stir in the Thai chili, ginger, and cumin powder and cook for another 1 minute or until fragrant. 5. Add the cooked chicken, tomato, vegetable broth, milk, coconut aminos, and curry paste to the Instant Pot and stir well. 6. Lock the lid. Select the Manual mode and set the cooking time for 10 minutes at High Pressure. 7. When the timer beeps, perform a quick pressure release. Carefully remove the lid. Season with salt and pepper to taste and serve.

Thai Yellow Curry with Chicken Meatballs

Prep time: 5 minutes | Cook time: 30 minutes | Serves 4

- 1 pound 95 percent lean ground chicken
- ⅓ cup gluten-free panko (Japanese bread crumbs)
- 1 egg white
- 1 tablespoon coconut oil
- 1 yellow onion, cut into 1-inch pieces
- One 14-ounce can light coconut milk
- 3 tablespoons yellow curry paste
- ¾ cup water
- 8 ounces carrots, halved lengthwise, then cut crosswise into 1-inch lengths (or quartered if very
- large)
- 8 ounces zucchini, quartered lengthwise, then cut crosswise into 1-inch lengths (or cut into halves, then thirds if large)
- 8 ounces cremini mushrooms, quartered
- Fresh Thai basil leaves for serving (optional)
- Fresno or jalapeño chile, thinly sliced, for serving (optional)
- 1 lime, cut into wedges
- Cooked cauliflower "rice" for serving

1. In a medium bowl, combine the chicken, panko, and egg white and mix until evenly combined. Set aside. 2. Select the Sauté setting on the Instant Pot and heat the oil for 2 minutes. Add the onion and sauté for 5 minutes, until it begins to soften and brown. Add ½ cup of the coconut milk and the curry paste and sauté for 1 minute more, until bubbling and fragrant. Press the Cancel button to turn off the pot, then stir in the water. 3. Using a 1½-tablespoon cookie scoop, shape and drop meatballs into the pot in a single layer. 4. Secure the lid and set the Pressure Release to Sealing. Select the Pressure Cook or Manual setting and set the cooking time for 5 minutes at high pressure. (The pot will take about 5 minutes to come up to pressure before the cooking program begins.) 5. When the cooking program ends, perform a quick pressure release by moving the Pressure Release to Venting, or let the pressure release naturally. Open the pot and stir in the carrots, zucchini, mushrooms, and remaining 1¼ cups coconut milk. 6. Press the Cancel button to reset the cooking program, then select the Sauté setting. Bring the curry to a simmer (this will take about 2 minutes), then let cook, uncovered, for about 8 minutes, until the carrots are fork-tender. Press the Cancel button to turn off the pot. 7. Ladle the curry into bowls. Serve piping hot, topped with basil leaves and chile slices, if desired, and the lime wedges and cauliflower "rice" on the side.

Tuscan Chicken Drumsticks

Prep time: 15 minutes | Cook time: 12 minutes | Serves 4

- 4 chicken drumsticks
- 1 cup chopped spinach
- 1 teaspoon minced garlic
- 1 teaspoon ground paprika
- 1 cup heavy cream
- 1 teaspoon cayenne pepper
- 1 ounce (28 g) sun-dried tomatoes, chopped

1. Put all ingredients in the instant pot. 2. Close and seal the lid. 3. Cook the meal on Manual mode (High Pressure) for 12 minutes. 4. Then allow the natural pressure release for 10 minutes. 5. Serve the chicken with hot sauce from the instant pot.

Authentic Chicken Shawarma

Prep time: 15 minutes | Cook time: 17 minutes | Serves 4

- 1 pound (454 g) chicken fillet
- ½ teaspoon ground coriander
- ½ teaspoon smoked paprika
- ½ teaspoon dried thyme
- 1 tablespoon tahini sauce
- 1 teaspoon lemon juice
- 1 teaspoon heavy cream
- 1 cup water, for cooking

1. Rub the chicken fillet with ground coriander, smoked paprika, thyme, and wrap in the foil. 2. Then pour water and insert the steamer rack in the instant pot. 3. Place the wrapped chicken in the steamer; close and seal the lid. 4. Cook the chicken on Manual mode (High Pressure) for 17 minutes. Make a quick pressure release. 5. Make the sauce: Mix up heavy cream, lemon juice, and tahini paste. 6. Slice the chicken and sprinkle it with sauce.

Chicken and Bacon Ranch Casserole

Prep time: 5 minutes | Cook time: 30 minutes | Serves 4

- 4 slices bacon
- 4 (6-ounce / 170-g) boneless, skinless chicken breasts, cut into 1-inch cubes
- ½ teaspoon salt
- ¼ teaspoon pepper

- 1 tablespoon coconut oil
- ½ cup chicken broth
- ½ cup ranch dressing
- ½ cup shredded Cheddar cheese
- 2 ounces (57 g) cream cheese

1. Press the Sauté button to heat your Instant Pot. 2. Add the bacon slices and cook for about 7 minutes until crisp, flipping occasionally. 3. Remove from the pot and place on a paper towel to drain. Set aside. 4. Season the chicken cubes with salt and pepper. 5. Set your Instant Pot to Sauté and melt the coconut oil. 6. Add the chicken cubes and brown for 3 to 4 minutes until golden brown. 7. Stir in the broth and ranch dressing. 8. Secure the lid. Select the Manual mode and set the cooking time for 20 minutes at High Pressure. 9. Once cooking is complete, do a quick pressure release. Carefully open the lid. 10. Stir in the Cheddar and cream cheese. Crumble the cooked bacon and scatter on top. Serve immediately.

Chapter 3 Beef, Pork, and Lamb

Easy Pot Roast and Vegetables

Prep time: 20 minutes | Cook time: 35 minutes | Serves 6

- 3–4 pound chuck roast, trimmed of fat and cut into serving-sized chunks
- 4 medium potatoes, cubed, unpeeled
- 4 medium carrots, sliced, or
- 1 pound baby carrots
- 2 celery ribs, sliced thin
- 1 envelope dry onion soup mix
- 3 cups water

1. Place the pot roast chunks and vegetables into the Instant Pot along with the potatoes, carrots and celery. 2. Mix together the onion soup mix and water and pour over the contents of the Instant Pot. 3. Secure the lid and make sure the vent is set to sealing. Set the Instant Pot to Manual mode for 35 minutes. Let pressure release naturally when cook time is up.

Korean Short Rib Lettuce Wraps

Prep time: 7 minutes | Cook time: 25 minutes | Serves 4

- ¼ cup coconut aminos, or 1 tablespoon wheat-free tamari
- 2 tablespoons coconut vinegar
- 2 tablespoons sesame oil
- 3 green onions, thinly sliced, plus more for garnish
- 2 teaspoons peeled and grated fresh ginger
- 2 teaspoons minced garlic
- ½ teaspoon fine sea salt
- ½ teaspoon red pepper flakes, plus more for garnish
- 1 pound (454 g) boneless beef short ribs, sliced ½ inch thick
- For Serving:
- 1 head radicchio, thinly sliced
- Butter lettuce leaves

1. Place the coconut aminos, vinegar, sesame oil, green onions, ginger, garlic, salt, and red pepper flakes in the Instant Pot and stir to combine. Add the short ribs and toss to coat well. 2. Seal the lid, press Manual, and set the timer for 20 minutes. Once finished, let the pressure release naturally. 3. Remove the ribs from the Instant Pot and set aside on a warm plate, leaving the sauce in the pot. 4. Press Sauté and cook the sauce, whisking often, until thickened to your liking, about 5 minutes. 5. Put the sliced radicchio on a serving platter, then lay the short ribs on top. Pour the thickened sauce over the ribs. Garnish with more sliced green onions and red pepper flakes. Serve wrapped in lettuce leaves.

Cilantro Lime Shredded Pork

Prep time: 5 minutes | Cook time: 30 minutes | Serves 4

- 1 tablespoon chili adobo sauce
- 1 tablespoon chili powder
- 2 teaspoons salt
- 1 teaspoon garlic powder
- 1 teaspoon cumin
- ½ teaspoon pepper
- 1 (2½ to 3 pounds / 1.1 to 1.4 kg) cubed pork butt
- 1 tablespoon coconut oil
- 2 cups beef broth
- 1 lime, cut into wedges
- ¼ cup chopped cilantro

1. In a small bowl, mix adobo sauce, chili powder, salt, garlic powder, cumin, and pepper. 2. Press the Sauté button on Instant Pot and add coconut oil to pot. Rub spice mixture onto cubed pork butt. Place pork into pot and sear for 3 to 5 minutes per side. Add broth. 3. Press the Cancel button. Lock Lid. Press the Manual button and adjust time to 30 minutes. 4. When timer beeps, let pressure naturally release until the float valve drops, and unlock lid. 5. Shred pork with fork. Pork should easily fall apart. For extra-crispy pork, place single layer in skillet on stove over medium heat. Cook for 10 to 15 minutes or until water has cooked out and pork becomes brown and crisp. Serve warm with fresh lime wedges and cilantro garnish.

Steak Bites with Garlic Dipping Sauce

Prep time: 5 minutes | Cook time: 10 minutes | Serves 4

Steak Bites:
- 1 pound (454 g) sirloin steak
- 1 teaspoon salt

Dipping Sauce:
- ½ cup mayonnaise
- 1 teaspoon lemon juice
- 1 roasted garlic clove,
- ¼ teaspoon pepper
- 4 tablespoons butter

- mashed
- ⅛ teaspoon red pepper flakes

1. Cut steak into 1-inch cubes. Sprinkle with salt and pepper. Press the Sauté button and add butter to Instant Pot. When butter is melted, add steak and sear each side until desired doneness, about 10 minutes. Press the Cancel button and place steak bites into dish. 2. In medium bowl, mix mayo, lemon juice, roasted garlic, and red pepper flakes. Serve steak bites with dipping sauce.

Korean Beef and Pickled Vegetable Bowls

Prep time: 15 minutes | Cook time: 10 minutes | Serves 6

- 1 tablespoon vegetable oil
- 5 garlic cloves, thinly sliced
- 1 tablespoon julienned fresh ginger
- 2 dried red chiles
- 1 cup sliced onions
- 1 pound (454 g) 80% lean ground beef
- 1 tablespoon gochujang, adjusted to taste
- 1 cup fresh basil leaves, divided
- 1 tablespoon coconut aminos
- 1 teaspoon Swerve
- 2 tablespoons freshly squeezed lime juice
- 1 teaspoon salt
- 1 teaspoon freshly ground pepper
- ¼ cup water
- 1 teaspoon sesame oil
- For the Pickled Vegetables:
- 1 cucumber, peeled, coarsely grated
- 1 turnip, coarsely grated
- ¼ cup white vinegar
- ½ teaspoon salt
- ½ teaspoon Swerve

1. Select Sauté mode of the Instant Pot. When the pot is hot, add the oil and heat until it is shimmering. 2. Add the garlic, ginger, and chiles and sauté for 1 minute. 3. Add the onions and sauté for 1 minute. 4. Add the ground beef and cooking for 4 minutes.. 5. Add the gochujang, ½ cup of basil, coconut aminos, sweetener, lime juice, salt, pepper, water, and sesame oil, and stir to combine. 6. Lock the lid. Select Manual mode. Set the time for 4 minutes on High Pressure. 7. When cooking is complete, let the pressure release naturally for 5 minutes, then release any remaining pressure. Unlock the lid and stir in the remaining ½ cup of basil. 8. Meanwhile, put the cucumber and turnip in a medium bowl and mix with the vinegar, salt, and sweetener. To serve, portion the basil beef into individual bowls and serve with the pickled salad.

Bacon-Wrapped Pork Bites

Prep time: 15 minutes | Cook time: 20 minutes | Serves 4

- 3 tablespoons butter
- 10 ounces (283 g) pork tenderloin, cubed
- 6 ounces (170 g) bacon,
- sliced
- ½ teaspoon white pepper
- ¾ cup chicken stock

1. Melt the butter on Sauté mode in the Instant Pot. 2. Meanwhile, wrap the pork tenderloin cubes in the sliced bacon and sprinkle with white pepper. Secure with toothpicks, if necessary. 3. Put the wrapped pork tenderloin in the melted butter and cook for 3 minutes on each side. 4. Add the chicken stock and close the lid. 5. Select Manual mode and set cooking time for 14 minutes on High Pressure. 6. When timer beeps, use a natural pressure release for 5 minutes, then release any remaining pressure. Open the lid. 7. Discard the toothpicks and serve immediately.

Beef Shami Kabob

Prep time: 15 minutes | Cook time: 35 minutes | Serves 4

- 1 pound (454 g) beef chunks, chopped
- 1 teaspoon ginger paste
- ½ teaspoon ground cumin
- 2 cups water
- ¼ cup almond flour
- 1 egg, beaten
- 1 tablespoon coconut oil

1. Put the beef chunks, ginger paste, ground cumin, and water in the Instant Pot. 2. Select Manual mode and set cooking time for 30 minutes on High Pressure. 3. When timer beeps, make a quick pressure release. Open the lid. 4. Drain the water from the meat. Transfer the beef in the blender. Add the almond flour and beaten egg. Blend until smooth. Shape the mixture into small meatballs. 5. Heat the coconut oil on Sauté mode and put the meatballs inside. 6. Cook for 2 minutes on each side or until golden brown. 7. Serve immediately.

Peppercorn Pork with Salsa Verde

Prep time: 10 minutes | Cook time: 40 minutes | Serves 3

- 12 ounces (340 g) pork shoulder, sliced
- ½ cup salsa verde
- ½ cup water
- ¾ teaspoon peppercorns
- ½ teaspoon salt

1. Toss the butter in the instant pot and sauté it for 1 minute or until it is melted. 2. After this, add pork shoulder, salt, and peppercorns; sauté the ingredients for 10 minutes. 3. After this, add water and salsa verde. 4. Set the Bean/Chili mode and set the timer on 30 minutes (High Pressure). 5. When the time is over, make a natural pressure release.

Low Carb Pork Tenderloin

Prep time: 15 minutes | Cook time: 30 minutes | Serves 2

- 9 ounces (255 g) pork tenderloin
- 1 teaspoon erythritol
- ½ teaspoon dried dill
- ½ teaspoon white pepper
- 1 garlic clove, minced
- 3 tablespoons butter
- ¼ cup water

1. Rub the pork tenderloin with erythritol, dried dill, white pepper, and minced garlic. 2. Then melt the butter in the instant pot on Sauté mode. 3. Add pork tenderloin and cook it for 8 minutes from each side (use Sauté mode). 4. Then add water and close the lid. 5. Cook the meat on Sauté mode for 10 minutes. 6. Cool the cooked tenderloin for 10 to 15 minutes and slice.

Beef and Broccoli with Cheddar

Prep time: 5 minutes | Cook time: 10 minutes | Serves 4

- 1 pound (454 g) 85% lean ground beef
- 1 teaspoon salt
- ½ teaspoon garlic powder
- ½ teaspoon dried parsley
- ¼ teaspoon dried oregano
- 2 tablespoons butter
- ¾ cup beef broth
- 2 cups broccoli florets
- ¼ cup heavy cream
- 1 cup shredded mild Cheddar cheese

1. Press the Sauté button and brown ground beef in Instant Pot until there's no more pink. Press the Cancel button. Sprinkle seasonings over meat and add butter, broth, and broccoli. Click lid closed. 2. Press the Manual button and set time for 2 minutes. When timer beeps, press the Cancel button. Stir in heavy cream and Cheddar until completely melted.

Carnitas Burrito Bowls

Prep time: 10 minutes | Cook time: 1 hour | Serves 6

Carnitas
- 1 tablespoon chili powder
- ½ teaspoon garlic powder
- 1 teaspoon ground coriander
- 1 teaspoon fine sea salt
- ½ cup water

Rice and Beans
- 1 cup Minute brand brown rice (see Note)
- 1½ cups drained cooked

Pico de Gallo
- 8 ounces tomatoes (see Note), diced
- ½ small yellow onion, diced
- 1 jalapeño chile, seeded and

Pinch of fine sea salt
- ¼ cup sliced green onions, white and green parts
- 2 tablespoons chopped fresh cilantro
- 3 hearts romaine lettuce, cut

- ¼ cup fresh lime juice
- One 2-pound boneless pork shoulder butt roast, cut into 2-inch cubes

  black beans, or one 15-ounce can black beans, rinsed and drained

  finely diced
- 1 tablespoon chopped fresh cilantro
- 1 teaspoon fresh lime juice

  into ¼-inch-wide ribbons
- 2 large avocados, pitted, peeled, and sliced
- Hot sauce (such as Cholula or Tapatío) for serving

1. To make the carnitas: In a small bowl, combine the chili powder, garlic powder, coriander, and salt and mix well. 2. Pour the water and lime juice into the Instant Pot. Add the pork, arranging the pieces in a single layer. Sprinkle the chili powder mixture evenly over the pork. 3. Secure the lid and set the Pressure Release to Sealing. Select the Meat/Stew setting and set the cooking time for 30 minutes at high pressure. (The pot will take about 10 minutes to come up to pressure before the cooking program begins.) 4. When the cooking program ends, let the pressure release naturally for at least 15 minutes, then move the Pressure Release to Venting to release any remaining steam. Open the pot and, using tongs, transfer the pork to a plate or cutting board. 5. While the pressure is releasing, preheat the oven to 400°F. 6. Wearing heat-resistant mitts, lift out the inner pot and pour the cooking liquid into a fat separator. Pour the defatted cooking liquid into a liquid measuring cup and discard the fat. (Alternatively, use a ladle or large spoon to skim the fat off the surface of the liquid.) Add water as needed to the cooking liquid to total 1 cup (you may have enough without adding water). 7. To make the rice and beans: Pour the 1 cup cooking liquid into the Instant Pot and add the rice, making sure it is in an even layer. Place a tall steam rack into the pot. Add the black beans to a 1½-quart stainless-steel bowl and place the bowl on top of the rack. (The bowl should not touch the lid once the pot is closed.) 8. Secure the lid and set the Pressure Release to Sealing. Press the Cancel button to reset the cooking program, then select the Pressure Cook or Manual setting and set the cooking time for 15 minutes at high pressure. (The pot will take about 5 minutes to come to pressure before the cooking program begins.) 9. While the rice and beans are cooking, using two forks, shred the meat into bite-size pieces. Transfer the pork to a sheet pan, spreading it out in an even layer. Place in the oven for 20 minutes, until crispy and browned. 10. To make the pico de gallo: While the carnitas, rice, and beans are cooking, in a medium bowl, combine the tomatoes, onion, jalapeño, cilantro, lime juice, and salt and mix well. Set aside. 11. When the cooking program ends, let the pressure release naturally for 5 minutes, then move the Pressure Release to Venting to release any remaining steam. Open the pot and, wearing heat-resistant mitts, remove the bowl of beans and then the steam rack from the pot. Then remove the inner pot. Add the green onions and cilantro to the rice and, using a fork, fluff the rice and mix in the green onions and cilantro. 12. Divide the rice, beans, carnitas, pico de gallo, lettuce, and avocados evenly among six bowls. Serve warm, with the hot sauce on the side.

Beef Chili with Kale

Prep time: 10 minutes | Cook time: 10 minutes | Serves 6

- 2 tablespoons olive oil
- 1½ pounds (680 g) ground chuck
- 1 green bell pepper, chopped
- 1 red bell pepper, chopped
- 2 red chilies, minced
- 1 red onion
- 2 garlic cloves, smashed
- 1 teaspoon cumin
- 1 teaspoon Mexican oregano
- 1 teaspoon cayenne pepper
- 1 teaspoon smoked paprika
- Salt and freshly ground black pepper, to taste
- 1½ cups puréed tomatoes
- 4 cups fresh kale

1. Press the Sauté button to heat up the Instant Pot. Then, heat the oil; once hot, cook the ground chuck for 2 minutes, crumbling it with a fork or a wide spatula. 2. Add the pepper, onions, and garlic; cook an additional 2 minutes or until fragrant. Stir in the remaining ingredients, minus kale leaves. 3. Choose the Manual setting and cook for 6 minutes at High Pressure. Once cooking is complete, use a natural pressure release; carefully remove the lid. 4. Add kale, cover with the lid and allow the kale leaves to wilt completely. Bon appétit!

Beef Masala Curry

Prep time: 10 minutes | Cook time: 20 minutes | Serves 4

- 2 tomatoes, quartered
- 1 small onion, quartered
- 4 garlic cloves, chopped
- ½ cup fresh cilantro leaves
- 1 teaspoon garam masala
- ½ teaspoon ground coriander
- 1 teaspoon ground cumin
- ½ teaspoon cayenne
- 1 teaspoon salt
- 1 pound (454 g) beef chuck roast, cut into 1-inch cubes

1. In a blender, combine the tomatoes, onion, garlic, and cilantro. 2. Process until the vegetables are puréed. Add the garam masala, coriander, cumin, cayenne, and salt. Process for several more seconds. 3. To the Instant Pot, add the beef and pour the vegetable purée on top. 4. Lock the lid. Select Manual mode and set cooking time for 20 minutes on High Pressure. 5. When timer beeps, let the pressure release naturally for 10 minutes, then release any remaining pressure. Unlock the lid. 6. Stir and serve immediately.

Creamy Pork Liver

Prep time: 5 minutes | Cook time: 7 minutes | Serves 3

- 14 ounces (397 g) pork liver, chopped
- 1 teaspoon salt
- 1 teaspoon butter
- ½ cup heavy cream
- 3 tablespoons scallions, chopped

1. Rub the liver with the salt on a clean work surface. 2. Put the butter in the Instant Pot and melt on the Sauté mode. 3. Add the heavy cream, scallions, and liver. 4. Stir and close the lid. Select Manual mode and set cooking time for 12 minutes on High Pressure. 5. When timer beeps, perform a natural pressure release for 5 minutes, then release any remaining pressure. Open the lid. 6. Serve immediately.

Spanish Pork Shoulder

Prep time: 10 minutes | Cook time: 40 minutes | Serves 3

- 12 ounces (340 g) pork shoulder
- ½ cup chili verde
- 1 tablespoon butter
- ¼ cup beef broth
- ¾ teaspoon ground black pepper
- ½ teaspoon salt

1. Chop the pork shoulder and sprinkle the meat with the ground black pepper and salt. 2. Toss the butter in the instant pot and sauté it for 1 minute or until it is melted. 3. After this, add pork shoulder and sauté it for 10 minutes. 4. After this, add beef broth and chili Verde. 5. Lock the instant pot lid and seal it. 6. Set the Bean/Chili mode and set the timer on 30 minutes (High Pressure). 7. When the time is over, make a natural pressure release. 8. Serve it!

Beery Boston-Style Butt

Prep time: 10 minutes | Cook time: 1 hour 1 minutes | Serves 4

- 1 tablespoon butter
- 1 pound (454 g) Boston-style butt
- ½ cup leeks, chopped
- ¼ cup beer
- ½ cup chicken stock
- Pinch of grated nutmeg
- Sea salt, to taste
- ¼ teaspoon ground black pepper
- ¼ cup water

1. Press the Sauté button to heat up the Instant Pot. Once hot, melt the butter. 2. Cook the Boston-style butt for 3 minutes on each side. Remove from the pot and reserve. 3. Sauté the leeks for 5 minutes or until fragrant. Add the remaining ingredients and stir to combine. 4. Secure the lid. Choose the Manual mode and set cooking time for 50 minutes on High pressure. 5. Once cooking is complete, use a natural pressure release for 20 minutes, then release any remaining pressure. Carefully remove the lid. 6. Serve immediately.

5-Ingredient Mexican Lasagna

Prep time: 15 minutes | Cook time: 15 minutes | Serves 4

- Nonstick cooking spray
- ½ (15 ounces) can light red kidney beans, rinsed and drained
- 4 (6-inch) gluten-free corn tortillas
- 1½ cups cooked shredded beef, pork, or chicken
- 1⅓ cups salsa
- 1⅓ cups shredded Mexican cheese blend

1. Spray a 6-inch springform pan with nonstick spray. Wrap the bottom in foil. 2. In a medium bowl, mash the beans with a fork. 3. Place 1 tortilla in the bottom of the pan. Add about ⅓ of the beans, ½ cup of meat, ⅓ cup of salsa, and ⅓ cup of cheese. Press down. Repeat for 2 more layers. Add the remaining tortilla and press down. Top with the remaining salsa and cheese. There are no beans or meat on the top layer. 4. Tear off a piece of foil big enough to cover the pan, and spray it with nonstick spray. Line the pan with the foil, sprayed-side down. 5. Pour 1 cup of water into the electric pressure cooker. 6. Place the pan on the wire rack and carefully lower it into the pot. Close and lock the lid of the pressure cooker. Set the valve to sealing. 7. Cook on high pressure for 15 minutes. 8. When the cooking is complete, hit Cancel. Allow the pressure to release naturally for 10 minutes, then quick release any remaining pressure. 9. Once the pin drops, unlock and remove the lid. 10. Using the handles of the wire rack, carefully remove the pan from the pot. Let the lasagna sit for 5 minutes. Carefully remove the ring. 11. Slice into quarters and serve.

Coconut Pork Muffins

Prep time: 5 minutes | Cook time: 9 minutes | Serves 2

- 1 egg, beaten
- 2 tablespoons coconut flour
- 1 teaspoon parsley
- ¼ teaspoon salt
- 1 tablespoon coconut cream
- 4 ounces (113 g) ground pork, fried
- 1 cup water

1. Whisk together the egg, coconut flour, parsley, salt, and coconut cream. Add the fried ground pork. Mix the the mixture until homogenous. 2. Pour the mixture into a muffin pan. 3. Pour the water in the Instant Pot and place in the trivet. 4. Lower the muffin pan on the trivet and close the Instant Pot lid. 5. Set the Manual mode and set cooking time for 4 minutes on High Pressure. 6. When timer beeps, perform a natural pressure release for 5 minutes, then release any remaining pressure. Open the lid. 7. Serve warm.

Cinnamon Beef with Blackberries

Prep time: 15 minutes | Cook time: 30 minutes | Serves 2

- 15 ounces (425 g) beef loin, chopped
- 1 tablespoon blackberries
- 1 cup water
- ½ teaspoon ground
- cinnamon
- ⅓ teaspoon ground black pepper
- ½ teaspoon salt
- 1 tablespoon butter

1. Pour water in the instant pot bowl. 2. Add chopped beef loin, blackberries, ground cinnamon, salt, and ground black pepper. Add butter. 3. Close the instant pot lid and set the Meat/Stew mode. 4. Cook the meat for 30 minutes. Then remove the meat from the instant pot. Blend the remaining blackberry mixture. 5. Pour it over the meat.

Cilantro Pork Meatballs

Prep time: 10 minutes | Cook time: 15 minutes | Serves 3

- 1 cup ground pork
- 1 ounce (28 g) fresh cilantro, chopped
- 1 garlic clove, diced
- ½ teaspoon salt
- 1 teaspoon ground coriander
- 2 tablespoons butter
- 1 tablespoon coconut cream

1. Blend the fresh cilantro until it is smooth and mix it up with ground pork, diced garlic, salt, and ground coriander. 2. Make the small meatballs and press them gently with the help of the hand palms. 3. Then melt the butter in the instant pot on Sauté mode and add the meatballs. 4. Cook them for 3 minutes from each side. Add coconut cream and close the lid. 5. Cook the meal on Sauté mode for 5 minutes.

Pork Meatballs with Thyme

Prep time: 15 minutes | Cook time: 16 minutes | Serves 8

- 2 cups ground pork
- 1 teaspoon dried thyme
- ½ teaspoon chili flakes
- ½ teaspoon garlic powder
- 1 tablespoon coconut oil
- ¼ teaspoon ground ginger
- 3 tablespoons almond flour
- ¼ cup water

1. In the mixing bowl, mix up ground pork, dried thyme, chili flakes, garlic powder, ground ginger, and almond flour. 2. Make the meatballs. 3. Melt the coconut oil in the instant pot on Sauté mode. 4. Arrange the meatballs in the instant pot in one layer and cook them for 3 minutes from each side. 5. Then add water and cook the meatballs for 10 minutes.

Bone Broth Brisket with Tomatoes

Prep time: 5 minutes | Cook time: 75 minutes | Serves 4 to 5

- 2 tablespoons coconut oil
- ½ teaspoon garlic salt
- ½ teaspoon crushed red pepper
- ½ teaspoon dried basil
- ½ teaspoon kosher salt
- ½ teaspoon freshly ground
- black pepper
- 1 (14-ounce / 397-g) can sugar-free or low-sugar diced tomatoes
- 1 cup grass-fed bone broth
- 1 pound (454 g) beef brisket, chopped

1. Set the Instant Pot to Sauté and melt the oil. Mix the garlic salt, red pepper, basil, kosher salt, black pepper, and tomatoes in a medium bowl. 2. Pour bone broth into the Instant Pot, then add the brisket, and top with the premixed sauce. Close the lid, set the pressure release to Sealing, and hit Cancel to stop the current program. Select Manual, set the Instant Pot to 75 minutes on High Pressure, and let cook. 3. Once cooked, carefully switch the pressure release to Venting. Open the Instant Pot, and serve. You can pour remaining sauce over brisket, if desired.

Pork Butt Roast

Prep time: 10 minutes | Cook time: 9 minutes | Serves 6 to 8

- 3 to 4 pounds pork butt roast
- 2 to 3 tablespoons of your
- favorite rub
- 2 cups water

1. Place pork in the inner pot of the Instant Pot. 2. Sprinkle in the rub all over the roast and add the water, being careful not to wash off the rub. 3. Secure the lid and set the vent to sealing. Cook for 9 minutes on the Manual setting. 4. Let the pressure release naturally.

Ginger Pork Meatballs

Prep time: 10 minutes | Cook time: 7 minutes | Serves 3

- 11 ounces (312 g) ground pork
- 1 teaspoon ginger paste
- 1 teaspoon lemon juice
- ¼ teaspoon chili flakes
- 1 tablespoon butter
- ¼ cup water

1. Combine the ground pork and ginger paste in a large bowl. 2. Mix in the lemon juice and chili flakes. 3. Put the butter in the Instant Pot and melt on Sauté mode. 4. Meanwhile, shape the mixture into small meatballs. 5. Place the meatballs in the Instant Pot and cook for 2 minutes on each side. 6. Add water and lock the lid. 7. Set the Manual mode and set cooking time for 3 minutes on High Pressure. 8. When timer beeps, perform a quick pressure release. Open the lid. 9. Serve warm.

Pork Chops Pomodoro

Prep time: 0 minutes | Cook time: 30 minutes | Serves 6

- 2 pounds boneless pork loin chops, each about 5⅓ ounces and ½ inch thick
- ¾ teaspoon fine sea salt
- ½ teaspoon freshly ground black pepper
- 2 tablespoons extra-virgin olive oil
- 2 garlic cloves, chopped
- ½ cup low-sodium chicken broth or vegetable broth
- ½ teaspoon Italian seasoning
- 1 tablespoon capers, drained
- 2 cups cherry tomatoes
- 2 tablespoons chopped fresh basil or flat-leaf parsley
- Spiralized zucchini noodles, cooked cauliflower "rice," or cooked whole-grain pasta for serving
- Lemon wedges for serving

1. Pat the pork chops dry with paper towels, then season them all over with the salt and pepper. 2. Select the Sauté setting on the Instant Pot and heat 1 tablespoon of the oil for 2 minutes. Swirl the oil to coat the bottom of the pot. Using tongs, add half of the pork chops in a single layer and sear for about 3 minutes, until lightly browned on the first side. Flip the chops and sear for about 3 minutes more, until lightly browned on the second side. Transfer the chops to a plate. Repeat with the remaining 1 tablespoon oil and pork chops. 3. Add the garlic to the pot and sauté for about 1 minute, until bubbling but not browned. Stir in the broth, Italian seasoning, and capers, using a wooden spoon to nudge any browned bits from the bottom of the pot and working quickly so not too much liquid evaporates. Using the tongs, transfer the pork chops to the pot. Add the tomatoes in an even layer on top of the chops. 4. Secure the lid and set the Pressure Release to Sealing. Press the Cancel button to reset the cooking program, then select the Pressure Cook or Manual setting and set the cooking time for 10 minutes at high pressure. (The pot will take about 5 minutes to come up to pressure before the cooking program begins.) 5. When the cooking program ends, let the pressure release naturally for at least 10 minutes, then move the Pressure Release to Venting to release any remaining steam. Open the pot and, using the tongs, transfer the pork chops to a serving dish. 6. Spoon the tomatoes and some of the cooking liquid on top of the pork chops. Sprinkle with the basil and serve right away, with zucchini noodles and lemon wedges on the side.

French Dip Chuck Roast

Prep time: 5 minutes | Cook time: 70 minutes | Serves 6

- 2 tablespoons avocado oil
- 2 to 2½ pounds (907 g to 1.1 kg) chuck roast
- 2 cups beef broth
- 2 tablespoons dried rosemary
- 3 cloves garlic, minced
- 1 teaspoon salt
- ½ teaspoon black pepper
- ¼ teaspoon dried thyme
- ½ onion, quartered
- 2 bay leaves

1. Turn the pot to Sauté mode. Once hot, add the avocado oil. Add the roast and sear it on each side. This should take about 5 minutes. Press Cancel. 2. Add the broth to the pot. 3. Add the rosemary, garlic, salt, pepper, and thyme to the top of the roast. Add the onion and bay leaves. 4. Close the lid and seal the vent. Cook on High Pressure for 50 minutes. Let the steam naturally release for 15 minutes before Manually releasing. 5. Remove the roast to a plate and shred with two forks. Strain the jus though a fine-mesh sieve. Serve the roast au jus for dipping.

Albóndigas Sinaloenses

Prep time: 15 minutes | Cook time: 10 minutes | Serves 6

- 1 pound (454 g) ground pork
- ½ pound (227 g) Italian sausage, crumbled
- 2 tablespoons yellow onion, finely chopped
- ½ teaspoon dried oregano
- 1 sprig fresh mint, finely minced
- ½ teaspoon ground cumin
- 2 garlic cloves, finely minced
- ¼ teaspoon fresh ginger, grated
- Seasoned salt and ground black pepper, to taste
- 1 tablespoon olive oil
- ½ cup yellow onions, finely chopped
- 2 chipotle chilies in adobo
- 2 tomatoes, puréed
- 2 tablespoons tomato passata
- 1 cup chicken broth

1. In a mixing bowl, combine the pork, sausage, 2 tablespoons of yellow onion, oregano, mint, cumin, garlic, ginger, salt, and black pepper. 2. Roll the mixture into meatballs and reserve. 3. Press the Sauté button to heat up the Instant Pot. Heat the olive oil and cook the meatballs for 4 minutes, stirring continuously. 4. Stir in ½ cup of yellow onions, chilies in adobo, tomatoes passata, and broth. Add reserved meatballs. 5. Secure the lid. Choose the Manual mode and set cooking time for 6 minutes at High pressure. 6. Once cooking is complete, use a quick pressure release. Carefully remove the lid. 7. Serve immediately.

Creamed Beef Brisket

Prep time: 6 minutes | Cook time: 20 minutes | Serves 3

- ½ teaspoon salt
- 14 ounces (397 g) beef brisket, cut into the strips
- ½ cup water
- ½ cup heavy cream
- ½ teaspoon ground black pepper
- 1 tablespoon avocado oil

1. Preheat the instant pot on the Sauté mode. 2. When it is displayed "Hot", pour avocado oil inside and heat it up. 3. Add the meat. 4. Sprinkle the meat with the ground black pepper and salt. 5. Sauté it for 5 minutes. Stir it once per cooking time. 6. Add water and heavy cream. 7. Seal the lid and set the Manual mode. 8. Put the timer on 15 minutes (High Pressure). 9. Make a quick pressure release.

Greek Lamb Leg

Prep time: 10 minutes | Cook time: 50 minutes | Serves 4

- 1 pound (454 g) lamb leg
- ½ teaspoon dried thyme
- 1 teaspoon paprika powder
- ¼ teaspoon cumin seeds
- 1 tablespoon softened butter
- 2 garlic cloves
- ¼ cup water

1. Rub the lamb leg with dried thyme, paprika powder, and cumin seeds on a clean work surface. 2. Brush the leg with softened butter and transfer to the Instant Pot. Add garlic cloves and water. 3. Close the lid. Select Manual mode and set cooking time for 50 minutes on High Pressure. 4. When timer beeps, use a quick pressure release. Open the lid. 5. Serve warm.

Pork Taco Casserole

Prep time: 15 minutes | Cook time: 30 minutes | Serves 6

- ½ cup water
- 2 eggs
- 3 ounces (85 g) Cottage cheese, at room temperature
- ¼ cup heavy cream
- 1 teaspoon taco seasoning
- 6 ounces (170 g) Cotija cheese, crumbled
- ¾ pound (340 g) ground pork
- ½ cup tomatoes, puréed
- 1 tablespoon taco seasoning
- 3 ounces (85 g) chopped green chilies
- 6 ounces (170 g) Queso Manchego cheese, shredded

1. Add the water in the Instant Pot and place in the trivet. 2. In a mixing bowl, combine the eggs, Cottage cheese, heavy cream, and taco seasoning. 3. Lightly grease a casserole dish. Spread the Cotija cheese over the bottom. Stir in the egg mixture. 4. Lower the casserole dish onto the trivet. 5. Secure the lid. Choose Manual mode and set cooking time for 20 minutes on High Pressure. 6. Once cooking is complete, use a quick pressure release. Carefully remove the lid. 7. In the meantime, heat a skillet over a medium-high heat. Brown the ground pork, crumbling with a fork. 8. Add the tomato purée, taco seasoning, and green chilies. Spread the mixture over the prepared cheese crust. 9. Top with shredded Queso Manchego. 10. Secure the lid. Choose Manual mode and set cooking time for 10 minutes on High Pressure. 11. Once cooking is complete, use a quick pressure release. Carefully remove the lid. Serve immediately.

Garlic Butter Italian Sausages

Prep time: 15 minutes | Cook time: 20 minutes | Serves 4

- 1 teaspoon garlic powder
- 1 cup water
- 1 teaspoon butter
- 12 ounces (340 g) Italian sausages, chopped
- ½ teaspoon Italian seasoning

1. Sprinkle the chopped Italian sausages with Italian seasoning and garlic powder and place in the instant pot. 2. Add butter and cook the sausages on Sauté mode for 10 minutes. Stir them from time to time with the help of the spatula. 3. Then add water and close the lid. 4. Cook the sausages on Manual mode (High Pressure) for 10 minutes. 5. Allow the natural pressure release for 10 minutes more.

Garlic Beef Stroganoff

Prep time: 20 minutes | Cook time: 25 minutes | Serves 6

- 2 tablespoons canola oil
- 1½ pounds boneless round steak, cut into thin strips, trimmed of fat
- 2 teaspoons sodium-free beef bouillon powder
- 1 cup mushroom juice, with water added to make a full cup
- 2 (4½-ounce) jars sliced mushrooms, drained with
- juice reserved
- 10¾-ounce can 98% fat-free, lower-sodium cream of mushroom soup
- 1 large onion, chopped
- 3 garlic cloves, minced
- 1 tablespoon Worcestershire sauce
- 6-ounces fat-free cream cheese, cubed and softened

1. Press the Sauté button and put the oil into the Instant Pot inner pot. 2. Once the oil is heated, sauté the beef until it is lightly browned, about 2 minutes on each side. Set the beef aside for a moment. Press Cancel and wipe out the Instant Pot with some paper towel. 3. Press Sauté again and dissolve the bouillon in the mushroom juice and water in inner pot of the Instant Pot. Once dissolved, press Cancel. 4. Add the mushrooms, soup, onion, garlic, and Worcestershire sauce and stir. Add the beef back to the pot. 5. Secure the lid and make sure the vent is set to sealing. Press Manual and set for 15 minutes. 6. When cook time is up, let the pressure release naturally for 15 minutes, then perform a quick release. 7. Press Cancel and remove the lid. Press Sauté. Stir in cream cheese until smooth. 8. Serve over noodles.

Chile Verde Pulled Pork with Tomatillos

Prep time: 15 minutes | Cook time: 1 hour 3 minutes | Serves 6

- 2 pounds (907 g) pork shoulder, cut into 6 equal-sized pieces
- 1 teaspoon sea salt
- ½ teaspoon ground black pepper
- 2 jalapeño peppers, deseeded and stemmed
- 1 pound (454 g) tomatillos, husks removed and quartered
- 3 garlic cloves
- 1 tablespoon lime juice
- 3 tablespoons fresh cilantro, chopped
- 1 medium white onion, chopped
- 1 teaspoon ground cumin
- ½ teaspoon dried oregano
- 1⅔ cups chicken broth
- 1½ tablespoons olive oil

1. Season the pork pieces with the salt and pepper. Gently rub the seasonings into the pork cuts. Set aside. 2. Combine the jalapeños, tomatillos, garlic cloves, lime juice, cilantro, onions, cumin, oregano, and chicken broth in the blender. Pulse until well combined. Set aside. 3. Select Sauté mode and add the olive oil to the pot. Once the oil is hot, add the pork cuts and sear for 4 minutes per side or until browned. 4. Pour the jalapeño sauce over the pork and lightly stir to coat well. 5. Lock the lid. Select Manual mode and set cooking time for 55 minutes on High Pressure. 6. When cooking is complete, allow the pressure to release naturally for 10 minutes and then release the remaining pressure. 7. Open the lid. Transfer the pork pieces to a cutting board and use two forks to shred the pork. 8. Transfer the shredded pork back to the pot and stir to combine the pork with the sauce. Transfer to a serving platter. Serve warm.

Lamb Chops with Shaved Zucchini Salad

Prep time: 20 minutes | Cook time: 40 minutes | Serves 4

- 4 (8- to 12-ounce/ 227- to 340-g) lamb shoulder chops (blade or round bone), about ¾ inch thick, trimmed
- ¾ teaspoon table salt, divided
- ¾ teaspoon pepper, divided
- 2 tablespoons extra-virgin olive oil, divided
- 1 onion, chopped
- 5 garlic cloves, minced
- ½ cup chicken broth
- 1 bay leaf
- 4 zucchini (6 ounces / 170 g each), sliced lengthwise into ribbons
- 1 teaspoon grated lemon zest plus 1 tablespoon juice
- 2 ounces (57 g) goat cheese, crumbled (½ cup)
- ¼ cup chopped fresh mint
- 2 tablespoons raisins

1. Pat lamb chops dry with paper towels and sprinkle with ½

teaspoon salt and ½ teaspoon pepper. Using highest sauté function, heat 1½ teaspoons oil in Instant Pot for 5 minutes (or until just smoking). Brown half of chops on both sides, 6 to 8 minutes; transfer to plate. Repeat with 1½ teaspoons oil and remaining chops; transfer to plate. 2. Add onion to fat left in pot and cook, using highest sauté function, until softened, about 5 minutes. Stir in garlic and cook until fragrant, about 30 seconds. Stir in broth and bay leaf, scraping up any browned bits. Return chops to pot along with any accumulated juices (chops will overlap). Lock lid in place and close pressure release valve. Select high pressure cook function and cook for 20 minutes. 3. Turn off Instant Pot and let pressure release naturally for 15 minutes. Quick-release any remaining pressure, then carefully remove lid, allowing steam to escape away from you. Transfer chops to serving dish. Gently toss zucchini with lemon zest and juice, remaining 1 tablespoon oil, remaining ¼ teaspoon salt, and remaining ¼ teaspoon pepper in bowl. Arrange zucchini on serving dish with lamb, and sprinkle with goat cheese, mint, and raisins. Serve.

Spicy Beef Stew with Butternut Squash

Prep time: 15 minutes | Cook time: 30 minutes | Serves 8

- 1½ tablespoons smoked paprika
- 2 teaspoons ground cinnamon
- 1½ teaspoons kosher salt
- 1 teaspoon ground ginger
- 1 teaspoon red pepper flakes
- ½ teaspoon freshly ground black pepper
- 2 pounds beef shoulder roast, cut into 1-inch cubes
- 2 tablespoons avocado oil, divided
- 1 cup low-sodium beef or vegetable broth
- 1 medium red onion, cut into wedges
- 8 garlic cloves, minced
- 1 (28-ounce) carton or can no-salt-added diced tomatoes
- 2 pounds butternut squash, peeled and cut into 1-inch pieces
- Chopped fresh cilantro or parsley, for serving

1. In a zip-top bag or medium bowl, combine the paprika, cinnamon, salt, ginger, red pepper, and black pepper. Add the beef and toss to coat. 2. Set the electric pressure cooker to the Sauté setting. When the pot is hot, pour in 1 tablespoon of avocado oil. 3. Add half of the beef to the pot and cook, stirring occasionally, for 3 to 5 minutes or until the beef is no longer pink. Transfer it to a plate, then add the remaining 1 tablespoon of avocado oil and brown the remaining beef. Transfer to the plate. Hit Cancel. 4. Stir in the broth and scrape up any brown bits from the bottom of the pot. Return the beef to the pot and add the onion, garlic, tomatoes and their juices, and squash. Stir well. 5. Close and lock lid of pressure cooker. Set the valve to sealing. 6. Cook on high pressure for 30 minutes. 7. When cooking is complete, hit Cancel. Allow the pressure to release naturally for 10 minutes, then quick release any remaining pressure. 8. Unlock and remove lid. 9. Spoon into serving bowls, sprinkle with cilantro or parsley, and serve.

Beef Shawarma and Veggie Salad Bowls

Prep time: 10 minutes | Cook time: 19 minutes | Serves 4

- 2 teaspoons olive oil
- 1½ pounds (680 g) beef flank steak, thinly sliced
- Sea salt and freshly ground black pepper, to taste
- 1 teaspoon cayenne pepper
- ½ teaspoon ground bay leaf
- ½ teaspoon ground allspice
- ½ teaspoon cumin, divided
- ½ cup Greek yogurt
- 2 tablespoons sesame oil
- 1 tablespoon fresh lime juice
- 2 English cucumbers, chopped
- 1 cup cherry tomatoes, halved
- 1 red onion, thinly sliced
- ½ head romaine lettuce, chopped

1. Press the Sauté button to heat up the Instant Pot. Then, heat the olive oil and cook the beef for about 4 minutes. 2. Add all seasonings, 1½ cups of water, and secure the lid. 3. Choose Manual mode. Set the cook time for 15 minutes on High Pressure. 4. Once cooking is complete, use a natural pressure release. Carefully remove the lid. 5. Allow the beef to cool completely. 6. To make the dressing, whisk Greek yogurt, sesame oil, and lime juice in a mixing bowl. 7. Then, divide cucumbers, tomatoes, red onion, and romaine lettuce among four serving bowls. Dress the salad and top with the reserved beef flank steak. Serve warm.

Osso Buco with Gremolata

Prep time: 35 minutes | Cook time: 1 hour 2 minutes | Serves 6

- 4 bone-in beef shanks
- Sea salt, to taste
- 2 tablespoons avocado oil
- 1 small turnip, diced
- 1 medium onion, diced
- 1 medium stalk celery, diced
- 4 cloves garlic, smashed
- 1 tablespoon unsweetened tomato purée
- ½ cup dry white wine
- 1 cup chicken broth
- 1 sprig fresh rosemary
- 2 sprigs fresh thyme
- 3 Roma tomatoes, diced
- For the Gremolata:
- ½ cup loosely packed parsley leaves
- 1 clove garlic, crushed
- Grated zest of 2 lemons

1. On a clean work surface, season the shanks all over with salt. 2. Set the Instant Pot to Sauté and add the oil. When the oil shimmers, add 2 shanks and sear for 4 minutes per side. Remove the shanks to a bowl and repeat with the remaining shanks. Set aside. 3. Add the turnip, onion, and celery to the pot and cook for 5 minutes or until softened. 4. Add the garlic and unsweetened tomato purée and cook 1 minute more, stirring frequently. 5. Deglaze the pot with the wine, scraping the bottom with a wooden spoon to loosen any browned bits. Bring to a boil. 6. Add the broth, rosemary, thyme, and shanks, then add the tomatoes on top of the shanks. 7. Secure the lid. Press the Manual button and set cooking time for 40 minutes on High Pressure. 8. Meanwhile, for the gremolata: In a small food processor, combine the parsley, garlic, and lemon zest and pulse until the parsley is finely chopped. Refrigerate until ready to use. 9. When timer beeps, allow the pressure to release naturally for 20 minutes, then release any remaining pressure. Open the lid. 10. To serve, transfer the shanks to large, shallow serving bowl. Ladle the braising sauce over the top and sprinkle with the gremolata.

Lamb Sirloin Masala

Prep time: 10 minutes | Cook time: 25 minutes | Serves 3

- 12 ounces (340 g) lamb sirloin, sliced
- 1 tablespoon garam masala
- 1 tablespoon lemon juice
- 1 tablespoon olive oil
- ¼ cup coconut cream

1. Sprinkle the sliced lamb sirloin with garam masala, lemon juice, olive oil, and coconut cream in a large bowl. Toss to mix well. 2. Transfer the mixture in the Instant Pot. Cook on Sauté mode for 25 minutes. Flip the lamb for every 5 minutes. 3. When cooking is complete, allow to cool for 10 minutes, then serve warm.

Pork Chops in Creamy Mushroom Gravy

Prep time: 5 minutes | Cook time: 15 minutes | Serves 4

- 4 (5-ounce / 142-g) pork chops
- 1 teaspoon salt
- ½ teaspoon pepper
- 2 tablespoons avocado oil
- 1 cup chopped button mushrooms
- ½ medium onion, sliced
- 1 clove garlic, minced
- 1 cup chicken broth
- ¼ cup heavy cream
- 4 tablespoons butter
- ¼ teaspoon xanthan gum
- 1 tablespoon chopped fresh parsley

1. Sprinkle pork chops with salt and pepper. Place avocado oil and mushrooms in Instant Pot and press the Sauté button. Sauté 3 to 5 minutes until mushrooms begin to soften. Add onions and pork chops. Sauté additional 3 minutes until pork chops reach a golden brown. 2. Add garlic and broth to Instant Pot. Click lid closed. Press the Manual button and adjust time for 15 minutes. When timer beeps, allow a 10-minute natural release. Quick-release the remaining pressure. 3. Remove lid and place pork chops on plate. Press the Sauté button and add heavy cream, butter, and xanthan gum. Reduce for 5 to 10 minutes or until sauce begins to thicken. Add pork chops back into pot. Serve warm topped with mushroom sauce and parsley.

Nutmeg Pork Tenderloin

Prep time: 10 minutes | Cook time: 20 minutes | Serves 6

- 1 pound (454 g) pork tenderloin, sliced
- ½ cup apple cider vinegar
- 1 teaspoon ground nutmeg
- 1 tablespoon butter
- ½ cup water

1. Mix up the sliced pork tenderloin with ground nutmeg and put it in the instant pot. 2. Add water, butter, and apple cider vinegar. 3. Close and seal the lid and cook the meat on Manual mode (High Pressure) for 20 minutes. 4. When the time is finished, make a quick pressure release and open the lid.

Chapter 4 Fish and Seafood

Cod Fillets with Cherry Tomatoes

Prep time: 2 minutes | Cook time: 15 minutes | Serves 4

- 2 tablespoons butter
- ¼ cup diced onion
- 1 clove garlic, minced
- 1 cup cherry tomatoes, halved
- ¼ cup chicken broth
- ¼ teaspoon dried thyme
- ¼ teaspoon salt
- ⅛ teaspoon pepper
- 4 (4-ounce / 113-g) cod fillets
- 1 cup water
- ¼ cup fresh chopped Italian parsley

1. Set your Instant Pot to Sauté. Add and melt the butter. Once hot, add the onions and cook until softened. Add the garlic and cook for another 30 seconds. 2. Add the tomatoes, chicken broth, thyme, salt, and pepper. Continue to cook for 5 to 7 minutes, or until the tomatoes start to soften. 3. Pour the sauce into a glass bowl. Add the fish fillets. Cover with foil. 4. Pour the water into the Instant Pot and insert a trivet. Place the bowl on top. 5. Lock the lid. Select the Manual mode and set the cooking time for 3 minutes at Low Pressure. 6. Once cooking is complete, do a quick pressure release. Carefully open the lid. 7. Sprinkle with the fresh parsley and serve.

Garlic Tuna Casserole

Prep time: 7 minutes | Cook time: 9 minutes | Serves 4

- 1 cup grated Parmesan or shredded Cheddar cheese, plus more for topping
- 1 (8-ounce / 227-g) package cream cheese (1 cup), softened
- ½ cup chicken broth
- 1 tablespoon unsalted butter
- ½ small head cauliflower, cut into 1-inch pieces
- 1 cup diced onions
- 2 cloves garlic, minced, or
- more to taste
- 2 (4-ounce / 113-g) cans chunk tuna packed in water, drained
- 1½ cups cold water
- For Garnish:
- Chopped fresh flat-leaf parsley
- Sliced green onions
- Cherry tomatoes, halved
- Ground black pepper

1. In a blender, add the Parmesan cheese, cream cheese, and broth and blitz until smooth. Set aside. 2. Set your Instant Pot to Sauté. Add and melt the butter. Add the cauliflower and onions and sauté for 4 minutes, or until the onions are softened. Fold in the garlic and sauté for an additional 1 minute. 3. Place the cheese sauce and

tuna in a large bowl. Mix in the veggies and stir well. Transfer the mixture to a casserole dish. 4. Place a trivet in the bottom of your Instant Pot and add the cold water. Use a foil sling, lower the casserole dish onto the trivet. Tuck in the sides of the sling. 5. Lock the lid. Select the Manual mode and set the cooking time for 5 minutes for al dente cauliflower or 8 minutes for softer cauliflower at High Pressure. 6. Once cooking is complete, do a quick pressure release. Carefully open the lid. 7. Serve topped with the cheese and garnished with the parsley, green onions, cherry tomatoes, and freshly ground pepper.

Cod with Warm Beet and Arugula Salad

Prep time: 15 minutes | Cook time: 8 minutes | Serves 4

- ¼ cup extra-virgin olive oil, divided, plus extra for drizzling
- 1 shallot, sliced thin
- 2 garlic cloves, minced
- 1½ pounds (680 g) small beets, scrubbed, trimmed, and cut into ½-inch wedges
- ½ cup chicken or vegetable
- broth
- 1 tablespoon dukkah, plus extra for sprinkling
- ¼ teaspoon table salt
- 4 (6-ounce / 170-g) skinless cod fillets, 1½ inches thick
- 1 tablespoon lemon juice
- 2 ounces (57 g) baby arugula

1. Using highest sauté function, heat 1 tablespoon oil in Instant Pot until shimmering. Add shallot and cook until softened, about 2 minutes. Stir in garlic and cook until fragrant, about 30 seconds. Stir in beets and broth. Lock lid in place and close pressure release valve. Select high pressure cook function and cook for 3 minutes. Turn off Instant Pot and quick-release pressure. Carefully remove lid, allowing steam to escape away from you. 2. Fold sheet of aluminum foil into 16 by 6-inch sling. Combine 2 tablespoons oil, dukkah, and salt in bowl, then brush cod with oil mixture. Arrange cod skinned side down in center of sling. Using sling, lower cod into Instant Pot; allow narrow edges of sling to rest along sides of insert. Lock lid in place and close pressure release valve. Select high pressure cook function and cook for 2 minutes. 3. Turn off Instant Pot and quick-release pressure. Carefully remove lid, allowing steam to escape away from you. Using sling, transfer cod to large plate. Tent with foil and let rest while finishing beet salad. 4. Combine lemon juice and remaining 1 tablespoon oil in large bowl. Using slotted spoon, transfer beets to bowl with oil mixture. Add arugula and gently toss to combine. Season with salt and pepper to taste. 5 Serve cod with salad, sprinkling individual portions with extra dukkah and drizzling with extra oil.

Tuna Spinach Cakes

Prep time: 15 minutes | Cook time: 8 minutes | Serves 4

- 10 ounces (283 g) tuna, shredded
- 1 cup spinach
- 1 egg, beaten
- 1 teaspoon ground coriander
- 2 tablespoon coconut flakes
- 1 tablespoon avocado oil

1. Blend the spinach in the blender until smooth. 2. Then transfer it in the mixing bowl and add tuna, egg, and ground coriander. 3. Add coconut flakes and stir the mass with the help of the spoon. 4. Heat up avocado oil in the instant pot on Sauté mode for 2 minutes. 5. Then make the medium size cakes from the tuna mixture and place them in the hot oil. 6. Cook the tuna cakes on Sauté mode for 3 minutes. Then flip the on another side and cook for 3 minutes more or until they are light brown.

Rosemary Catfish

Prep time: 10 minutes | Cook time: 20 minutes | Serves 4

- 16 ounces (454 g) catfish fillet
- 1 tablespoon dried rosemary
- 1 teaspoon garlic powder
- 1 tablespoon avocado oil
- 1 teaspoon salt
- 1 cup water, for cooking

1. Cut the catfish fillet into 4 steaks. 2. Then sprinkle them with dried rosemary, garlic powder, avocado oil, and salt. 3. Place the fish steak in the baking mold in one layer. 4. After this, pour water and insert the steamer rack in the instant pot. 5. Put the baking mold with fish on the rack. Close and seal the lid. 6. Cook the meal on Manual (High Pressure) for 20 minutes. Make a quick pressure release.

Coconut Shrimp Curry

Prep time: 10 minutes | Cook time: 4 minutes | Serves 5

- 15 ounces (425 g) shrimp, peeled
- 1 teaspoon chili powder
- 1 teaspoon garam masala
- 1 cup coconut milk
- 1 teaspoon olive oil
- ½ teaspoon minced garlic

1. Heat up the instant pot on Sauté mode for 2 minutes. 2. Then add olive oil. Cook the ingredients for 1 minute. 3. Add shrimp and sprinkle them with chili powder, garam masala, minced garlic, and coconut milk. 4. Carefully stir the ingredients and close the lid. 5. Cook the shrimp curry on Manual mode for 1 minute. Make a quick pressure release.

Salmon with Dill Butter

Prep time: 7 minutes | Cook time: 8 minutes | Serves 2

- 1 teaspoon salt
- 2 tablespoons chopped fresh dill
- 10 ounces (283 g) salmon
- fillet
- ¼ cup butter
- ½ cup water

1. Put butter and salt in the baking pan. 2. Add salmon fillet and dill. Cover the pan with foil. 3. Pour water in the instant pot and insert the baking pan with fish inside. 4. Set the Steam mode and cook the salmon for 8 minutes. 5. Unwrap the cooked salmon and serve!

Cod Fillet with Olives

Prep time: 15 minutes | Cook time: 10 minutes | Serves 2

- 8 ounces (227 g) cod fillet
- ¼ cup sliced olives
- 1 teaspoon olive oil
- ¼ teaspoon salt
- 1 cup water, for cooking

1. Pour water and insert the steamer rack in the instant pot. 2. Then cut the cod fillet into 2 servings and sprinkle with salt and olive oil. 3. Then place the fish on the foil and top with the sliced olives. Wrap the fish and transfer it in the steamer rack. 4. Close and seal the lid. Cook the fish on Manual mode (High Pressure) for 10 minutes. 5. Allow the natural pressure release for 5 minutes.

Haddock and Veggie Foil Packets

Prep time: 5 minutes | Cook time: 10 minutes | Serves 4

- 1½ cups water
- 1 lemon, sliced
- 2 bell peppers, sliced
- 1 brown onion, sliced into rings
- 4 sprigs parsley
- 2 sprigs thyme
- 2 sprigs rosemary
- 4 haddock fillets
- Sea salt, to taste
- ⅓ teaspoon ground black pepper, or more to taste
- 2 tablespoons extra-virgin olive oil

1. Pour the water and lemon into your Instant Pot and insert a steamer basket. 2. Assemble the packets with large sheets of heavy-duty foil. 3. Place the peppers, onion rings, parsley, thyme, and rosemary in the center of each foil. Place the fish fillets on top of the veggies. 4. Sprinkle with the salt and black pepper and drizzle the olive oil over the fillets. Place the packets in the steamer basket. 5. Lock the lid. Select the Manual mode and set the cooking time for 10 minutes at Low Pressure. 6. When the timer beeps, perform a quick pressure release. Carefully remove the lid. 7. Serve warm.

Tuna Fillets with Lemon Butter

Prep time: 5 minutes | Cook time: 3 minutes | Serves 4

- 1 cup water
- ⅓ cup lemon juice
- 2 sprigs fresh thyme
- 2 sprigs fresh parsley
- 2 sprigs fresh rosemary
- 1 pound (454 g) tuna fillets
- 4 cloves garlic, pressed
- Sea salt, to taste
- ¼ teaspoon black pepper, or more to taste
- 2 tablespoons butter, melted
- 1 lemon, sliced

1. Pour the water into your Instant Pot. Add the lemon juice, thyme, parsley, and rosemary and insert a steamer basket. 2. Put the tuna fillets in the basket. Top with the garlic and season with the salt and black pepper. 3. Drizzle the melted butter over the fish fillets and place the lemon slices on top. 4. Lock the lid. Select the Manual mode and set the cooking time for 3 minutes at Low Pressure. 5. When the timer beeps, perform a quick pressure release. Carefully remove the lid. Serve immediately.

Braised Striped Bass with Zucchini and Tomatoes

Prep time: 20 minutes | Cook time: 16 minutes | Serves 4

- 2 tablespoons extra-virgin olive oil, divided, plus extra for drizzling
- 3 zucchini (8 ounces / 227 g each), halved lengthwise and sliced ¼ inch thick
- 1 onion, chopped
- ¾ teaspoon table salt, divided
- 3 garlic cloves, minced
- 1 teaspoon minced fresh oregano or ¼ teaspoon dried
- ¼ teaspoon red pepper flakes
- 1 (28-ounce / 794-g) can whole peeled tomatoes, drained with juice reserved, halved
- 1½ pounds (680 g) skinless striped bass, 1½ inches thick, cut into 2-inch pieces
- ¼ teaspoon pepper
- 2 tablespoons chopped pitted kalamata olives
- 2 tablespoons shredded fresh mint

1. Using highest sauté function, heat 1 tablespoon oil in Instant Pot for 5 minutes (or until just smoking). Add zucchini and cook until tender, about 5 minutes; transfer to bowl and set aside. 2. Add remaining 1 tablespoon oil, onion, and ¼ teaspoon salt to now-empty pot and cook, using highest sauté function, until onion is softened, about 5 minutes. Stir in garlic, oregano, and pepper flakes and cook until fragrant, about 30 seconds. Stir in tomatoes and reserved juice. 3. Sprinkle bass with remaining ½ teaspoon salt and pepper. Nestle bass into tomato mixture and spoon some of cooking liquid on top of pieces. Lock lid in place and close pressure release valve. Select high pressure cook function and set cook time for 0 minutes. Once Instant Pot has reached pressure, immediately turn off pot and quick-release pressure. Carefully remove lid, allowing steam to escape away from you. 4. Transfer bass to plate, tent with aluminum foil, and let rest while finishing vegetables. Stir zucchini

into pot and let sit until heated through, about 5 minutes. Stir in olives and season with salt and pepper to taste. Serve bass with vegetables, sprinkling individual portions with mint and drizzling with extra oil.

Fish Bake with Veggies

Prep time: 10 minutes | Cook time: 5 minutes | Serves 4

- 1½ cups water
- Cooking spray
- 2 ripe tomatoes, sliced
- 2 cloves garlic, minced
- 1 teaspoon dried oregano
- 1 teaspoon dried basil
- ½ teaspoon dried rosemary
- 1 red onion, sliced
- 1 head cauliflower, cut into
- florets
- 1 pound (454 g) tilapia fillets, sliced
- Sea salt, to taste
- 1 tablespoon olive oil
- 1 cup crumbled feta cheese
- ⅓ cup Kalamata olives, pitted and halved

1. Pour the water into your Instant Pot and insert a trivet. 2. Spritz a casserole dish with cooking spray. Add the tomato slices to the dish. Scatter the top with the garlic, oregano, basil, and rosemary. 3. Mix in the onion and cauliflower. Arrange the fish fillets on top. Sprinkle with the salt and drizzle with the olive oil. 4. Place the feta cheese and Kalamata olives on top. Lower the dish onto the trivet. 5. Lock the lid. Select the Manual mode and set the cooking time for 5 minutes at High Pressure. 6. When the timer beeps, perform a quick pressure release. Carefully remove the lid. 7. Allow to cool for 5 minutes before serving.

Snapper in Spicy Tomato Sauce

Prep time: 5 minutes | Cook time: 5 minutes | Serves 6

- 2 teaspoons coconut oil, melted
- 1 teaspoon celery seeds
- ½ teaspoon fresh grated ginger
- ½ teaspoon cumin seeds
- 1 yellow onion, chopped
- 2 cloves garlic, minced
- 1½ pounds (680 g) snapper fillets
- ¾ cup vegetable broth
- 1 (4-ounce / 113-g) can fire-roasted diced tomatoes
- 1 bell pepper, sliced
- 1 jalapeño pepper, minced
- Sea salt and ground black pepper, to taste
- ¼ teaspoon chili flakes
- ½ teaspoon turmeric powder

1. Set the Instant Pot to Sauté. Add and heat the sesame oil until hot. Sauté the celery seeds, fresh ginger, and cumin seeds. 2. Add the onion and continue to sauté until softened and fragrant. 3. Mix in the minced garlic and continue to cook for 30 seconds. Add the remaining ingredients and stir well. 4. Lock the lid. Select the Manual mode and set the cooking time for 3 minutes at Low Pressure. 5. When the timer beeps, perform a quick pressure release. Carefully remove the lid. 6. Serve warm

Turmeric Salmon

Prep time: 10 minutes | Cook time: 4 minutes | Serves 3

- 1 pound (454 g) salmon fillet
- 1 teaspoon ground black pepper
- ½ teaspoon salt
- 1 teaspoon ground turmeric
- 1 teaspoon lemon juice
- 1 cup water

1. In the shallow bowl, mix up salt, ground black pepper, and ground turmeric. 2. Sprinkle the salmon fillet with lemon juice and rub with the spice mixture. 3. Then pour water in the instant pot and insert the steamer rack. 4. Wrap the salmon fillet in the foil and place it on the rack. 5. Close and seal the lid. 6. Cook the fish on Manual mode (High Pressure) for 4 minutes. 7. Make a quick pressure release and cut the fish on servings.

Almond Milk Curried Fish

Prep time: 10 minutes | Cook time: 3 minutes | Serves 2

- 8 ounces (227 g) cod fillet, chopped
- 1 teaspoon curry paste
- 1 cup organic almond milk

1. Mix up curry paste and almond milk and pour the liquid in the instant pot. 2. Add chopped cod fillet and close the lid. 3. Cook the fish curry on Manual mode (High Pressure) for 3 minutes. 4. Then make the quick pressure release for 5 minutes.

Shrimp and Asparagus Risotto

Prep time: 15 minutes | Cook time: 20 minutes | Serves 4

- ¼ cup extra-virgin olive oil, divided
- 8 ounces (227 g) asparagus, trimmed and cut on bias into 1-inch lengths
- ½ onion, chopped fine
- ¼ teaspoon table salt
- 1½ cups Arborio rice
- 3 garlic cloves, minced
- ½ cup dry white wine
- 3 cups chicken or vegetable broth, plus extra as needed
- 1 pound (454 g) large shrimp (26 to 30 per pound), peeled and deveined
- 2 ounces (57 g) Parmesan cheese, grated (1 cup)
- 1 tablespoon lemon juice
- 1 tablespoon minced fresh chives

1. Using highest sauté function, heat 1 tablespoon oil in Instant Pot until shimmering. Add asparagus, partially cover, and cook until just crisp-tender, about 4 minutes. Using slotted spoon, transfer asparagus to bowl; set aside. 2. Add onion, 2 tablespoons oil, and salt to now-empty pot and cook, using highest sauté function, until onion is softened, about 5 minutes. Stir in rice and garlic and cook until grains are translucent around edges, about 3 minutes. Stir in wine and cook until nearly evaporated, about 1 minute. 3. Stir in broth, scraping up any rice that sticks to bottom of pot. Lock lid in place and close pressure release valve. Select high pressure cook function and cook for 7 minutes. 4. Turn off Instant Pot and quick-release pressure. Carefully remove lid, allowing steam to escape away from you. Stir shrimp and asparagus into risotto, cover, and let sit until shrimp are opaque throughout, 5 to 7 minutes. Add Parmesan and remaining 1 tablespoon oil, and stir vigorously until risotto becomes creamy. Adjust consistency with extra hot broth as needed. Stir in lemon juice and season with salt and pepper to taste. Sprinkle individual portions with chives before serving.

Salmon Steaks with Garlicky Yogurt

Prep time: 2 minutes | Cook time: 4 minutes | Serves 4

- 1 cup water
- 2 tablespoons olive oil
- 4 salmon steaks
- Coarse sea salt and ground black pepper, to taste
- Garlicky Yogurt:
- 1 (8-ounce / 227-g) container full-fat Greek yogurt
- 2 cloves garlic, minced
- 2 tablespoons mayonnaise
- ⅓ teaspoon Dijon mustard

1. Pour the water into the Instant Pot and insert a trivet. 2. Rub the olive oil into the fish and sprinkle with the salt and black pepper on all sides. Put the fish on the trivet. 3. Lock the lid. Select the Manual mode and set the cooking time for 4 minutes at High Pressure. 4. When the timer beeps, perform a quick pressure release. Carefully remove the lid. 5. Meanwhile, stir together all the ingredients for the garlicky yogurt in a bowl. 6. Serve the salmon steaks alongside the garlicky yogurt.

Perch Fillets with Red Curry

Prep time: 5 minutes | Cook time: 6 minutes | Serves 4

- 1 cup water
- 2 sprigs rosemary
- 1 large-sized lemon, sliced
- 1 pound (454 g) perch fillets
- 1 teaspoon cayenne pepper
- Sea salt and ground black pepper, to taste
- 1 tablespoon red curry paste
- 1 tablespoons butter

1. Add the water, rosemary, and lemon slices to the Instant Pot and insert a trivet. 2. Season the perch fillets with the cayenne pepper, salt, and black pepper. Spread the red curry paste and butter over the fillets. 3. Arrange the fish fillets on the trivet. 4. Lock the lid. Select the Manual mode and set the cooking time for 6 minutes at Low Pressure. 5. When the timer beeps, perform a quick pressure release. Carefully remove the lid. Serve with your favorite keto sides.

Dill Salmon Cakes

Prep time: 15 minutes | Cook time: 10 minutes | Serves 4

- 1 pound (454 g) salmon fillet, chopped
- 1 tablespoon chopped dill
- 2 eggs, beaten
- ½ cup almond flour
- 1 tablespoon coconut oil

1. Put the chopped salmon, dill, eggs, and almond flour in the food processor. 2. Blend the mixture until it is smooth. 3. Then make the small balls (cakes) from the salmon mixture. 4. After this, heat up the coconut oil on Sauté mode for 3 minutes. 5. Put the salmon cakes in the instant pot in one layer and cook them on Sauté mode for 2 minutes from each side or until they are light brown.

Cajun Cod Fillet

Prep time: 10 minutes | Cook time: 4 minutes | Serves 2

- 10 ounces (283 g) cod fillet
- 1 tablespoon olive oil
- 1 teaspoon Cajun seasoning
- 2 tablespoons coconut aminos

1. Sprinkle the cod fillet with coconut aminos and Cajun seasoning. 2. Then heat up olive oil in the instant pot on Sauté mode. 3. Add the spiced cod fillet and cook it for 4 minutes from each side. 4. Then cut it into halves and sprinkle with the oily liquid from the instant pot.

Fish Packets with Pesto and Cheese

Prep time: 8 minutes | Cook time: 6 minutes | Serves 4

- 1½ cups cold water.
- 4 (4-ounce / 113-g) white fish fillets, such as cod or haddock
- 1 teaspoon fine sea salt
- ½ teaspoon ground black pepper
- 1 (4-ounce / 113-g) jar pesto
- ½ cup shredded Parmesan cheese (about 2 ounces / 57 g)
- Halved cherry tomatoes, for garnish

1. Pour the water into your Instant Pot and insert a steamer basket. 2. Sprinkle the fish on all sides with the salt and pepper. Take four sheets of parchment paper and place a fillet in the center of each sheet. 3. Dollop 2 tablespoons of the pesto on top of each fillet and sprinkle with 2 tablespoons of the Parmesan cheese. 4. Wrap the fish in the parchment by folding in the edges and folding down the top like an envelope to close tightly. 5. Stack the packets in the steamer basket, seam-side down. 6. Lock the lid. Select the Manual

mode and set the cooking time for 6 minutes at Low Pressure. 7. Once cooking is complete, do a natural pressure release for 10 minutes, then release any remaining pressure. Carefully open the lid. 8. Remove the fish packets from the pot. Transfer to a serving plate and garnish with the cherry tomatoes. 9. Serve immediately.

Ahi Tuna and Cherry Tomato Salad

Prep time: 5 minutes | Cook time: 4 minutes | Serves 4

- 1 cup water
- 2 sprigs thyme
- 2 sprigs rosemary
- 2 sprigs parsley
- 1 lemon, sliced
- 1 pound (454 g) ahi tuna
- ⅓ teaspoon ground black pepper
- 1 head lettuce
- 1 cup cherry tomatoes, halved
- 1 red bell pepper, julienned
- 2 tablespoons extra-virgin olive oil
- 1 teaspoon Dijon mustard
- Sea salt, to taste

1. Pour the water into your Instant Pot. Add the thyme, rosemary, parsley, and lemon and insert a trivet. 2. Lay the fish on the trivet and season with the ground black pepper. 3. Lock the lid. Select the Manual mode and set the cooking time for 4 minutes at High Pressure. 4. When the timer beeps, perform a quick pressure release. Carefully remove the lid. 5. In a salad bowl, place the remaining ingredients and toss well. Add the flaked tuna and toss again. 6. Serve chilled.

Ahi Tuna and Cherry Tomato Salad

Prep time: 5 minutes | Cook time: 4 minutes | Serves 4

- 1 cup water
- 2 sprigs thyme
- 2 sprigs rosemary
- 2 sprigs parsley
- 1 lemon, sliced
- 1 pound (454 g) ahi tuna
- ⅓ teaspoon ground black pepper
- 1 head lettuce
- 1 cup cherry tomatoes, halved
- 1 red bell pepper, julienned
- 2 tablespoons extra-virgin olive oil
- 1 teaspoon Dijon mustard
- Sea salt, to taste

1. Pour the water into your Instant Pot. Add the thyme, rosemary, parsley, and lemon and insert a trivet. 2. Lay the fish on the trivet and season with the ground black pepper. 3. Lock the lid. Select the Manual mode and set the cooking time for 4 minutes at High Pressure. 4. When the timer beeps, perform a quick pressure release. Carefully remove the lid. 5. In a salad bowl, place the remaining ingredients and toss well. Add the flaked tuna and toss again. 6. Serve chilled.

Italian Salmon

Prep time: 10 minutes | Cook time: 4 minutes | Serves 2

- 10 ounces (283 g) salmon fillet
- 1 teaspoon Italian seasoning
- 1 cup water

1. Pour water and insert the trivet in the instant pot. 2. Then rub the salmon fillet with Italian seasoning and wrap in the foil. 3. Place the wrapped fish on the trivet and close the lid. 4. Cook the meal on Manual mode (High Pressure) for 4 minutes. 5. Make a quick pressure release and remove the fish from the foil. 6. Cut it into servings.

Salade Niçoise with Oil-Packed Tuna

Prep time: 5 minutes | Cook time: 20 minutes | Serves 4

- 8 ounces small red potatoes, quartered
- 8 ounces green beans, trimmed
- 4 large eggs
- french vinaigrette
- 2 tablespoons extra-virgin olive oil
- 2 tablespoons cold-pressed avocado oil
- 2 tablespoons white wine vinegar
- 1 tablespoon water
- 1 teaspoon Dijon mustard
- ½ teaspoon dried oregano
- ¼ teaspoon fine sea salt
- 1 tablespoon minced shallot
- 2 hearts romaine lettuce, leaves separated and torn into bite-size pieces
- ½ cup grape tomatoes, halved
- ¼ cup pitted Niçoise or Greek olives
- One 7 ounces can oil-packed tuna, drained and flaked
- Freshly ground black pepper
- 1 tablespoon chopped fresh flat-leaf parsley

1. Pour 1 cup water into the Instant Pot and place a steamer basket into the pot. Add the potatoes, green beans, and eggs to the basket. 2. Secure the lid and set the Pressure Release to Sealing. Select the Steam setting and set the cooking time for 3 minutes at high pressure. (The pot will take about 15 minutes to come up to pressure before the cooking program begins.) 3. To make the vinaigrette: While the vegetables and eggs are steaming, in a small jar or other small container with a tight-fitting lid, combine the olive oil, avocado oil, vinegar, water, mustard, oregano, salt, and shallot and shake vigorously to emulsify. Set aside. 4. Prepare an ice bath. 5. When the cooking program ends, perform a quick release by moving the Pressure Release to Venting. Open the pot and, wearing heat-resistant mitts, lift out the steamer basket. Using tongs, transfer the eggs and green beans to the ice bath, leaving the potatoes in the steamer basket. 6. While the eggs and green beans are cooling, divide the lettuce, tomatoes, olives, and tuna among four shallow individual bowls. Drain the eggs and green beans. Peel and halve the eggs lengthwise, then arrange them on the salads along with the green beans and potatoes. 7. Spoon the vinaigrette over the salads and sprinkle with the pepper and parsley. Serve right away.

Chili and Turmeric Haddock

Prep time: 10 minutes | Cook time: 5 minutes | Serves 4

- 1 chili pepper, minced
- 1 pound (454 g) haddock, chopped
- ½ teaspoon ground turmeric
- ½ cup fish stock
- 1 cup water

1. In the mixing bowl mix up chili pepper, ground turmeric, and fish stock. 2. Then add chopped haddock and transfer the mixture in the baking mold. 3. Pour water in the instant pot and insert the trivet. 4. Place the baking mold with fish on the trivet and close the lid. 5. Cook the meal on Manual (High Pressure) for 5 minutes. Make a quick pressure release.

Lemon Pepper Tilapia with Broccoli and Carrots

Prep time: 0 minutes | Cook time: 15 minutes | Serves 4

- 1 pound tilapia fillets
- 1 teaspoon lemon pepper seasoning
- ¼ teaspoon fine sea salt
- 2 tablespoons extra-virgin olive oil
- 2 garlic cloves, minced
- 1 small yellow onion, sliced
- ½ cup low-sodium vegetable broth
- 2 tablespoons fresh lemon juice
- 1 pound broccoli crowns, cut into bite-size florets
- 8 ounces carrots, cut into ¼-inch thick rounds

1. Sprinkle the tilapia fillets all over with the lemon pepper seasoning and salt. 2. Select the Sauté setting on the Instant Pot and heat the oil and garlic for 2 minutes, until the garlic is bubbling but not browned. Add the onion and sauté for about 3 minutes more, until it begins to soften. 3. Pour in the broth and lemon juice, then use a wooden spoon to nudge any browned bits from the bottom of the pot. Using tongs, add the fish fillets to the pot in a single layer; it's fine if they overlap slightly. Place the broccoli and carrots on top. 4. Secure the lid and set the Pressure Release to Sealing. Press the Cancel button to reset the cooking program, then select the Pressure Cook or Manual setting and set the cooking time for 1 minute at low pressure. (The pot will take about 10 minutes to come up to pressure before the cooking program begins.) 5. When the cooking program ends, let the pressure release naturally for 10 minutes (don't open the pot before the 10 minutes are up, even if the float valve has gone down), then move the Pressure Release to Venting to release any remaining steam. Open the pot. Use a fish spatula to transfer the vegetables and fillets to plates. Serve right away.

Clam Chowder with Bacon and Celery

Prep time: 10 minutes | Cook time: 4 minutes | Serves 2

- 5 ounces (142 g) clams
- 1 ounce (28 g) bacon, chopped
- 3 ounces (85 g) celery,
- chopped
- ½ cup water
- ½ cup heavy cream

1. Cook the bacon on Sauté mode for 1 minute. 2. Then add clams, celery, water, and heavy cream. 3. Close and seal the lid. 4. Cook the seafood on steam mode (High Pressure) for 3 minutes. Make a quick pressure release. 5. Ladle the clams with the heavy cream mixture in the bowls.

Salmon with Garlicky Broccoli Rabe and White Beans

Prep time: 20 minutes | Cook time: 10 minutes | Serves 4

- 2 tablespoons extra-virgin olive oil, plus extra for drizzling
- 4 garlic cloves, sliced thin
- ½ cup chicken or vegetable broth
- ¼ teaspoon red pepper flakes
- 1 lemon, sliced ¼ inch thick, plus lemon wedges for serving
- 4 (6-ounce / 170-g) skinless salmon fillets, 1½ inches thick
- ½ teaspoon table salt
- ¼ teaspoon pepper
- 1 pound (454 g) broccoli rabe, trimmed and cut into 1-inch pieces
- 1 (15-ounce / 425-g) can cannellini beans, rinsed

1. Using highest sauté function, cook oil and garlic in Instant Pot until garlic is fragrant and light golden brown, about 3 minutes. Using slotted spoon, transfer garlic to paper towel–lined plate and season with salt to taste; set aside for serving. Turn off Instant Pot, then stir in broth and pepper flakes. 2. Fold sheet of aluminum foil into 16 by 6-inch sling. Arrange lemon slices widthwise in 2 rows across center of sling. Sprinkle flesh side of salmon with salt and pepper, then arrange skinned side down on top of lemon slices. Using sling, lower salmon into Instant Pot; allow narrow edges of sling to rest along sides of insert. Lock lid in place and close pressure release valve. Select high pressure cook function and cook for 3 minutes. 3. Turn off Instant Pot and quick-release pressure. Carefully remove lid, allowing steam to escape away from you. Using sling, transfer salmon to large plate. Tent with foil and let rest while preparing broccoli rabe mixture. 4. Stir broccoli rabe and beans into cooking liquid, partially cover, and cook, using highest sauté function, until broccoli rabe is tender, about 5 minutes. Season with salt and pepper to taste. Gently lift and tilt salmon fillets with spatula to remove lemon slices. Serve salmon with broccoli rabe mixture and lemon wedges, sprinkling individual portions with garlic chips and drizzling with extra oil.

Tuna Stuffed Poblano Peppers

Prep time: 15 minutes | Cook time: 12 minutes | Serves 4

- 7 ounces (198 g) canned tuna, shredded
- 1 teaspoon cream cheese
- ¼ teaspoon minced garlic
- 2 ounces (57 g) Provolone cheese, grated
- 4 poblano pepper
- 1 cup water, for cooking

1. Remove the seeds from poblano peppers. 2. In the mixing bowl, mix up shredded tuna, cream cheese, minced garlic, and grated cheese. 3. Then fill the peppers with tuna mixture and put it in the baking pan. 4. Pour water and insert the baking pan in the instant pot. 5. Cook the meal on Manual mode (High Pressure) for 12 minutes. Then make a quick pressure release.

Foil-Pack Haddock with Spinach

Prep time: 15 minutes | Cook time: 15 minutes | Serves 4

- 12 ounces (340 g) haddock fillet
- 1 cup spinach
- 1 tablespoon avocado oil
- 1 teaspoon minced garlic
- ½ teaspoon ground coriander
- 1 cup water, for cooking

1. Blend the spinach until smooth and mix up with avocado oil, ground coriander, and minced garlic. 2. Then cut the haddock into 4 fillets and place on the foil. 3. Top the fish fillets with spinach mixture and place them on the rack. 4. Pour water and insert the rack in the instant pot. 5. Close and seal the lid and cook the haddock on Manual (High Pressure) for 15 minutes. 6. Do a quick pressure release.

Baked Flounder with Artichoke

Prep time: 10 minutes | Cook time: 10 minutes | Serves 2

- 8 ounces (227 g) flounder fillet
- 1 lemon slice, chopped
- 1 teaspoon ground black pepper
- ¼ teaspoon salt
- ½ large artichoke, chopped
- 1 tablespoon sesame oil
- 1 cup water, for cooking

1. Brush the round baking pan with sesame oil. 2. Then place the chopped artichoke in the baking pan and flatten it. 3. Sprinkle the flounder fillet with ground black pepper and salt and put over the artichoke. 4. Add chopped lemon. 5. Pour water and insert the steamer rack in the instant pot. 6. Place the pan with fish in the steamer. Close and seal the lid. 7. Cook the meal on Manual (High Pressure) for 10 minutes. Make a quick pressure release.

Rosemary Baked Haddock

Prep time: 7 minutes | Cook time: 10 minutes | Serves 2

- 2 eggs, beaten
- 12 ounces (340 g) haddock fillet, chopped
- 1 tablespoon cream cheese
- ¾ teaspoon dried rosemary
- 2 ounces (57 g) Parmesan, grated
- 1 teaspoon butter

1. Whisk the beaten eggs until homogenous. Add the cream cheese, dried rosemary, and dill. 2. Grease the springform with the butter and place the haddock inside. 3. Pour the egg mixture over the fish and add sprinkle with Parmesan. 4. Set the Manual mode (High Pressure) and cook for 5 minutes. Then make a natural release pressure for 5 minutes.

Mediterranean Salmon with Whole-Wheat Couscous

Prep time: 5 minutes | Cook time: 30 minutes | Serves 4

Couscous
- 1 cup whole-wheat couscous
- 1 cup water
- 1 tablespoon extra-virgin olive oil
- 1 teaspoon dried basil
- ¼ teaspoon fine sea salt

Salmon
- 1 pound skinless salmon fillet
- 2 teaspoons extra-virgin olive oil
- 1 tablespoon fresh lemon juice
- 1 garlic clove, minced

- 1 pint cherry or grape tomatoes, halved
- 8 ounces zucchini, halved lengthwise, then sliced crosswise ¼ inch thick

- ¼ teaspoon dried oregano
- ¼ teaspoon fine sea salt
- ¼ teaspoon freshly ground black pepper
- 1 tablespoon capers, drained
- Lemon wedges for serving

1. Pour 1 cup water into the Instant Pot. Have ready two-tier stackable stainless-steel containers. 2. To make the couscous: In one of the containers, stir together the couscous, water, oil, basil, and salt. Sprinkle the tomatoes and zucchini over the top. 3. To make the salmon: Place the salmon fillet in the second container. In a small bowl, whisk together the oil, lemon juice, garlic, oregano, salt, pepper, and capers. Spoon the oil mixture over the top of the salmon. 4. Place the container with the couscous and vegetables on the bottom and the salmon container on top. Cover the top container with its lid and then latch the containers together. Grasping the handle, lower the containers into the Instant Pot. 5. Secure the lid and set the Pressure Release to Sealing. Select the Pressure Cook or Manual setting and set the cooking time for 20 minutes at high pressure. (The pot will take about 10 minutes to come up to pressure before the cooking program begins.) 6. When the cooking program ends, let the pressure release naturally for 5 minutes, then move the Pressure Release to Venting to release any remaining steam. Open the pot and, wearing heat-resistant mitts, lift out the stacked containers. Unlatch, unstack, and open the containers, taking care not to get burned by the steam. 7. Using a fork, fluff the couscous and mix in the vegetables. Spoon the couscous onto plates, then use a spatula to cut the salmon into four pieces and place a piece on top of each couscous serving. Serve right away, with lemon wedges on the side.

Dill Lemon Salmon

Prep time: 10 minutes | Cook time: 4 minutes | Serves 4

- 1 pound (454 g) salmon fillet
- 1 tablespoon butter, melted
- 2 tablespoons lemon juice
- 1 teaspoon dried dill
- 1 cup water

1. Cut the salmon fillet on 4 servings. 2. Line the instant pot baking pan with foil and put the salmon fillets inside in one layer. 3. Then sprinkle the fish with dried dill, lemon juice, and butter. 4. Pour water in the instant pot and insert the rack. 5. Place the baking pan with salmon on the rack and close the lid. 6. Cook the meal on Manual mode (High Pressure) for 4 minutes. Allow the natural pressure release for 5 minutes and remove the fish from the instant pot.

Lemony Fish and Asparagus

Prep time: 5 minutes | Cook time: 3 minutes | Serves 4

- 2 lemons
- 2 cups cold water
- 2 tablespoons extra-virgin olive oil
- 4 (4-ounce / 113-g) white fish fillets, such as cod or haddock
- 1 teaspoon fine sea salt
- 1 teaspoon ground black pepper
- 1 bundle asparagus, ends trimmed
- 2 tablespoons lemon juice
- Fresh dill, for garnish

1. Grate the zest off the lemons until you have about 1 tablespoon and set the zest aside. Slice the lemons into ⅛-inch slices. 2. Pour the water into the Instant Pot. Add 1 tablespoon of the olive oil to each of two stackable steamer pans. 3. Sprinkle the fish on all sides with the lemon zest, salt, and pepper. 4. Arrange two fillets in each steamer pan and top each with the lemon slices and then the asparagus. Sprinkle the asparagus with the salt and drizzle the lemon juice over the top. 5. Stack the steamer pans in the Instant Pot. Cover the top steamer pan with its lid. 6. Lock the lid. Select the Manual mode and set the cooking time for 3 minutes at High Pressure. 7. Once cooking is complete, do a natural pressure release for 7 minutes, then release any remaining pressure. Carefully open the lid. 8. Lift the steamer pans out of the Instant Pot. 9. Transfer the fish and asparagus to a serving plate. Garnish with the lemon slices and dill. 10. Serve immediately.

Steamed Lobster Tails with Thyme

Prep time: 10 minutes | Cook time: 4 minutes | Serves 4

- 4 lobster tails
- 1 tablespoon butter, softened
- 1 teaspoon dried thyme
- 1 cup water

1. Pour water and insert the steamer rack in the instant pot. 2. Put the lobster tails on the rack and close the lid. 3. Cook the meal on Manual mode (High Pressure) for 4 minutes. Make a quick pressure release. 4. After this, mix up butter and dried thyme. Peel the lobsters and rub them with thyme butter.

Aromatic Monkfish Stew

Prep time: 5 minutes | Cook time: 6 minutes | Serves 6

- Juice of 1 lemon
- 1 tablespoon fresh basil
- 1 tablespoon fresh parsley
- 1 tablespoon olive oil
- 1 teaspoon garlic, minced
- 1½ pounds (680 g) monkfish
- 1 tablespoon butter
- 1 bell pepper, chopped
- 1 onion, sliced
- ½ teaspoon cayenne pepper
- ½ teaspoon mixed
- peppercorns
- ¼ teaspoon turmeric powder
- ¼ teaspoon ground cumin
- Sea salt and ground black pepper, to taste
- 2 cups fish stock
- ½ cup water
- ¼ cup dry white wine
- 2 bay leaves
- 1 ripe tomato, crushed

1. Stir together the lemon juice, basil, parsley, olive oil, and garlic in a ceramic dish. Add the monkfish and marinate for 30 minutes. 2. Set your Instant Pot to Sauté. Add and melt the butter. Once hot, cook the bell pepper and onion until fragrant. 3. Stir in the remaining ingredients. 4. Lock the lid. Select the Manual mode and set the cooking time for 6 minutes at High Pressure. 5. When the timer beeps, perform a quick pressure release. Carefully remove the lid. 6. Discard the bay leaves and divide your stew into serving bowls. Serve hot.

Louisiana Shrimp Gumbo

Prep time: 10 minutes | Cook time: 4 minutes | Serves 6

- 1 pound (454 g) shrimp
- ¼ cup chopped celery stalk
- 1 chili pepper, chopped
- ¼ cup chopped okra
- 1 tablespoon coconut oil
- 2 cups chicken broth
- 1 teaspoon sugar-free tomato paste

1. Put all ingredients in the instant pot and stir until you get a light red color. 2. Then close and seal the lid. 3. Cook the meal on

Manual mode (High Pressure) for 4 minutes. 4. When the time is finished, allow the natural pressure release for 10 minutes.

Greek Shrimp with Tomatoes and Feta

Prep time: 10 minutes | Cook time: 2 minutes | Serves 6

- 3 tablespoons unsalted butter
- 1 tablespoon garlic
- ½ teaspoon red pepper flakes, or more as needed
- 1½ cups chopped onion
- 1 (14½-ounce / 411-g) can diced tomatoes, undrained
- 1 teaspoon dried oregano
- 1 teaspoon salt
- 1 pound (454 g) frozen shrimp, peeled
- 1 cup crumbled feta cheese
- ½ cup sliced black olives
- ¼ cup chopped parsley

1. Preheat the Instant Pot by selecting Sauté and adjusting to high heat. When the inner cooking pot is hot, add the butter and heat until it foams. Add the garlic and red pepper flakes, and cook just until fragrant, about 1 minute. 2. Add the onion, tomatoes, oregano, and salt, and stir to combine. 3. Add the frozen shrimp. 4. Lock the lid into place. Select Manual and adjust the pressure to Low. Cook for 1 minute. When the cooking is complete, quick-release the pressure. Unlock the lid. 5. Mix the shrimp in with the lovely tomato broth. 6. Allow the mixture to cool slightly. Right before serving, sprinkle with the feta cheese, olives, and parsley. This dish makes a soupy broth, so it's great over mashed cauliflower.

Mussels with Fennel and Leeks

Prep time: 20 minutes | Cook time: 6 minutes | Serves 4

- 1 tablespoon extra-virgin olive oil, plus extra for drizzling
- 1 fennel bulb, 1 tablespoon fronds minced, stalks discarded, bulb halved, cored, and sliced thin
- 1 leek, ends trimmed, leek halved lengthwise, sliced
- 1 inch thick, and washed thoroughly
- 4 garlic cloves, minced
- 3 sprigs fresh thyme
- ¼ teaspoon red pepper flakes
- ½ cup dry white wine
- 3 pounds (1.4 kg) mussels, scrubbed and debearded

1. Using highest sauté function, heat oil in Instant Pot until shimmering. Add fennel and leek and cook until softened, about 5 minutes. Stir in garlic, thyme sprigs, and pepper flakes and cook until fragrant, about 30 seconds. Stir in wine, then add mussels. 2. Lock lid in place and close pressure release valve. Select high pressure cook function and set cook time for 0 minutes. Once Instant Pot has reached pressure, immediately turn off pot and quick-release pressure. Carefully remove lid, allowing steam to escape away from you. 3. Discard thyme sprigs and any mussels that have not opened. Transfer mussels to individual serving bowls, sprinkle with fennel fronds, and drizzle with extra oil. Serve.

Chapter 5 VegetablesandSides

Simple Cauliflower Gnocchi

Prep time: 5 minutes | Cook time: 2 minutes | Serves 4

- 2 cups cauliflower, boiled
- ½ cup almond flour
- 1 tablespoon sesame oil
- 1 teaspoon salt
- 1 cup water

1. In a bowl, mash the cauliflower until puréed. Mix it up with the almond flour, sesame oil and salt. 2. Make the log from the cauliflower dough and cut it into small pieces. 3. Pour the water in the Instant Pot and add the gnocchi. 4. Lock the lid. Select the Manual mode and set the cooking time for 2 minutes on High Pressure. Once the timer goes off, perform a natural pressure release for 5 minutes, then release any remaining pressure. Carefully open the lid. 5. Remove the cooked gnocchi from the water and serve.

Beet and Watercress Salad with Orange and Dill

Prep time: 20 minutes | Cook time: 8 minutes | Serves 4

- 2 pounds (907 g) beets, scrubbed, trimmed, and cut into ¾-inch pieces
- ½ cup water
- 1 teaspoon caraway seeds
- ½ teaspoon table salt
- 1 cup plain Greek yogurt
- 1 small garlic clove, minced to paste
- 5 ounces (142 g) watercress, torn into bite-size pieces
- 1 tablespoon extra-virgin
- olive oil, divided, plus extra for drizzling
- 1 tablespoon white wine vinegar, divided
- 1 teaspoon grated orange zest plus 2 tablespoons juice
- ¼ cup hazelnuts, toasted, skinned, and chopped
- ¼ cup coarsely chopped fresh dill
- Coarse sea salt

1. Combine beets, water, caraway seeds, and table salt in Instant Pot. Lock lid in place and close pressure release valve. Select high pressure cook function and cook for 8 minutes. Turn off Instant Pot and quick-release pressure. Carefully remove lid, allowing steam to escape away from you. 2. Using slotted spoon, transfer beets to plate; set aside to cool slightly. Combine yogurt, garlic, and 3 tablespoons beet cooking liquid in bowl; discard remaining cooking liquid. In large bowl toss watercress with 2 teaspoons oil and 1 teaspoon vinegar. Season with table salt and pepper to taste. 3. Spread yogurt mixture over surface of serving dish. Arrange watercress on top of yogurt mixture, leaving 1-inch border of yogurt mixture. Add beets to now-empty large bowl and toss with orange zest and juice, remaining 2 teaspoons vinegar, and remaining 1 teaspoon oil. Season with table salt and pepper to taste. Arrange beets on top of watercress mixture. Drizzle with extra oil and sprinkle with hazelnuts, dill, and sea salt. Serve.

Steamed Tomato with Halloumi Cheese

Prep time: 5 minutes | Cook time: 3 minutes | Serves 4

- 8 tomatoes, sliced
- 1 cup water
- ½ cup crumbled Halloumi cheese
- 2 tablespoons extra-virgin
- olive oil
- 2 tablespoons snipped fresh basil
- 2 garlic cloves, smashed

1. Pour the water into the Instant Pot and put the trivet in the pot. Place the tomatoes in the trivet. 2. Lock the lid. Select the Manual mode and set the cooking time for 3 minutes on High Pressure. When the timer goes off, perform a quick pressure release. Carefully open the lid. 3. Toss the tomatoes with the remaining ingredients and serve.

Green Cabbage Turmeric Stew

Prep time: 5 minutes | Cook time: 4 minutes | Serves 4

- 2 tablespoons olive oil
- ½ cup sliced yellow onion
- 1 teaspoon crushed garlic
- Sea salt and freshly ground black pepper, to taste
- 1 teaspoon turmeric powder
- 1 serrano pepper, chopped
- 1 pound (454 g) green cabbage, shredded
- 1 celery stalk, chopped
- 2 tablespoons rice wine
- 1 cup roasted vegetable broth

1. Place all of the above ingredients in the Instant Pot. 2. Secure the lid. Choose Manual mode and High Pressure; cook for 4 minutes. Once cooking is complete, use a quick pressure release; carefully remove the lid. 3. Divide between individual bowls and serve warm. Bon appétit!

Satarash with Eggs

Prep time: 10 minutes | Cook time: 5 minutes | Serves 4

- 2 tablespoons olive oil
- 1 white onion, chopped
- 2 cloves garlic
- 2 ripe tomatoes, puréed
- 1 green bell pepper, deseeded and sliced
- 1 red bell pepper, deseeded and sliced
- 1 teaspoon paprika
- ½ teaspoon dried oregano
- ½ teaspoon turmeric
- Kosher salt and ground black pepper, to taste
- 1 cup water
- 4 large eggs, lightly whisked

1. Press the Sauté button on the Instant Pot and heat the olive oil. Add the onion and garlic to the pot and sauté for 2 minutes, or until fragrant. Stir in the remaining ingredients, except for the eggs. 2. Lock the lid. Select the Manual mode and set the cooking time for 3 minutes on High Pressure. When the timer goes off, perform a quick pressure release. Carefully open the lid. 3. Fold in the eggs and stir to combine. Lock the lid and let it sit in the residual heat for 5 minutes. Serve warm.

Braised Radishes with Sugar Snap Peas and Dukkah

Prep time: 20 minutes | Cook time: 5 minutes | Serves 4

- ¼ cup extra-virgin olive oil, divided
- 1 shallot, sliced thin
- 3 garlic cloves, sliced thin
- 1½ pounds (680 g) radishes, 2 cups greens reserved, radishes trimmed and halved if small or quartered if large
- ½ cup water
- ½ teaspoon table salt
- 8 ounces (227 g) sugar snap peas, strings removed, sliced thin on bias
- 8 ounces (227 g) cremini mushrooms, trimmed and sliced thin
- 2 teaspoons grated lemon zest plus 1 teaspoon juice
- 1 cup plain Greek yogurt
- ½ cup fresh cilantro leaves
- 3 tablespoons dukkah

1. Using highest sauté function, heat 2 tablespoons oil in Instant Pot until shimmering. Add shallot and cook until softened, about 2 minutes. Stir in garlic and cook until fragrant, about 30 seconds. Stir in radishes, water, and salt. Lock lid in place and close pressure release valve. Select high pressure cook function and cook for 1 minute. 2. Turn off Instant Pot and quick-release pressure. Carefully remove lid, allowing steam to escape away from you. Stir in snap peas, cover, and let sit until heated through, about 3 minutes. Add radish greens, mushrooms, lemon zest and juice, and remaining 2 tablespoons oil and gently toss to combine. Season with salt and pepper to taste. 3. Spread ¼ cup yogurt over bottom of 4 individual serving plates. Using slotted spoon, arrange vegetable mixture on top and sprinkle with cilantro and dukkah. Serve.

Indian Okra

Prep time: 8 minutes | Cook time: 7 minutes | Serves 6

- 1 pound (454 g) young okra
- 4 tablespoons ghee or avocado oil
- ½ teaspoon cumin seeds
- ¼ teaspoon ground turmeric
- Pinch of ground cinnamon
- ½ medium onion, diced
- 2 cloves garlic, minced
- 2 teaspoons minced fresh
- ginger
- 1 serrano chile, seeded and ribs removed, minced
- 1 small tomato, diced
- ½ teaspoon sea salt
- ¼ teaspoon cayenne pepper (optional)
- 1 cup vegetable stock or filtered water

1. Rinse and thoroughly dry the okra. Slice it on a diagonal into slices ½ to ¾ inch thick, discarding the stems. 2. Set the Instant Pot to Sauté. Once hot, add the ghee and heat until melted. Stir in the cumin seeds, turmeric, and cinnamon and cook until they are fragrant, about 1 minute. This may cause the cumin seeds to jump and pop. Add the onion and cook, stirring frequently, until soft and translucent, about 3 minutes. Add the garlic, ginger, and serrano chile and sauté for an additional minute. Press Cancel. 3. Stir in the tomato, okra, salt, cayenne (if using), and stock. Secure the lid and set the steam release valve to Sealing. Press the Manual button and set the cook time to 2 minutes. 4. When the Instant Pot beeps, carefully switch the steam release valve to Venting to quick-release the pressure. When fully released, open the lid. Stir gently and allow the okra to rest on the Keep Warm setting for a few minutes before serving.

Parmesan Cauliflower Mash

Prep time: 7 minutes | Cook time: 5 minutes | Serves 4

- 1 head cauliflower, cored and cut into large florets
- ½ teaspoon kosher salt
- ½ teaspoon garlic pepper
- 2 tablespoons plain Greek yogurt
- ¾ cup freshly grated Parmesan cheese
- 1 tablespoon unsalted butter or ghee (optional)
- Chopped fresh chives

1. Pour 1 cup of water into the electric pressure cooker and insert a steamer basket or wire rack. 2. Place the cauliflower in the basket. 3. Close and lock the lid of the pressure cooker. Set the valve to sealing. 4. Cook on high pressure for 5 minutes. 5. When the cooking is complete, hit Cancel and quick release the pressure. 6. Once the pin drops, unlock and remove the lid. 7. Remove the cauliflower from the pot and pour out the water. Return the cauliflower to the pot and add the salt, garlic pepper, yogurt, and cheese. Use an immersion blender or potato masher to purée or mash the cauliflower in the pot. 8. Spoon into a serving bowl, and garnish with butter (if using) and chives.

Parmesan Zoodles

Prep time: 5 minutes | Cook time: 5 minutes | Serves 2

- 1 large zucchini, trimmed and spiralized
- 1 tablespoon butter
- 1 garlic clove, diced
- ½ teaspoon chili flakes
- 3 ounces (85 g) Parmesan cheese, grated

1. Set the Instant Pot on the Sauté mode and melt the butter. Add the garlic and chili flakes to the pot. Sauté for 2 minutes, or until fragrant. 2. Stir in the zucchini spirals and sauté for 2 minutes, or until tender. 3. Add the grated Parmesan cheese to the pot and stir well. Continue to cook it for 1 minute, or until the cheese melts. 4. Transfer to a plate and serve immediately

Sesame Zoodles with Scallions

Prep time: 10 minutes | Cook time: 3 minutes | Serves 6

- 2 large zucchinis, trimmed and spiralized
- ¼ cup chicken broth
- 1 tablespoon chopped scallions
- 1 tablespoon coconut aminos
- 1 teaspoon sesame oil
- 1 teaspoon sesame seeds
- ¼ teaspoon chili flakes

1. Set the Instant Pot on the Sauté mode. Add the zucchini spirals to the pot and pour in the chicken broth. Sauté for 3 minutes and transfer to the serving bowls. 2. Sprinkle with the scallions, coconut aminos, sesame oil, sesame seeds and chili flakes. Gently stir the zoodles. 3. Serve immediately.

Vinegary Broccoli with Cheese

Prep time: 5 minutes | Cook time: 5 minutes | Serves 4

- 1 pound (454 g) broccoli, cut into florets
- 1 cup water
- 2 garlic cloves, minced
- 1 cup crumbled Cottage cheese
- 2 tablespoons balsamic vinegar
- 1 teaspoon cumin seeds
- 1 teaspoon mustard seeds
- Salt and pepper, to taste

1. Pour the water into the Instant Pot and put the steamer basket in the pot. Place the broccoli in the steamer basket. 2. Close and secure the lid. Select the Manual setting and set the cooking time for 5 minutes at High Pressure. Once the timer goes off, do a quick pressure release. Carefully open the lid. 3. Stir in the remaining ingredients. 4. Serve immediately.

Individual Asparagus and Goat Cheese Frittatas

Prep time: 15 minutes | Cook time: 15 minutes | Serves 4

- 1 tablespoon extra-virgin olive oil
- 8 ounces (227 g) asparagus, trimmed and sliced ¼ inch thick
- 1 red bell pepper, stemmed, seeded, and chopped
- 2 shallots, minced
- 2 ounces (57 g) goat cheese, crumbled (½ cup)
- 1 tablespoon minced fresh tarragon
- 1 teaspoon grated lemon zest
- 8 large eggs
- ½ teaspoon table salt

1. Using highest sauté function, heat oil in Instant Pot until shimmering. Add asparagus, bell pepper, and shallots; cook until softened, about 5 minutes. Turn off Instant Pot and transfer vegetables to bowl. Stir in goat cheese, tarragon, and lemon zest. 2. Arrange trivet included with Instant Pot in base of now-empty insert and add 1 cup water. Spray four 6-ounce ramekins with vegetable oil spray. Beat eggs, ¼ cup water, and salt in large bowl until thoroughly combined. Divide vegetable mixture between prepared ramekins, then pour egg mixture over top (you may have some left over). Set ramekins on trivet. Lock lid in place and close pressure release valve. Select high pressure cook function and cook for 10 minutes. 3. Turn off Instant Pot and quick-release pressure. Carefully remove lid, allowing steam to escape away from you. Using tongs, transfer ramekins to wire rack and let cool slightly. Run paring knife around inside edge of ramekins to loosen frittatas, then invert onto individual serving plates. Serve.

Lemon Cabbage and Tempeh

Prep time: 8 minutes | Cook time: 10 minutes | Serves 3

- 2 tablespoons sesame oil
- ½ cup chopped scallions
- 2 cups shredded cabbage
- 6 ounces (170 g) tempeh, cubed
- 1 tablespoon coconut aminos
- 1 cup vegetable stock
- 2 garlic cloves, minced
- 1 tablespoon lemon juice
- Salt and pepper, to taste
- ¼ teaspoon paprika
- ¼ cup roughly chopped fresh cilantro

1. Press the Sauté button to heat up your Instant Pot. Heat the sesame oil and sauté the scallions until tender and fragrant. 2. Then, add the cabbage, tempeh, coconut aminos, vegetable stock, garlic, lemon juice, salt, pepper, and paprika. 3. Secure the lid. Choose Manual mode and Low Pressure; cook for 3 minutes. Once cooking is complete, use a quick pressure release; carefully remove the lid. 4. Press the Sauté button to thicken the sauce if desired. Divide between serving bowls, garnish with fresh cilantro, and serve warm. Bon appétit!

Corn on the Cob

Prep time: 5 minutes | Cook time: 12 to 15 minutes | Serves 4

- 2 large ears fresh corn
- Olive oil for misting
- Salt, to taste (optional)

1. Shuck corn, remove silks, and wash. 2. Cut or break each ear in half crosswise. 3. Spray corn with olive oil. 4. Air fry at 390°F (199°C) for 12 to 15 minutes or until browned as much as you like. 5. Serve plain or with coarsely ground salt.

Asparagus with Copoundy Cheese

Prep time: 5 minutes | Cook time: 1 minute | Serves 4

- 1½ pounds (680 g) fresh asparagus
- 1 cup water
- 2 tablespoons olive oil
- 4 garlic cloves, minced
- Sea salt, to taste
- ¼ teaspoon ground black pepper
- ½ cup shredded Copoundy cheese

1. Pour the water into the Instant Pot and put the steamer basket in the pot. 2. Place the asparagus in the steamer basket. Drizzle the asparagus with the olive oil and sprinkle with the garlic on top. Season with salt and black pepper. 3. Close and secure the lid. Select the Manual mode and set the cooking time for 1 minute at High Pressure. Once cooking is complete, do a quick pressure release. Carefully open the lid. 4. Transfer the asparagus to a platter and served topped with the shredded cheese.

Masala Cauliflower

Prep time: 6 minutes | Cook time: 5 minutes | Serves 4

- 2 tablespoons olive oil
- ½ cup chopped scallions
- 2 cloves garlic, pressed
- 1 tablespoon garam masala
- 1 teaspoon curry powder
- 1 red chili pepper, minced
- ½ teaspoon ground cumin
- Sea salt and ground black
- pepper, to taste
- 1 tablespoon chopped fresh coriander
- 2 tomatoes, puréed
- 1 pound (454 g) cauliflower, broken into florets
- ½ cup water
- ½ cup almond yogurt

1. Press the Sauté button to heat up your Instant Pot. Now, heat the oil and sauté the scallions for 1 minute. 2. Add garlic and continue to cook an additional 30 seconds or until aromatic. 3. Add garam masala, curry powder, chili pepper, cumin, salt, black pepper, coriander, tomatoes, cauliflower, and water. 4. Secure the lid. Choose Manual mode and High Pressure; cook for 3 minutes. Once cooking is complete, use a quick pressure release; carefully remove the lid. 5. Pour in the almond yogurt, stir well and serve warm. Bon appétit!

Green Beans with Potatoes and Basil

Prep time: 20 minutes | Cook time: 10 minutes | Serves 4

- 2 tablespoons extra-virgin olive oil, plus extra for drizzling
- 1 onion, chopped fine
- 2 tablespoons minced fresh oregano or 2 teaspoons dried
- 2 tablespoons tomato paste
- 4 garlic cloves, minced
- 1 (14½-ounce / 411-g) can whole peeled tomatoes, drained with juice reserved, chopped
- 1 cup water
- 1 teaspoon table salt
- ¼ teaspoon pepper
- 1½ pounds (680 g) green beans, trimmed and cut into 2-inch lengths
- 1 pound (454 g) Yukon Gold potatoes, peeled and cut into 1-inch pieces
- 3 tablespoons chopped fresh basil or parsley
- 2 tablespoons toasted pine nuts
- Shaved Parmesan cheese

1. Using highest sauté function, heat oil in Instant Pot until shimmering. Add onion and cook until softened, about 5 minutes. Stir in oregano, tomato paste, and garlic and cook until fragrant, about 30 seconds. Stir in tomatoes and their juice, water, salt, and pepper, then stir in green beans and potatoes. Lock lid in place and close pressure release valve. Select high pressure cook function and cook for 5 minutes. 2. Turn off Instant Pot and quick-release pressure. Carefully remove lid, allowing steam to escape away from you. Season with salt and pepper to taste. Sprinkle individual portions with basil, pine nuts, and Parmesan and drizzle with extra oil. Serve.

Instant Pot Zucchini Sticks

Prep time: 5 minutes | Cook time: 8 minutes | Serves 2

- 2 zucchinis, trimmed and cut into sticks
- 2 teaspoons olive oil
- ½ teaspoon white pepper
- ½ teaspoon salt
- 1 cup water

1. Place the zucchini sticks in the Instant Pot pan and sprinkle with the olive oil, white pepper and salt. 2. Pour the water and put the trivet in the pot. Place the pan on the trivet. 3. Lock the lid. Select the Manual setting and set the cooking time for 8 minutes at High Pressure. Once the timer goes off, use a quick pressure release. Carefully open the lid. 4. Remove the zucchinis from the pot and serve.

Curried Cauliflower and Tomatoes

Prep time: 10 minutes | Cook time: 2 minutes | Serves 4 to 6

- 1 medium head cauliflower, cut into bite-size pieces
- 1 (14-ounce / 397-g) can sugar-free diced tomatoes, undrained
- 1 bell pepper, thinly sliced
- 1 (14-ounce / 397-g) can full-fat coconut milk
- ½ to 1 cup water
- 2 tablespoons red curry paste
- 1 teaspoon salt
- 1 teaspoon garlic powder
- ½ teaspoon onion powder
- ½ teaspoon ground ginger
- ¼ teaspoon chili powder
- Freshly ground black pepper, to taste

1. Add all the ingredients, except for the black pepper, to the Instant Pot and stir to combine. 2. Lock the lid. Select the Manual setting and set the cooking time for 2 minutes at High Pressure. Once the timer goes off, use a quick pressure release. Carefully open the lid. 3. Sprinkle the black pepper and stir well. Serve immediately.

Spiced Winter Squash with Halloumi and Shaved Brussels Sprouts

Prep time: 20 minutes | Cook time: 15 minutes | Serves 4

- 3 tablespoons extra-virgin olive oil, divided
- 2 tablespoons lemon juice
- 2 garlic cloves, minced, divided
- ⅛ teaspoon plus ½ teaspoon table salt, divided
- 8 ounces (227 g) Brussels sprouts, trimmed, halved, and sliced very thin
- 1 (8-ounce / 227-g) block halloumi cheese, sliced crosswise into ¾-inch-thick slabs
- 4 scallions, white parts
- minced, green parts sliced thin on bias
- ½ teaspoon ground cardamom
- ¼ teaspoon ground cumin
- ⅛ teaspoon cayenne pepper
- 2 pounds (907 g) butternut squash, peeled, seeded, and cut into 1-inch pieces
- ½ cup chicken or vegetable broth
- 2 teaspoons honey
- ¼ cup dried cherries
- 2 tablespoons roasted pepitas

1. Whisk 1 tablespoon oil, lemon juice, ¼ teaspoon garlic, and ⅛ teaspoon salt together in bowl. Add Brussels sprouts and toss to coat; let sit until ready to serve. 2. Using highest sauté function, heat remaining 2 tablespoons oil in Instant Pot until shimmering. Arrange halloumi around edges of pot and cook until browned, about 3 minutes per side; transfer to plate. Add scallion whites to fat left in pot and cook until softened, about 2 minutes. Stir in remaining garlic, cardamom, cumin, and cayenne and cook until fragrant, about 30 seconds. Stir in squash, broth, and remaining ½

teaspoon salt. Lock lid in place and close pressure release valve. Select high pressure cook function and cook for 6 minutes. 3. Turn off Instant Pot and quick-release pressure. Carefully remove lid, allowing steam to escape away from you. Using highest sauté function, continue to cook squash mixture, stirring occasionally until liquid is almost completely evaporated, about 5 minutes. Turn off Instant Pot. Using potato masher, mash squash until mostly smooth. Season with salt and pepper to taste. 4. Spread portion of squash over bottom of individual serving plates. Top with Brussels sprouts and halloumi. Drizzle with honey and sprinkle with cherries, pepitas, and scallion greens. Serve.

Gobi Masala

Prep time: 5 minutes | Cook time: 4 to 5 minutes | Serves 4 to 6

- 1 tablespoon olive oil
- 1 teaspoon cumin seeds
- 1 white onion, diced
- 1 garlic clove, minced
- 1 head cauliflower, chopped
- 1 tablespoon ground
- coriander
- 1 teaspoon ground cumin
- ½ teaspoon garam masala
- ½ teaspoon salt
- 1 cup water

1. Set the Instant Pot to the Sauté mode and heat the olive oil. Add the cumin seeds to the pot and sauté for 30 seconds, stirring constantly. Add the onion and sauté for 2 to 3 minutes, stirring constantly. Add the garlic and sauté for 30 seconds, stirring frequently. 2. Stir in the remaining ingredients. 3. Lock the lid. Select the Manual mode and set the cooking time for 1 minute on High Pressure. When the timer goes off, perform a quick pressure release. Carefully open the lid. 4. Serve immediately.

Savory and Rich Creamed Kale

Prep time: 10 minutes | Cook time: 5 minutes | Serves 4

- 2 tablespoons extra-virgin olive oil
- 2 cloves garlic, crushed
- 1 small onion, chopped
- 12 ounces (340 g) kale, finely chopped
- ½ cup chicken broth
- 1 teaspoon Herbes de Provence
- 4 ounces (113 g) cream cheese
- ½ cup full-fat heavy cream
- 1 teaspoon dried tarragon

1. Press the Sauté button on the Instant Pot and heat the olive oil. Add the garlic and onion to the pot and sauté for 2 minutes, or until the onion is soft. Stir in the kale, chicken broth and Herbes de Provence. 2. Lock the lid. Select the Manual mode and set the cooking time for 3 minutes at High Pressure. When the timer goes off, perform a quick pressure release. Carefully open the lid. 3. Stir in the cream cheese, heavy cream and tarragon. Stir well to thicken the dish. Serve immediately.

Chinese-Style Pe-Tsai with Onion

Prep time: 5 minutes | Cook time: 8 minutes | Serves 4

- 2 tablespoons sesame oil
- 1 yellow onion, chopped
- 1 pound (454 g) pe-tsai cabbage, shredded
- ¼ cup rice wine vinegar
- 1 tablespoon coconut aminos
- 1 teaspoon finely minced garlic
- ½ teaspoon salt
- ¼ teaspoon Szechuan pepper

1. Set the Instant Pot on the Sauté mode and heat the sesame oil. Add the onion to the pot and sauté for 5 minutes, or until tender. Stir in the remaining ingredients. 2. Lock the lid. Select the Manual mode and set the cooking time for 3 minutes on High Pressure. When the timer goes off, perform a quick pressure release. Carefully open the lid. 3. Transfer the cabbage mixture to a bowl and serve immediately.

Lemony Asparagus with Gremolata

Prep time: 15 minutes | Cook time: 2 minutes | Serves 2 to 4

Gremolata:
- 1 cup finely chopped fresh Italian flat-leaf parsley leaves

Asparagus:
- 1½ pounds (680 g) asparagus, trimmed

Lemony Vinaigrette:
- 1½ tablespoons fresh lemon juice
- 1 teaspoon Swerve
- 1 teaspoon Dijon mustard
- 2 tablespoons extra-virgin

Garnish:
- 3 tablespoons slivered almonds

- 3 garlic cloves, peeled and grated
- Zest of 2 small lemons

- 1 cup water

  olive oil
- Kosher salt and freshly ground black pepper, to taste

1. In a small bowl, stir together all the ingredients for the gremolata. 2. Pour the water into the Instant Pot. Arrange the asparagus in a steamer basket. Lower the steamer basket into the pot. 3. Lock the lid. Select the Steam mode and set the cooking time for 2 minutes on Low Pressure. 4. Meanwhile, prepare the lemony vinaigrette: In a bowl, combine the lemon juice, swerve and mustard and whisk to combine. Slowly drizzle in the olive oil and continue to whisk. Season generously with salt and pepper. 5. When the timer goes off, perform a quick pressure release. Carefully open the lid. Remove the steamer basket from the Instant Pot. 6. Transfer the asparagus to a serving platter. Drizzle with the vinaigrette and sprinkle with the gremolata. Serve the asparagus topped with the slivered almonds.

Spicy Cauliflower Head

Prep time: 5 minutes | Cook time: 7 minutes | Serves 4

- 13 ounces (369 g) cauliflower head
- 1 cup water
- 1 tablespoon coconut cream
- 1 tablespoon avocado oil
- 1 teaspoon ground paprika
- 1 teaspoon ground turmeric
- ½ teaspoon ground cumin
- ½ teaspoon salt

1. Pour the water in the Instant Pot and insert the trivet. 2. In the mixing bowl, stir together the coconut cream, avocado oil, paprika, turmeric, cumin and salt. 3. Carefully brush the cauliflower head with the coconut cream mixture. Sprinkle the remaining coconut cream mixture over the cauliflower. 4. Transfer the cauliflower head onto the trivet. 5. Lock the lid. Select the Manual mode and set the cooking time for 7 minutes at High Pressure. When the timer goes off, use a natural pressure release for 10 minutes, then release any remaining pressure. Carefully open the lid. 6. Serve immediately.

Thyme Cabbage

Prep time: 10 minutes | Cook time: 5 minutes | Serves 4

- 1 pound (454 g) white cabbage
- 2 tablespoons butter
- 1 teaspoon dried thyme
- ½ teaspoon salt
- 1 cup water

1. Cut the white cabbage on medium size petals and sprinkle with the butter, dried thyme and salt. Place the cabbage petals in the Instant Pot pan. 2. Pour the water and insert the trivet in the Instant Pot. Put the pan on the trivet. 3. Set the lid in place. Select the Manual mode and set the cooking time for 5 minutes on High Pressure. When the timer goes off, do a quick pressure release. Carefully open the lid. 4. Serve immediately.

Best Brown Rice

Prep time: 5 minutes | Cook time: 22 minutes | Serves 6 to 12

- 2 cups brown rice
- 2½ cups water

1. Rinse brown rice in a fine-mesh strainer. 2. Add rice and water to the inner pot of the Instant Pot. 3. Secure the lid and make sure vent is on sealing. 4. Use Manual setting and select 22 minutes cooking time on high pressure. 5. When cooking time is done, let the pressure release naturally for 10 minutes, then press Cancel and manually release any remaining pressure.

Caramelized Onions

Prep time: 10 minutes | Cook time: 35 minutes | Serves 8

- 4 tablespoons margarine
- 6 large Vidalia or other sweet onions, sliced into thin half rings
- 10-ounce can chicken, or vegetable, broth

1. Press Sauté on the Instant Pot. Add in the margarine and let melt. 2. Once the margarine is melted, stir in the onions and sauté for about 5 minutes. Pour in the broth and then press Cancel. 3. Secure the lid and make sure vent is set to sealing. Press Manual and set time for 20 minutes. 4. When cook time is up, release the pressure manually. Remove the lid and press Sauté. Stir the onion mixture for about 10 more minutes, allowing extra liquid to cook off.

Almond Butter Zucchini Noodles

Prep time: 10 minutes | Cook time: 4 minutes | Serves 4

- 2 tablespoons coconut oil
- 1 yellow onion, chopped
- 2 zucchini, julienned
- 1 cup shredded Chinese cabbage
- 2 garlic cloves, minced
- 2 tablespoons almond butter
- Sea salt and freshly ground black pepper, to taste
- 1 teaspoon cayenne pepper

1. Press the Sauté button to heat up your Instant Pot. Heat the coconut oil and sweat the onion for 2 minutes. 2. Add the other ingredients. 3. Secure the lid. Choose Manual mode and High Pressure; cook for 2 minutes. Once cooking is complete, use a quick pressure release; carefully remove the lid. Bon appétit!

Garlicky Broccoli with Roasted Almonds

Prep time: 10 minutes | Cook time: 4 minutes | Serves 4 to 6

- 6 cups broccoli florets
- 1 cup water
- 1½ tablespoons olive oil
- 8 garlic cloves, thinly sliced
- 2 shallots, thinly sliced
- ½ teaspoon crushed red pepper flakes
- Grated zest and juice of 1 medium lemon
- ½ teaspoon kosher salt
- Freshly ground black pepper, to taste
- ¼ cup chopped roasted almonds
- ¼ cup finely slivered fresh basil

1. Pour the water into the Instant Pot. Place the broccoli florets in a steamer basket and lower into the pot. 2. Close and secure the lid. Select the Steam setting and set the cooking time for 2 minutes at Low Pressure. Once the timer goes off, use a quick pressure release. Carefully open the lid. 3. Transfer the broccoli to a large bowl filled with cold water and ice. Once cooled, drain the broccoli and pat dry. 4. Select the Sauté mode on the Instant Pot and heat the olive oil. Add the garlic to the pot and sauté for 30 seconds, tossing constantly. Add the shallots and pepper flakes to the pot and sauté for 1 minute. 5. Stir in the cooked broccoli, lemon juice, salt and black pepper. Toss the ingredients together and cook for 1 minute. 6. Transfer the broccoli to a serving platter and sprinkle with the chopped almonds, lemon zest and basil. Serve immediately.

Mushroom Stroganoff with Vodka

Prep time: 8 minutes | Cook time: 8 minutes | Serves 4

- 2 tablespoons olive oil
- ½ teaspoon crushed caraway seeds
- ½ cup chopped onion
- 2 garlic cloves, smashed
- ¼ cup vodka
- ¾ pound (340 g) button mushrooms, chopped
- 1 celery stalk, chopped
- 1 ripe tomato, puréed
- 1 teaspoon mustard seeds
- Sea salt and freshly ground pepper, to taste
- 2 cups vegetable broth

1. Press the Sauté button to heat up your Instant Pot. Now, heat the oil and sauté caraway seeds until fragrant, about 40 seconds. 2. Then, add the onion and garlic, and continue sautéing for 1 to 2 minutes more, stirring frequently. 3. After that, add the remaining ingredients and stir to combine. 4. Secure the lid. Choose Manual mode and High Pressure; cook for 5 minutes. Once cooking is complete, use a quick pressure release; carefully remove the lid. 5. Ladle into individual bowls and serve warm. Bon appétit!

Vegetable Curry

Prep time: 25 minutes | Cook time: 3 minutes | Serves 10

- 16-ounce package baby carrots
- 3 medium potatoes, unpeeled, cubed
- 1 pound fresh or frozen green beans, cut in 2-inch pieces
- 1 medium green pepper, chopped
- 1 medium onion, chopped
- 1–2 cloves garlic, minced
- 15-ounce can garbanzo beans, drained
- 28-ounce can crushed tomatoes
- 3 teaspoons curry powder
- 1½ teaspoons chicken bouillon granules
- 1¾ cups boiling water
- 3 tablespoons minute tapioca

1. Combine carrots, potatoes, green beans, pepper, onion, garlic, garbanzo beans, crushed tomatoes, and curry powder in the Instant Pot. 2. Dissolve bouillon in boiling water, then stir in tapicoa. Pour over the contents of the Instant Pot and stir. 3. Secure the lid and make sure vent is set to sealing. Press Manual and set for 3 minutes. 4. When cook time is up, manually release the pressure.

Braised Fennel with radicchio, Pear, and Pecorino

Prep time: 20 minutes | Cook time: 12 minutes | Serves 4

- 6 tablespoons extra-virgin olive oil, divided
- 2 fennel bulbs (12 ounces / 340 g each), 2 tablespoons fronds chopped, stalks discarded, bulbs halved, each half cut into 1-inch-thick wedges
- ¾ teaspoon table salt, divided
- ½ teaspoon grated lemon zest plus 4 teaspoons juice

- 5 ounces (142 g) baby arugula
- 1 small head radicchio (6 ounces/ 170 g), shredded
- 1 Bosc or Bartlett pear, quartered, cored, and sliced thin
- ¼ cup whole almonds, toasted and chopped
- Shaved Pecorino Romano cheese

1. Using highest sauté function, heat 2 tablespoons oil in Instant Pot for 5 minutes (or until just smoking). Brown half of fennel, about 3 minutes per side; transfer to plate. Repeat with 1 tablespoon oil and remaining fennel; do not remove from pot. 2. Return first batch of fennel to pot along with ½ cup water and ½ teaspoon salt. Lock lid in place and close pressure release valve. Select high pressure cook function and cook for 2 minutes. Turn off Instant Pot and quick-release pressure. Carefully remove lid, allowing steam to escape away from you. Using slotted spoon, transfer fennel to plate; discard cooking liquid. 3. Whisk remaining 3 tablespoons oil, lemon zest and juice, and remaining ¼ teaspoon salt together in large bowl. Add arugula, radicchio, and pear and toss to coat. Transfer arugula mixture to serving dish and arrange fennel wedges on top. Sprinkle with almonds, fennel fronds, and Pecorino. Serve.

Buttery Whole Cauliflower

Prep time: 5 minutes | Cook time: 8 minutes | Serves 4

- 1 large cauliflower, rinsed and patted dry
- 1 cup water
- 4 tablespoons melted butter
- 2 cloves garlic, minced

- Pinch of sea salt
- Pinch of fresh ground black pepper
- 1 tablespoon chopped fresh flat leaf parsley, for garnish

1. Pour the water into the Instant Pot and put the trivet in the pot. Place the cauliflower on the trivet. 2. Lock the lid. Select the Manual mode and set the cooking time for 3 minutes at High Pressure. 3. Preheat the oven to 550ºF (288ºC). Line a baking sheet with parchment paper. 4. In a small bowl, whisk together the butter, garlic, sea salt and black pepper. Set aside. 5. When the timer beeps, use a quick pressure release. Carefully open the lid. 6. Transfer the cauliflower to the lined baking sheet. Dab and dry the surface with a clean kitchen towel. Brush the cauliflower with the garlic butter.

7. Place the baking sheet with the cauliflower in the preheated oven and roast for 5 minutes, or until the cauliflower is golden brown. Drizzle with any remaining garlic butter and sprinkle with the chopped parsley. Serve immediately.

Perfect Sweet Potatoes

Prep time: 5 minutes | Cook time: 15 minutes | Serves 4 to 6

- 4–6 medium sweet potatoes
- 1 cup of water

1. Scrub skin of sweet potatoes with a brush until clean. Pour water into inner pot of the Instant Pot. Place steamer basket in the bottom of the inner pot. Place sweet potatoes on top of steamer basket. 2. Secure the lid and turn valve to seal. 3. Select the Manual mode and set to pressure cook on high for 15 minutes. 4. Allow pressure to release naturally (about 10 minutes). 5. Once the pressure valve lowers, remove lid and serve immediately.

Braised Whole Cauliflower with North African Spices

Prep time: 15 minutes | Cook time: 10 minutes | Serves 4

- 2 tablespoons extra-virgin olive oil
- 6 garlic cloves, minced
- 3 anchovy fillets, rinsed and minced (optional)
- 2 teaspoons ras el hanout
- ⅛ teaspoon red pepper flakes
- 1 (28 ounces / 794 g) can whole peeled tomatoes, drained with juice reserved,

- chopped coarse
- 1 large head cauliflower (3 pounds / 1.4 kg)
- ½ cup pitted brine-cured green olives, chopped coarse
- ¼ cup golden raisins
- ¼ cup fresh cilantro leaves
- ¼ cup pine nuts, toasted

1. Using highest sauté function, cook oil, garlic, anchovies (if using), ras el hanout, and pepper flakes in Instant Pot until fragrant, about 3 minutes. Turn off Instant Pot, then stir in tomatoes and reserved juice. 2. Trim outer leaves of cauliflower and cut stem flush with bottom florets. Using paring knife, cut 4-inch-deep cross in stem. Nestle cauliflower stem side down into pot and spoon some of sauce over top. Lock lid in place and close pressure release valve. Select high pressure cook function and cook for 3 minutes. 3. Turn off Instant Pot and quick-release pressure. Carefully remove lid, allowing steam to escape away from you. Using tongs and slotted spoon, transfer cauliflower to serving dish and tent with aluminum foil. Stir olives and raisins into sauce and cook, using highest sauté function, until sauce has thickened slightly, about 5 minutes. Season with salt and pepper to taste. Cut cauliflower into wedges and spoon some of sauce over top. Sprinkle with cilantro and pine nuts. Serve, passing remaining sauce separately.

Chapter6 Snacksand Appetizers

Brussels Sprouts with Aioli Sauce

Prep time: 5 minutes | Cook time: 7 minutes | Serves 4

- 1 tablespoon butter
- ½ cup chopped scallions

Aioli Sauce:
- ¼ cup mayonnaise
- 1 tablespoon fresh lemon juice

- ¾ pound (340 g) Brussels sprouts

- 1 garlic clove, minced
- ½ teaspoon Dijon mustard

1. Set your Instant Pot to Sauté and melt the butter. 2. Add the scallions and sauté for 2 minutes until softened. Add the Brussels sprouts and cook for another 1 minute. 3. Lock the lid. Select the Manual mode and set the cooking time for 4 minutes at High Pressure. 4. Meanwhile, whisk together all the ingredients for the Aioli sauce in a small bowl until well incorporated. 5. When the timer beeps, perform a quick pressure release. Carefully remove the lid. 6. Serve the Brussels sprouts with the Aioli sauce on the side.

Green Goddess White Bean Dip

Prep time: 1 minutes | Cook time: 45 minutes | Makes 3 cups

- 1 cup dried navy, great Northern, or cannellini beans
- 4 cups water
- 2 teaspoons fine sea salt
- 3 tablespoons fresh lemon juice
- ¼ cup extra-virgin olive oil,

- plus 1 tablespoon
- ¼ cup firmly packed fresh flat-leaf parsley leaves
- 1 bunch chives, chopped
- Leaves from 2 tarragon sprigs
- Freshly ground black pepper

1. Combine the beans, water, and 1 teaspoon of the salt in the Instant Pot and stir to dissolve the salt. 2. Secure the lid and set the Pressure Release to Sealing. Select the Bean/Chili, Pressure Cook, or Manual setting and set the cooking time for 30 minutes at high pressure if using navy or Great Northern beans or 40 minutes at high pressure if using cannellini beans. (The pot will take about 15 minutes to come up to pressure before the cooking program begins.) 3. When the cooking program ends, let the pressure release naturally for 15 minutes, then move the Pressure Release to Venting to release any remaining steam. Open the pot and scoop out and reserve ½ cup of the cooking liquid. Wearing heat-resistant mitts, lift out the inner pot and drain the beans in a colander. 4. In a food processor or blender, combine the beans, ½ cup cooking liquid, lemon juice, ¼ cup olive oil, ½ teaspoon parsley, chives, tarragon, remaining 1 teaspoon salt, and ½ teaspoon pepper. Process or blend on medium speed, stopping to scrape down the sides of the container as needed, for about 1 minute, until the mixture is smooth. 5. Transfer the dip to a serving bowl. Drizzle with the remaining 1 tablespoon olive oil and sprinkle with a few grinds of pepper. The dip will keep in an airtight container in the refrigerator for up to 1 week. Serve at room temperature or chilled.

Rosemary Chicken Wings

Prep time: 10 minutes | Cook time: 16 minutes | Serves 4

- 4 boneless chicken wings
- 1 tablespoon olive oil
- 1 teaspoon dried rosemary

- ½ teaspoon garlic powder
- ¼ teaspoon salt

1. In the mixing bowl, mix up olive oil, dried rosemary, garlic powder, and salt. 2. Then rub the chicken wings with the rosemary mixture and leave for 10 minutes to marinate. 3. After this, put the chicken wings in the instant pot, add the remaining rosemary marinade and cook them on Sauté mode for 8 minutes from each side.

Cauliflower Fritters with Cheese

Prep time: 10 minutes | Cook time: 8 minutes | Serves 4

- 1 cup cauliflower, boiled
- 2 eggs, beaten
- 2 tablespoons almond flour
- 2 ounces (57 g) Cheddar

- cheese, shredded
- ½ teaspoon garlic powder
- 1 tablespoon avocado oil

1. In a medium bowl, mash the cauliflower. Add the beaten eggs, flour, cheese, and garlic powder and stir until well incorporated. Make the fritters from the cauliflower mixture. 2. Set your Instant Pot to Sauté and heat the avocado oil. 3. Add the fritters to the hot oil and cook each side for 3 minutes until golden brown. 4. Serve hot.

Cheddar Chips

Prep time: 10 minutes | Cook time: 5 minutes | Serves 4

- 1 cup shredded Cheddar cheese
- 1 tablespoon almond flour

1. Mix up Cheddar cheese and almond flour. 2. Then preheat the instant pot on Sauté mode. 3. Line the instant pot bowl with baking paper. 4. After this, make the small rounds from the cheese in the instant pot (on the baking paper) and close the lid. 5. Cook them for 5 minutes on Sauté mode or until the cheese is melted. 6. Then switch off the instant pot and remove the baking paper with cheese rounds from it. 7. Cool the chips well and remove them from the baking paper.

Lemon Artichokes

Prep time: 5 minutes | Cook time: 5 to 15 minutes | Serves 4

- 4 artichokes
- 1 cup water
- 2 tablespoons lemon juice
- 1 teaspoon salt

1. Wash and trim artichokes by cutting off the stems flush with the bottoms of the artichokes and by cutting ¾–1 inch off the tops. Stand upright in the bottom of the inner pot of the Instant Pot. 2. Pour water, lemon juice, and salt over artichokes. 3. Secure the lid and make sure the vent is set to sealing. On Manual, set the Instant Pot for 15 minutes for large artichokes, 10 minutes for medium artichokes, or 5 minutes for small artichokes. 4. When cook time is up, perform a quick release by releasing the pressure manually.

Creamy Spinach Dip

Prep time: 13 minutes | Cook time: 5 minutes | Serves 11

- 8 ounces low-fat cream cheese
- 1 cup low-fat sour cream
- ½ cup finely chopped onion
- ½ cup no-sodium vegetable broth
- 5 cloves garlic, minced
- ½ teaspoon salt
- ¼ teaspoon black pepper
- 10 ounces frozen spinach
- 12 ounces reduced-fat shredded Monterey Jack cheese
- 12 ounces reduced-fat shredded Parmesan cheese

1. Add cream cheese, sour cream, onion, vegetable broth, garlic, salt, pepper, and spinach to the inner pot of the Instant Pot. 2. Secure lid, make sure vent is set to sealing, and set to the Bean/Chili setting on high pressure for 5 minutes. 3. When done, do a manual release. 4. Add the cheeses and mix well until creamy and well combined.

Italian Tomatillos

Prep time: 10 minutes | Cook time: 10 minutes | Serves 4

- 1 tablespoon Italian seasoning
- 4 tomatillos, sliced
- 4 teaspoons olive oil
- 4 tablespoons water

1. Sprinkle the tomatillos with Italian seasoning. 2. Then pour the olive oil in the instant pot and heat it up on Sauté mode for 1 minute. 3. Put the tomatillos in the instant pot in one layer and cook them for 2 minutes from each side. 4. Then add water and close the lid. 5. Sauté the vegetables for 3 minutes more.

Herbed Shrimp

Prep time: 5 minutes | Cook time: 5 minutes | Serves 4

- 2 tablespoons olive oil
- ¾ pound (340 g) shrimp, peeled and deveined
- 1 teaspoon paprika
- 1 teaspoon garlic powder
- 1 teaspoon onion powder
- 1 teaspoon dried parsley flakes
- ½ teaspoon dried oregano
- ½ teaspoon dried thyme
- ½ teaspoon dried basil
- ½ teaspoon dried rosemary
- ¼ teaspoon red pepper flakes
- Coarse sea salt and ground black pepper, to taste
- 1 cup chicken broth

1. Set your Instant Pot to Sauté and heat the olive oil. 2. Add the shrimp and sauté for 2 to 3 minutes. 3. Add the remaining ingredients to the Instant Pot and stir to combine. 4. Secure the lid. Select the Manual mode and set the cooking time for 2 minutes at Low Pressure. 5. When the timer beeps, perform a quick pressure release. Carefully remove the lid. 6. Transfer the shrimp to a plate and serve.

Parmesan Zucchini Fries

Prep time: 15 minutes | Cook time: 5 minutes | Serves 4

- 1 zucchini
- 1 ounce (28 g) Parmesan, grated
- 1 tablespoon almond flour
- ½ teaspoon Italian seasoning
- 1 tablespoon coconut oil

1. Trim the zucchini and cut it into the French fries. 2. Then sprinkle them with grated Parmesan, almond flour, and Italian seasoning. 3. Put coconut oil in the instant pot and melt it on Sauté mode. 4. Put the zucchini in the hot oil in one layer and cook for 2 minutes from each side or until they are golden brown. 5. Dry the zucchini fries with paper towels.

Sesame Mushrooms

Prep time: 2 minutes | Cook time: 10 minutes | Serves 6

- 3 tablespoons sesame oil
- ¾ pound (340 g) small button mushrooms
- 1 teaspoon minced garlic
- ½ teaspoon smoked paprika
- ½ teaspoon cayenne pepper
- Salt and ground black pepper, to taste

1. Set your Instant Pot to Sauté and heat the sesame oil. 2. Add the mushrooms and sauté for 4 minutes until just tender, stirring occasionally. 3. Add the remaining ingredients to the Instant Pot and stir to mix well. 4. Lock the lid. Select the Manual mode and set the cooking time for 5 minutes at High Pressure. 5. When the timer beeps, perform a quick pressure release. Carefully remove the lid. 6. Serve warm.

Fast Spring Kale Appetizer

Prep time: 5 minutes | Cook time: 2 minutes | Serves 6

- 3 teaspoons butter
- 1 cup chopped spring onions
- 1 pound (454 g) kale, torn into pieces
- 1 cup water
- ½ teaspoon cayenne pepper
- Himalayan salt and ground black pepper, to taste
- ½ cup shredded Colby cheese, for serving

1. Set your Instant Pot to Sauté and melt the butter. 2. Add the spring onions and sauté for 1 minute until wilted. 3. Add the remaining ingredients except the cheese to the Instant Pot and mix well. 4. Lock the lid. Select the Manual mode and set the cooking time for 1 minute at High Pressure. 5. When the timer beeps, perform a quick pressure release. Carefully remove the lid. 6. Transfer the kale mixture to a bowl and serve topped with the cheese.

Oregano Sausage Balls

Prep time: 10 minutes | Cook time: 16 minutes | Serves 10

- 15 ounces (425 g) ground pork sausage
- 1 teaspoon dried oregano
- 4 ounces (113 g) Mozzarella, shredded
- 1 cup coconut flour
- 1 garlic clove, grated
- 1 teaspoon coconut oil, melted

1. In the bowl mix up ground pork sausages, dried oregano, shredded Mozzarella, coconut flour, and garlic clove. 2. When the mixture is homogenous, make the balls. 3. After this, pour coconut oil in the instant pot. 4. Arrange the balls in the instant pot and cook them on Sauté mode for 8 minutes from each side.

Creamy Scallion Dip

Prep time: 10 minutes | Cook time: 11 minutes | Serves 4

- 5 ounces (142 g) scallions, diced
- 4 tablespoons cream cheese
- 1 tablespoon chopped fresh parsley
- 1 teaspoon garlic powder
- 2 tablespoons coconut cream
- ½ teaspoon salt
- 1 teaspoon coconut oil

1. Heat up the instant pot on Sauté mode. 2. Then add coconut oil and melt it. 3. Add diced scallions and sauté it for 6 to 7 minutes or until it is light brown. 4. Add cream cheese, parsley, garlic powder, salt, and coconut cream. 5. Close the instant pot lid and cook the scallions dip for 5 minutes on Manual mode (High Pressure). 6. Make a quick pressure release. Blend the dip will it is smooth if desired.

Broccoli Cheese Dip

Prep time: 5 minutes | Cook time: 10 minutes | Serves 6

- 4 tablespoons butter
- ½ medium onion, diced
- 1½ cups chopped broccoli
- 8 ounces (227 g) cream cheese
- ½ cup mayonnaise
- ½ cup chicken broth
- 1 cup shredded Cheddar cheese

1. Press the Sauté button and then press the Adjust button to set heat to Less. Add butter to Instant Pot. Add onion and sauté until softened, about 5 minutes. Press the Cancel button. 2. Add broccoli, cream cheese, mayo, and broth to pot. Press the Manual button and adjust time for 4 minutes. 3. When timer beeps, quick-release the pressure and stir in Cheddar. Serve warm.

Creamy Spinach

Prep time: 5 minutes | Cook time: 4 minutes | Serves 4

- 2 cups chopped spinach
- 2 ounces (57 g) Monterey Jack cheese, shredded
- 1 cup almond milk
- 1 tablespoon butter
- 1 teaspoon minced garlic
- ½ teaspoon salt

1. Combine all the ingredients in the Instant Pot. 2. Secure the lid. Select the Manual mode and set the cooking time for 4 minutes at High Pressure. 3. Once cooking is complete, do a quick pressure release. Carefully open the lid. 4. Give the mixture a good stir and serve warm.

Cabbage and Broccoli Slaw

Prep time: 5 minutes | Cook time: 10 minutes | Serves 6

- 2 cups broccoli slaw
- ½ head cabbage, thinly sliced
- ¼ cup chopped kale
- 4 tablespoons butter
- 1 teaspoon salt
- ¼ teaspoon pepper

1. Press the Sauté button and add all ingredients to Instant Pot. Stir-fry for 7 to 10 minutes until cabbage softens. Serve warm.

Lemon-Butter Mushrooms

Prep time: 10 minutes | Cook time: 4 minutes | Serves 2

- 1 cup cremini mushrooms, sliced
- ½ cup water
- 1 tablespoon lemon juice
- 1 teaspoon almond butter
- 1 teaspoon grated lemon zest
- ½ teaspoon salt
- ½ teaspoon dried thyme

1. Combine all the ingredients in the Instant Pot. 2. Secure the lid. Select the Manual mode and set the cooking time for 4 minutes at High Pressure. 3. Once cooking is complete, do a natural pressure release for 5 minutes, then release any remaining pressure. Carefully open the lid. 4. Serve warm.

Hummus with Chickpeas and Tahini Sauce

Prep time: 10 minutes | Cook time: 55 minutes | Makes 4 cups

- 4 cups water
- 1 cup dried chickpeas
- 2½ teaspoons fine sea salt
- ½ cup tahini
- 3 tablespoons fresh lemon juice
- 1 garlic clove
- ¼ teaspoon ground cumin

1. Combine the water, chickpeas, and 1 teaspoon of the salt in the Instant Pot and stir to dissolve the salt. 2. Secure the lid and set the Pressure Release to Sealing. Select the Bean/Chili, Pressure Cook, or Manual setting and set the cooking time for 40 minutes at high pressure. (The pot will take about 15 minutes to come up to pressure before the cooking program begins.) 3. When the cooking program ends, let the pressure release naturally for 15 minutes, then move the Pressure Release to Venting to release any remaining steam. 4. Place a colander over a bowl. Open the pot and, wearing heat-resistant mitts, lift out the inner pot and drain the beans in the colander. Return the chickpeas to the inner pot and place it back in the Instant Pot housing on the Keep Warm setting. Reserve the cooking liquid. 5. In a blender or food processor, combine 1 cup of the cooking liquid, the tahini, lemon juice, garlic, cumin, and 1 teaspoon salt. Blend or process on high speed, stopping to scrape down the sides of the container as needed, for about 30 seconds, until smooth and a little fluffy. Scoop out and set aside ½ cup of this sauce for the topping. 6. Set aside ½ cup of the chickpeas for the topping. Add the remaining chickpeas to the tahini sauce in the blender or food processor along with ½ cup of the cooking liquid and the remaining ½ teaspoon salt. Blend or process on high speed, stopping to scrape down the sides of the container as needed, for about 1 minute, until very smooth. 7. Transfer the hummus to a shallow serving bowl. Spoon the reserved tahini mixture over the top, then sprinkle on the reserved chickpeas. The hummus will keep in an airtight container in the refrigerator for up to 3 days. Serve at room temperature or chilled.

Herbed Zucchini Slices

Prep time: 5 minutes | Cook time: 5 minutes | Serves 4

- 2 tablespoons olive oil
- 2 garlic cloves, chopped
- 1 pound (454 g) zucchini, sliced
- ½ cup water
- ½ cup sugar-free tomato purée
- 1 teaspoon dried thyme
- ½ teaspoon dried rosemary
- ½ teaspoon dried oregano

1. Set your Instant Pot to Sauté and heat the olive oil. 2. Add the garlic and sauté for 2 minutes until fragrant. 3. Add the remaining ingredients to the Instant Pot and stir well. 4. Lock the lid. Select the Manual mode and set the cooking time for 3 minutes at Low Pressure. 5. When the timer beeps, perform a quick pressure release. Carefully remove the lid. 6. Serve warm.

Crispy Brussels Sprouts with Bacon

Prep time: 5 minutes | Cook time: 10 minutes | Serves 4

- ½ pound (227 g) bacon
- 1 pound (454 g) Brussels sprouts
- 4 tablespoons butter
- 1 teaspoon salt
- ½ teaspoon pepper
- ½ cup water

1. Press the Sauté button and press the Adjust button to lower heat to Less. Add bacon to Instant Pot and fry for 3 to 5 minutes or until fat begins to render. Press the Cancel button. 2. Press the Sauté button, with heat set to Normal, and continue frying bacon until crispy. While bacon is frying, wash Brussels sprouts and remove damaged outer leaves. Cut in half or quarters. 3. When bacon is done, remove and set aside. Add Brussels sprouts to hot bacon grease and add butter. Sprinkle with salt and pepper. Sauté for 8 to 10 minutes until caramelized and crispy, adding a few tablespoons of water at a time as needed to deglaze pan. Serve warm.

Creamy Jalapeño Chicken Dip

Prep time: 5 minutes | Cook time: 12 minutes | Serves 10

- 1 pound boneless chicken breast
- 8 ounces low-fat cream cheese
- 3 jalapeños, seeded and sliced
- ½ cup water
- 8 ounces reduced-fat shredded cheddar cheese
- ¾ cup low-fat sour cream

1. Place the chicken, cream cheese, jalapeños, and water in the inner pot of the Instant Pot. 2. Secure the lid so it's locked and turn the vent to sealing. 3. Press Manual and set the Instant Pot for 12 minutes on high pressure. 4. When cooking time is up, turn off Instant Pot, do a quick release of the remaining pressure, then remove lid. 5. Shred the chicken between 2 forks, either in the pot or on a cutting board, then place back in the inner pot. 6. Stir in the shredded cheese and sour cream.

Ground Turkey Lettuce Cups

Prep time: 5 minutes | Cook time: 30 minutes | Serves 8

- 3 tablespoons water
- 2 tablespoons soy sauce, tamari, or coconut aminos
- 3 tablespoons fresh lime juice
- 2 teaspoons Sriracha, plus more for serving
- 2 tablespoons cold-pressed avocado oil
- 2 teaspoons toasted sesame oil
- 4 garlic cloves, minced
- 1-inch piece fresh ginger, peeled and minced
- 2 carrots, diced
- 2 celery stalks, diced
- 1 yellow onion, diced
- 2 pounds 93 percent lean ground turkey
- ½ teaspoon fine sea salt
- Two 8-ounce cans sliced water chestnuts, drained and chopped
- 1 tablespoon cornstarch
- 2 hearts romaine lettuce or 2 heads butter lettuce, leaves separated
- ½ cup roasted cashews (whole or halves and pieces), chopped
- 1 cup loosely packed fresh cilantro leaves

1. In a small bowl, combine the water, soy sauce, 2 tablespoons of the lime juice, and the Sriracha and mix well. Set aside. 2. Select the Sauté setting on the Instant Pot and heat the avocado oil, sesame oil, garlic, and ginger for 2 minutes, until the garlic is bubbling but not browned. Add the carrots, celery, and onion and sauté for about 3 minutes, until the onion begins to soften. 3. Add the turkey and salt and sauté, using a wooden spoon or spatula to break up the meat as it cooks, for about 5 minutes, until cooked through and no streaks of pink remain. Add the water chestnuts and soy sauce mixture and stir to combine, working quickly so not too much steam escapes. 4. Secure the lid and set the Pressure Release to Sealing. Press the Cancel button to reset the cooking program, then select the Pressure Cook or Manual setting and set the cooking time for 5 minutes at high pressure. (The pot will take about 10 minutes to come up to pressure before the cooking program begins.) 5. When the cooking program ends, perform a quick pressure release by moving the Pressure Release to Venting, or let the pressure release naturally. Open the pot. 6. In a small bowl, stir together the remaining 1 tablespoon lime juice and the cornstarch, add the mixture to the pot, and stir to combine. Press the Cancel button to reset the cooking program, then select the Sauté setting. Let the mixture come to a boil and thicken, stirring often, for about 2 minutes, then press the Cancel button to turn off the pot. 7. Spoon the turkey mixture onto the lettuce leaves and sprinkle the cashews and cilantro on top. Serve right away, with additional Sriracha at the table.

Jalapeño Poppers with Bacon

Prep time: 10 minutes | Cook time: 3 minutes | Serves 4

- 6 jalapeños
- 4 ounces (113 g) cream cheese
- ¼ cup shredded sharp
- Cheddar cheese
- 1 cup water
- ¼ cup cooked crumbled bacon

1. Cut jalapeños lengthwise and scoop out seeds and membrane, then set aside. 2. In small bowl, mix cream cheese and Cheddar. Spoon into emptied jalapeños. Pour water into Instant Pot and place steamer basket in bottom. 3. Place stuffed jalapeños on steamer rack. Click lid closed. Press the Manual button and adjust time for 3 minutes. When timer beeps, quick-release the pressure. Serve topped with crumbled bacon.

Herbed Mushrooms

Prep time: 5 minutes | Cook time: 10 minutes | Serves 4

- 2 tablespoons butter
- 2 cloves garlic, minced
- 20 ounces (567 g) button mushrooms
- 1 tablespoon coconut aminos
- 1 teaspoon dried rosemary
- 1 teaspoon dried basil
- 1 teaspoon dried sage
- 1 bay leaf
- Sea salt, to taste
- ½ teaspoon freshly ground black pepper
- ½ cup chicken broth
- ½ cup water
- 1 tablespoon roughly chopped fresh parsley leaves, for garnish

1. Set your Instant Pot to Sauté and melt the butter. 2. Add the garlic and mushrooms and sauté for 3 to 4 minutes until the garlic is fragrant. 3. Add the remaining ingredients except the parsley to the Instant Pot and stir well. 4. Lock the lid. Select the Manual mode and set the cooking time for 5 minutes at High Pressure. 5. When the timer beeps, perform a quick pressure release. Carefully open the lid. 6. Remove the mushrooms from the pot to a platter. Serve garnished with the fresh parsley leaves.

Coconut Cajun Shrimp

Prep time: 10 minutes | Cook time: 6 minutes | Serves 2

- 4 Royal tiger shrimps
- 3 tablespoons coconut shred
- 2 eggs, beaten
- ½ teaspoon Cajun seasoning
- 1 teaspoon olive oil

1. Heat up olive oil in the instant pot on Sauté mode. 2. Meanwhile, mix up Cajun seasoning and coconut shred. 3. Dip the shrimps in the eggs and coat in the coconut shred mixture. 4. After this, place the shrimps in the hot olive oil and cook them on Sauté mode for 3 minutes from each side.

Candied Pecans

Prep time: 5 minutes | Cook time: 20 minutes | Serves 10

- 4 cups raw pecans
- 1½ teaspoons liquid stevia
- ½ cup plus 1 tablespoon water, divided
- 1 teaspoon vanilla extract
- 1 teaspoon cinnamon
- ¼ teaspoon nutmeg
- ⅛ teaspoon ground ginger
- ⅛ teaspoon sea salt

1. Place the raw pecans, liquid stevia, 1 tablespoon water, vanilla, cinnamon, nutmeg, ground ginger, and sea salt into the inner pot of the Instant Pot. 2. Press the Sauté button on the Instant Pot and sauté the pecans and other ingredients until the pecans are soft. 3. Pour in the ½ cup water and secure the lid to the locked position. Set the vent to sealing. 4. Press Manual and set the Instant Pot for 15 minutes. 5. Preheat the oven to 350°F. 6. When cooking time is up, turn off the Instant Pot, then do a quick release. 7. Spread the pecans onto a greased, lined baking sheet. 8. Bake the pecans for 5 minutes or less in the oven, checking on them frequently so they do not burn.

Spinach and Artichoke Dip

Prep time: 5 minutes | Cook time: 4 minutes | Serves 11

- 8 ounces low-fat cream cheese
- 10-ounce box frozen spinach
- ½ cup no-sodium chicken broth
- 14-ounce can artichoke hearts, drained
- ½ cup low-fat sour cream
- ½ cup low-fat mayo
- 3 cloves of garlic, minced
- 1 teaspoon onion powder
- 16 ounces reduced-fat shredded Parmesan cheese
- 8 ounces reduced-fat shredded mozzarella

1. Put all ingredients in the inner pot of the Instant Pot, except the Parmesan cheese and the mozzarella cheese. 2. Secure the lid and set vent to sealing. Place on Manual high pressure for 4 minutes. 3. Do a quick release of steam. 4. Immediately stir in the cheeses.

7-Layer Dip

Prep time: 10 minutes | Cook time: 35 minutes | Serves 6

Cashew Sour Cream
- 1 cup raw whole cashews, soaked in water to cover for 1 to 2 hours and then drained
- ½ cup avocado oil

Beans
- ½ cup dried black beans
- 2 cups water
- ½ teaspoon fine sea salt
- ½ teaspoon chili powder
- ¼ teaspoon garlic powder
- ½ cup grape or cherry tomatoes, halved
- 1 avocado, diced
- ¼ cup chopped yellow onion
- ½ cup water
- ¼ cup fresh lemon juice
- 2 tablespoons nutritional yeast
- 1 teaspoon fine sea salt
- 1 jalapeño chile, sliced
- 2 tablespoons chopped cilantro
- 6 ounces baked corn tortilla chips
- 1 English cucumber, sliced
- 2 carrots, sliced
- 6 celery stalks, cut into sticks

1. To make the cashew sour cream: In a blender, combine the cashews, oil, water, lemon juice, nutritional yeast, and salt. Blend on high speed, stopping to scrape down the sides of the container as needed, for about 2 minutes, until very smooth. (The sour cream can be made in advance and stored in an airtight container in the refrigerator for up to 5 days.) 2. To make the beans: Pour 1 cup water into the Instant Pot. In a 1½-quart stainless-steel bowl, combine the beans, the 2 cups water, and salt and stir to dissolve the salt. Place the bowl on a long-handled silicone steam rack, then, holding the handles of the steam rack, lower it into the Instant Pot. (If you don't have the long-handled rack, use the wire metal steam rack and a homemade sling) 3. Secure the lid and set the Pressure Release to Sealing. Select the Bean/Chili, Pressure Cook, or Manual setting and set the cooking time for 25 minutes at high pressure. (The pot will take about 10 minutes to come up to pressure before the cooking program begins.) 4. When the cooking program ends, let the pressure release naturally for at least 20 minutes, then move the Pressure Release to Venting to release any remaining steam. 5. Place a colander over a bowl. Open the pot and, wearing heat-resistant mitts, lift out the inner pot and drain the beans in the colander. Transfer the liquid captured in the bowl to a measuring cup, and pour the beans into the bowl. Add ¼ cup of the cooking liquid to the beans and, using a potato masher or fork, mash the beans to your desired consistency, adding more cooking liquid as needed. Stir in the chili powder and garlic powder. 6. Using a rubber spatula, spread the black beans in an even layer in a clear-glass serving dish. Spread the cashew sour cream in an even layer on top of the beans. Add layers of the tomatoes, avocado, onion, jalapeño, and cilantro. (At this point, you can cover and refrigerate the assembled dip for up to 1 day.) Serve accompanied with the tortilla chips, cucumber, carrots, and celery on the side.

Creamed Onion Spinach

Prep time: 3 minutes | Cook time: 5 minutes | Serves 6

- 4 tablespoons butter
- ¼ cup diced onion
- 8 ounces (227 g) cream cheese
- 1 (12 ounces / 340 g) bag
- frozen spinach
- ½ cup chicken broth
- 1 cup shredded whole-milk Mozzarella cheese

1. Press the Sauté button and add butter. Once butter is melted, add onion to Instant Pot and sauté for 2 minutes or until onion begins to turn translucent. 2. Break cream cheese into pieces and add to Instant Pot. Press the Cancel button. Add frozen spinach and broth. Click lid closed. Press the Manual button and adjust time for 5 minutes. When timer beeps, quick-release the pressure and stir in shredded Mozzarella. If mixture is too watery, press the Sauté button and reduce for additional 5 minutes, stirring constantly.

Buttered Cabbage

Prep time: 5 minutes | Cook time: 5 minutes | Serves 4

- 1 medium head white cabbage, sliced into strips
- 4 tablespoons butter
- ½ teaspoon salt
- ¼ teaspoon pepper
- 1 cup water

1. Place cabbage in 7-cup glass bowl with butter, salt, and pepper. 2. Pour water into Instant Pot and place steam rack on bottom. Place bowl on steam rack. Click lid closed. Press the Manual button and adjust time for 5 minutes. When timer beeps, quick-release the pressure.

Lemon-Cheese Cauliflower Bites

Prep time: 5 minutes | Cook time: 8 minutes | Serves 6

- 1 cup water
- 1 pound (454 g) cauliflower, broken into florets
- Sea salt and ground black pepper, to taste
- 2 tablespoons extra-virgin olive oil
- 2 tablespoons lemon juice
- 1 cup grated Cheddar cheese

1. Pour the water into the Instant Pot and insert a steamer basket. Place the cauliflower florets in the basket. 2. Lock the lid. Select the Manual mode and set the cooking time for 3 minutes at Low Pressure. 3. When the timer beeps, perform a quick pressure release. Carefully remove the lid. 4. Season the cauliflower with salt and pepper. Drizzle with olive oil and lemon juice. Sprinkle the grated cheese all over the cauliflower. 5. Press the Sauté button to heat the Instant Pot. Allow to cook for about 5 minutes, or until the cheese melts. Serve warm.

Cayenne Beef Bites

Prep time: 5 minutes | Cook time: 23 minutes | Serves 6

- 2 tablespoons olive oil
- 1 pound (454 g) beef steak, cut into cubes
- 1 cup beef bone broth
- ¼ cup dry white wine
- 1 teaspoon cayenne pepper
- ½ teaspoon dried marjoram
- Sea salt and ground black pepper, to taste

1. Set your Instant Pot to Sauté and heat the olive oil. 2. Add the beef and sauté for 2 to 3 minutes, stirring occasionally. 3. Add the remaining ingredients to the Instant Pot and combine well. 4. Lock the lid. Select the Manual mode and set the cooking time for 20 minutes at High Pressure. 5. When the timer beeps, perform a natural pressure release for 10 minutes, then release any remaining pressure. Carefully remove the lid. 6. Remove the beef from the Instant Pot to a platter and serve warm.

Creole Pancetta and Cheese Balls

Prep time: 5 minutes | Cook time: 5 minutes | Serves 6

- 1 cup water
- 6 eggs
- 4 slices pancetta, chopped
- ⅓ cup grated Cheddar cheese
- ¼ cup cream cheese
- ¼ cup mayonnaise
- 1 teaspoon Creole seasonings
- Sea salt and ground black pepper, to taste

1. Pour the water into the Instant Pot and insert a steamer basket. Place the eggs in the basket. 2. Lock the lid. Select the Manual mode and set the cooking time for 5 minutes at Low Pressure. 3. When the timer beeps, perform a quick pressure release. Carefully remove the lid. 4. Allow the eggs to cool for 10 to 15 minutes. Peel the eggs and chop them, then transfer to a bowl. Add the remaining ingredients and stir to combine well. 5. Shape the mixture into balls with your hands. Serve chilled.

Curried Broccoli Skewers

Prep time: 15 minutes | Cook time: 1 minute | Serves 2

- 1 cup broccoli florets
- ½ teaspoon curry paste
- 2 tablespoons coconut cream
- 1 cup water, for cooking

1. In the shallow bowl mix up curry paste and coconut cream. 2. Then sprinkle the broccoli florets with curry paste mixture and string on the skewers. 3. Pour water and insert the steamer rack in the instant pot. 4. Place the broccoli skewers on the rack. Close and seal the lid. 5. Cook the meal on Manual mode (High Pressure) for 1 minute. 6. Make a quick pressure release.

Cheese Stuffed Bell Peppers

Prep time: 10 minutes | Cook time: 5 minutes | Serves 5

- 1 cup water
- 10 baby bell peppers, seeded and sliced lengthwise
- 4 ounces (113 g) Monterey Jack cheese, shredded
- 4 ounces (113 g) cream cheese
- 2 tablespoons chopped scallions
- 1 tablespoon olive oil
- 1 teaspoon minced garlic
- ½ teaspoon cayenne pepper
- ¼ teaspoon ground black pepper, or more to taste

1. Pour the water into the Instant Pot and insert a steamer basket. 2. Stir together the remaining ingredients except the bell peppers in a mixing bowl until combined. Stuff the peppers evenly with the mixture. Arrange the stuffed peppers in the basket. 3. Lock the lid. Select the Manual mode and set the cooking time for 5 minutes at High Pressure. 4. When the timer beeps, perform a quick pressure release. Carefully remove the lid. 5. Cool for 5 minutes and serve.

Garlic Herb Butter

Prep time: 10 minutes | Cook time: 8 minutes | Serves 4

- ⅓ cup butter
- 1 teaspoon dried parsley
- 1 tablespoon dried dill
- ½ teaspoon minced garlic
- ¼ teaspoon dried thyme

1. Preheat the instant pot on Sauté mode. 2. Then add butter and melt it. 3. Add dried parsley, dill, minced garlic, and thyme. Stir the butter mixture well. 4. Transfer it in the butter mold and refrigerate until it is solid.

Southern Boiled Peanuts

Prep time: 5 minutes | Cook time: 1 hour 20 minutes | Makes 8 cups

- 1 pound raw jumbo peanuts in the shell
- 3 tablespoons fine sea salt

1. Remove the inner pot from the Instant Pot and add the peanuts to it. Cover the peanuts with water and use your hands to agitate them, loosening any dirt. Drain the peanuts in a colander, rinse out the pot, and return the peanuts to it. Return the inner pot to the Instant Pot housing. 2. Add the salt and 9 cups water to the pot and stir to dissolve the salt. Select a salad plate just small enough to fit inside the pot and set it on top of the peanuts to weight them down, submerging them all in the water. 3. Secure the lid and set the Pressure Release to Sealing. Select the Steam setting and set the cooking time for 1 hour at low pressure. (The pot will take about 20 minutes to come up to pressure before the cooking program begins.) 4. When the cooking program ends, let the pressure release naturally (this will take about 1 hour). Open the pot and, wearing heat-resistant mitts, remove the inner pot from the housing. Let the peanuts cool to room temperature in the brine (this will take about 1½ hours). 5. Serve at room temperature or chilled. Transfer the peanuts with their brine to an airtight container and refrigerate for up to 1 week.

Mayo Chicken Celery

Prep time: 15 minutes | Cook time: 15 minutes | Serves 4

- 14 ounces (397 g) chicken breast, skinless, boneless
- 1 cup water
- 4 celery stalks
- 1 teaspoon salt
- ½ teaspoon onion powder
- 1 teaspoon mayonnaise

1. Combine all the ingredients except the mayo in the Instant Pot. 2. Secure the lid. Select the Manual mode and set the cooking time for 15 minutes at High Pressure. 3. Once cooking is complete, do a natural pressure release for 6 minutes, then release any remaining pressure. Carefully open the lid. 4. Remove the chicken and shred with two forks, then return to the Instant Pot. 5. Add the mayo and stir well. Serve immediately.

Parmesan Chicken Balls with Chives

Prep time: 10 minutes | Cook time: 15 minutes | Serves 4

- 1 teaspoon coconut oil, softened
- 1 cup ground chicken
- ¼ cup chicken broth
- 1 tablespoon chopped chives
- 1 teaspoon cayenne pepper
- 3 ounces (85 g) Parmesan cheese, grated

1. Set your Instant Pot to Sauté and heat the coconut oil. 2. Add the remaining ingredients except the cheese to the Instant Pot and stir to mix well. 3. Secure the lid. Select the Manual mode and set the cooking time for 15 minutes at High Pressure. 4. Once cooking is complete, do a quick pressure release. Carefully open the lid. 5. Add the grated cheese and stir until combined. Form the balls from the cooked chicken mixture and allow to cool for 10 minutes, then serve.

Chapter 7 Desserts

Coconut Squares

Prep time: 15 minutes | Cook time: 4 minutes | Serves 2

- ⅓ cup coconut flakes
- 1 tablespoon butter
- 1 egg, beaten
- 1 cup water, for cooking

1. Mix up together coconut flakes, butter, and egg. 2. Then put the mixture into the square shape mold and flatten well. 3. Pour water and insert the steamer rack in the instant pot. 4. Put the mold with dessert on the rack. Close and seal the lid. 5. Cook the meal on Manual mode (High Pressure) for 4 minutes. Make a quick pressure release. 6. Cool the cooked dessert little and cut into the squares.

Vanilla Cream Pie

Prep time: 20 minutes | Cook time: 35 minutes | Serves 12

- 1 cup heavy cream
- 3 eggs, beaten
- 1 teaspoon vanilla extract
- ¼ cup erythritol
- 1 cup coconut flour
- 1 tablespoon butter, melted
- 1 cup water, for cooking

1. In the mixing bowl, mix up coconut flour, erythritol, vanilla extract, eggs, and heavy cream. 2. Grease the baking pan with melted butter. 3. Pour the coconut mixture in the baking pan. 4. Pour water and insert the steamer rack in the instant pot. 5. Place the pie on the rack. Close and seal the lid. 6. Cook the pie on Manual mode (High Pressure) for 35 minutes. 7. Allow the natural pressure release for 10 minutes.

Blackberry Crisp

Prep time: 5 minutes | Cook time: 5 minutes | Serves 1

- 10 blackberries
- ½ teaspoon vanilla extract
- 2 tablespoons powdered erythritol
- ⅛ teaspoon xanthan gum
- 1 tablespoon butter
- ¼ cup chopped pecans
- 3 teaspoons almond flour
- ½ teaspoon cinnamon
- 2 teaspoons powdered erythritol
- 1 cup water

1. Place blackberries, vanilla, erythritol, and xanthan gum in 4-inch

ramekin. Stir gently to coat blackberries. 2. In small bowl, mix remaining ingredients. Sprinkle over blackberries and cover with foil. Press the Manual button and set time for 4 minutes. When timer beeps, quick-release the pressure. Serve warm. Feel free to add scoop of whipped cream on top.

Candied Mixed Nuts

Prep time: 5 minutes | Cook time: 15 minutes | Serves 8

- 1 cup pecan halves
- 1 cup chopped walnuts
- ⅓ cup Swerve, or more to
- taste
- ⅓ cup grass-fed butter
- 1 teaspoon ground cinnamon

1. Preheat your oven to 350ºF (180ºC), and line a baking sheet with aluminum foil. 2. While your oven is warming, pour ½ cup of filtered water into the inner pot of the Instant Pot, followed by the pecans, walnuts, Swerve, butter, and cinnamon. Stir nut mixture, close the lid, and then set the pressure valve to Sealing. Use the Manual mode to cook at High Pressure, for 5 minutes. 3. Once cooked, perform a quick release by carefully switching the pressure valve to Venting, and strain the nuts. Pour the nuts onto the baking sheet, spreading them out in an even layer. Place in the oven for 5 to 10 minutes (or until crisp, being careful not to overcook). Cool before serving. Store leftovers in the refrigerator or freezer.

Chai Pear-Fig Compote

Prep time: 20 minutes | Cook time: 3 minutes | Serves 4

- 1 vanilla chai tea bag
- 1 (3-inch) cinnamon stick
- 1 strip lemon peel (about 2-by-½ inches)
- 1½ pounds pears, peeled and chopped (about 3 cups)
- ½ cup chopped dried figs
- 2 tablespoons raisins

1. Pour 1 cup of water into the electric pressure cooker and hit Sauté/More. When the water comes to a boil, add the tea bag and cinnamon stick. Hit Cancel. Let the tea steep for 5 minutes, then remove and discard the tea bag. 2. Add the lemon peel, pears, figs, and raisins to the pot. 3. Close and lock the lid of the pressure cooker. Set the valve to sealing. 4. Cook on high pressure for 3 minutes. 5. When the cooking is complete, hit Cancel and quick release the pressure. 6. Once the pin drops, unlock and remove the lid. 7. Remove the lemon peel and cinnamon stick. Serve warm or cool to room temperature and refrigerate.

Goat Cheese–Stuffed Pears

Prep time: 6 minutes | Cook time: 2 minutes | Serves 4

- 2 ounces goat cheese, at room temperature
- 2 teaspoons pure maple syrup
- 2 ripe, firm pears, halved lengthwise and cored
- 2 tablespoons chopped pistachios, toasted

1. Pour 1 cup of water into the electric pressure cooker and insert a wire rack or trivet. 2. In a small bowl, combine the goat cheese and maple syrup. 3. Spoon the goat cheese mixture into the cored pear halves. Place the pears on the rack inside the pot, cut-side up. 4. Close and lock the lid of the pressure cooker. Set the valve to sealing. 5. Cook on high pressure for 2 minutes. 6. When the cooking is complete, hit Cancel and quick release the pressure. 7. Once the pin drops, unlock and remove the lid. 8. Using tongs, carefully transfer the pears to serving plates. 9. Sprinkle with pistachios and serve immediately.

Vanilla Butter Curd

Prep time: 5 minutes | Cook time: 6 hours | Serves 3

- 4 egg yolks, whisked
- 2 tablespoon butter
- 1 tablespoon erythritol
- ½ cup organic almond milk
- 1 teaspoon vanilla extract

1. Set the instant pot to Sauté mode and when the "Hot" is displayed, add butter. 2. Melt the butter but not boil it and add whisked egg yolks, almond milk, and vanilla extract. 3. Add erythritol. Whisk the mixture. 4. Cook the meal on Low for 6 hours.

Lemon Vanilla Cheesecake

Prep time: 15 minutes | Cook time: 20 minutes | Serves 6

- 2 teaspoons freshly squeezed lemon juice
- 2 teaspoons vanilla extract or almond extract
- ½ cup sour cream, divided, at room temperature
- ½ cup plus 2 teaspoons Swerve
- 8 ounces (227 g) cream cheese, at room temperature
- 2 eggs, at room temperature

1. Pour 2 cups of water into the inner cooking pot of the Instant Pot, then place a trivet (preferably with handles) in the pot. Line the sides of a 6-inch springform pan with parchment paper. 2. In a food processor, put the lemon juice, vanilla, ¼ cup of sour cream, ½ cup of Swerve, and the cream cheese. 3. Gently but thoroughly blend all the ingredients, scraping down the sides of the bowl as needed. 4. Add the eggs and blend only as long as you need to in order to get them well incorporated, 20 to 30 seconds. Your mixture will be pourable by now. 5. Pour the mixture into the prepared pan. Cover the pan with aluminum foil and place on the trivet. (If your trivet doesn't have handles, you may wish to use a foil sling to make removing the pan easier.) 6. Lock the lid into place. Select Manual and adjust the pressure to High. Cook for 20 minutes. When the cooking is complete, let the pressure release naturally. Unlock the lid. 7. Meanwhile, in a small bowl, mix together the remaining ¼ cup of sour cream and 2 teaspoons of Swerve for the topping. 8. Take out the cheesecake and remove the foil. Spread the topping over the top. Doing this while the cheesecake is still hot helps melt the topping into the cheesecake. 9. Put the cheesecake in the refrigerator and leave it alone. Seriously. Leave it alone and let it chill for at least 6 to 8 hours. It won't taste right hot. 10. When you're ready to serve, open the sides of the pan and peel off the parchment paper. Slice and serve.

Lime Muffins

Prep time: 10 minutes | Cook time: 15 minutes | Serves 6

- 1 teaspoon lime zest
- 1 tablespoon lemon juice
- 1 teaspoon baking powder
- 1 cup almond flour
- 2 eggs, beaten
- 1 tablespoon Swerve
- ¼ cup heavy cream
- 1 cup water, for cooking

1. In the mixing bowl, mix up lemon juice, baking powder, almond flour, eggs, Swerve, and heavy cream. 2. When the muffin batter is smooth, add lime zest and mix it up. 3. Fill the muffin molds with batter. 4. Then pour water and insert the rack in the instant pot. 5. Place the muffins on the rack. Close and seal the lid. 6. Cook the muffins on Manual (High Pressure) for 15 minutes. 7. Then allow the natural pressure release.

Keto Brownies

Prep time: 15 minutes | Cook time: 15 minutes | Serves 8

- 1 cup coconut flour
- 1 tablespoon cocoa powder
- 1 tablespoon coconut oil
- 1 teaspoon vanilla extract
- 1 teaspoon baking powder
- 1 teaspoon apple cider vinegar
- ⅓ cup butter, melted
- 1 tablespoon erythritol
- 1 cup water, for cooking

1. In the mixing bowl, mix up erythritol, melted butter, apple cider vinegar, baking powder, vanilla extract, coconut oil, cocoa powder, and coconut flour. 2. Whisk the mixture until smooth and pour it in the baking pan. Flatten the surface of the batter. 3. Pour water and insert the steamer rack in the instant pot. 4. Put the pan with brownie batter on the rack. Close and seal the lid. 5. Cook the brownie on Manual mode (High Pressure) for 15 minutes. 6. Then allow the natural pressure release for 5 minutes. 7. Cut the cooked brownies into the bars.

Cardamom Rolls with Cream Cheese

Prep time: 20 minutes | Cook time: 18 minutes | Serves 5

- ½ cup coconut flour
- 1 tablespoon ground cardamom
- 2 tablespoon Swerve
- 1 egg, whisked
- ¼ cup almond milk
- 1 tablespoon butter, softened
- 1 tablespoon cream cheese
- ⅓ cup water

1. Combine together coconut flour, almond milk, and softened butter. 2. Knead the smooth dough. 3. Roll up the dough with the help of the rolling pin. 4. Then combine together Swerve and ground cardamom. 5. Sprinkle the surface of the dough with the ground cardamom mixture. 6. Roll the dough into one big roll and cut them into servings. 7. Place the rolls into the instant pot round mold. 8. Pour water in the instant pot (⅓ cup) and insert the mold inside. 9. Set Manual mode (High Pressure) for 18 minutes. 10. Then use the natural pressure release method for 15 minutes. 11. Chill the rolls to the room temperature and spread with cream cheese.

Cinnamon Roll Cheesecake

Prep time: 15 minutes | Cook time: 35 minutes | Serves 12

Crust:
- 3½ tablespoons unsalted butter or coconut oil
- 1½ ounces (43 g) unsweetened baking chocolate, chopped
- 1 large egg, beaten

Filling:
- 4 (8-ounce / 227-g) packages cream cheese, softened
- ¾ cup Swerve
- ½ cup unsweetened almond milk (or hemp milk for nut-free)

Cinnamon Swirl:
- 6 tablespoons (¾ stick) unsalted butter (or butter flavored coconut oil for dairy-free)
- ½ cup Swerve
- Seeds scraped from ½ vanilla bean (about 8 inches

- ⅓ cup Swerve
- 2 teaspoons ground cinnamon
- 1 teaspoon vanilla extract
- ¼ teaspoon fine sea salt

- 1 teaspoon vanilla extract
- ¼ teaspoon almond extract (omit for nut-free)
- ¼ teaspoon fine sea salt
- 3 large eggs

long), or 1 teaspoon vanilla extract
- 1 tablespoon ground cinnamon
- ¼ teaspoon fine sea salt
- 1 cup cold water

1. Line a baking pan with two layers of aluminum foil. 2. Make the crust: Melt the butter in a pan over medium-low heat. Slowly add the chocolate and stir until melted. Stir in the egg, sweetener, cinnamon, vanilla extract, and salt. 3. Transfer the crust mixture to the prepared baking pan, spreading it with your hands to cover the bottom completely. 4. Make the filling: In the bowl of a stand mixer, add the cream cheese, sweetener, milk, extracts, and salt and mix until well blended. Add the eggs, one at a time, mixing on low speed after each addition just until blended. Then blend until the filling is smooth. Pour half of the filling over the crust. 5. Make the cinnamon swirl: Heat the butter over high heat in a pan until the butter froths and brown flecks appear, stirring occasionally. Stir in the sweetener, vanilla seeds, cinnamon, and salt. Remove from the heat and allow to cool slightly. 6. Spoon half of the cinnamon swirl on top of the cheesecake filling in the baking pan. Use a knife to cut the cinnamon swirl through the filling several times for a marbled effect. Top with the rest of the cheesecake filling and cinnamon swirl. Cut the cinnamon swirl through the cheesecake filling again several times. 7. Place a trivet in the bottom of the Instant Pot and pour in the water. Use a foil sling to lower the baking pan onto the trivet. Cover the cheesecake with 3 large sheets of paper towel to ensure that condensation doesn't leak onto it. Tuck in the sides of the sling. 8. Lock the lid. Select the Manual mode and set the cooking time for 26 minutes at High Pressure. 9. When the timer beeps, use a natural pressure release for 10 minutes. Carefully remove the lid. 10. Use the foil sling to lift the pan out of the Instant Pot. 11. Let the cheesecake cool, then place in the refrigerator for 4 hours to chill and set completely before slicing and serving.

Pumpkin Pie Pudding

Prep time: 10 minutes | Cook time: 20 minutes | Serves 6

Nonstick cooking spray
- 2 eggs
- ½ cup heavy (whipping) cream or almond milk (for dairy-free)
- ¾ cup Swerve
- 1 (15-ounce / 425-g) can pumpkin purée
- 1 teaspoon pumpkin pie spice
- 1 teaspoon vanilla extract
- For Serving:
- ½ cup heavy (whipping) cream

1. Grease a 6-by-3-inch pan extremely well with the cooking spray, making sure it gets into all the nooks and crannies. 2. In a medium bowl, whisk the eggs. Add the cream, Swerve, pumpkin purée, pumpkin pie spice, and vanilla, and stir to mix thoroughly. 3. Pour the mixture into the prepared pan and cover it with a silicone lid or aluminum foil. 4. Pour 2 cups of water into the inner cooking pot of the Instant Pot, then place a trivet in the pot. Place the covered pan on the trivet. 5. Lock the lid into place. Select Manual and adjust the pressure to High. Cook for 20 minutes. When the cooking is complete, let the pressure release naturally for 10 minutes, then quick-release any remaining pressure. Unlock the lid. 6. Remove the pan and place it in the refrigerator. Chill for 6 to 8 hours. 8. When ready to serve, finish by making the whipped cream. Using a hand mixer, beat the heavy cream until it forms soft peaks. Do not overbeat and turn it to butter. Serve each pudding with a dollop of whipped cream.

Fast Chocolate Mousse

Prep time: 10 minutes | Cook time: 4 minutes | Serves 1

- 1 egg yolk
- 1 teaspoon erythritol
- 1 teaspoon cocoa powder
- 2 tablespoons coconut milk
- 1 tablespoon cream cheese
- 1 cup water, for cooking

1. Pour water and insert the steamer rack in the instant pot. 2. Then whisk the egg yolk with erythritol. 3. When the mixture turns into lemon color, add coconut milk, cream cheese, and cocoa powder. Whisk the mixture until smooth. 4. Then pour it in the glass jar and place it on the steamer rack. 5. Close and seal the lid. 6. Cook the dessert on Manual (High Pressure) for 4 minutes. Make a quick pressure release.

Crustless Key Lime Cheesecake

Prep time: 15 minutes | Cook time: 35 minutes | Serves 8

- Nonstick cooking spray
- 16 ounces light cream cheese (Neufchâtel), softened
- ⅔ cup granulated erythritol sweetener
- ¼ cup unsweetened Key lime juice (I like Nellie & Joe's Famous Key West

Lime Juice)
- ½ teaspoon vanilla extract
- ¼ cup plain Greek yogurt
- 1 teaspoon grated lime zest
- 2 large eggs
- Whipped cream, for garnish (optional)

1. Spray a 7-inch springform pan with nonstick cooking spray. Line the bottom and partway up the sides of the pan with foil. 2. Put the cream cheese in a large bowl. Use an electric mixer to whip the cream cheese until smooth, about 2 minutes. Add the erythritol, lime juice, vanilla, yogurt, and zest, and blend until smooth. Stop the mixer and scrape down the sides of the bowl with a rubber spatula. With the mixer on low speed, add the eggs, one at a time, blending until just mixed. (Don't overbeat the eggs.) 3. Pour the mixture into the prepared pan. Drape a paper towel over the top of the pan, not touching the cream cheese mixture, and tightly wrap the top of the pan in foil. (Your goal here is to keep out as much moisture as possible.) 4. Pour 1 cup of water into the electric pressure cooker. 5. Place the foil-covered pan onto the wire rack and carefully lower it into the pot. 6. Close and lock the lid of the pressure cooker. Set the valve to sealing. 7. Cook on high pressure for 35 minutes. 8. When the cooking is complete, hit Cancel. Allow the pressure to release naturally for 20 minutes, then quick release any remaining pressure. 9. Once the pin drops, unlock and remove the lid. 10. Using the handles of the wire rack, carefully transfer the pan to a cooling rack. Cool to room temperature, then refrigerate for at least 3 hours. 11. When ready to serve, run a thin rubber spatula around the rim of the cheesecake to loosen it, then remove the ring. 12. Slice into wedges and serve with whipped cream (if using).

Egg Custard Tarts

Prep time: 10 minutes | Cook time: 20 minutes | Serves 2

- ¼ cup almond flour
- 1 tablespoon coconut oil
- 2 egg yolks
- ¼ cup coconut milk
- 1 tablespoon erythritol
- 1 teaspoon vanilla extract
- 1 cup water, for cooking

1. Make the dough: Mix up almond flour and coconut oil. 2. Then place the dough into 2 mini tart molds and flatten well in the shape of cups. 3. Pour water in the instant pot. Insert the steamer rack. 4. Place the tart mold in the instant pot. Close and seal the lid. 5. Cook them for 3 minutes on Manual mode (High Pressure). Make a quick pressure release. 6. Then whisk together vanilla extract, erythritol, coconut milk, and egg yolks. 7. Pour the liquid in the tart molds and close the lid. 8. Cook the dessert for 7 minutes on Manual mode (High Pressure). 9. Then allow the natural pressure release for 10 minutes more.

Espresso Cheesecake with Raspberries

Prep time: 5 minutes | Cook time: 35 minutes | Serves 8

- 1 cup blanched almond flour
- ½ cup plus 2 tablespoons Swerve
- 3 tablespoons espresso powder, divided
- 2 tablespoons butter
- 1 egg
- ½ cup full-fat heavy cream
- 16 ounces (454 g) cream

cheese
- 1 cup water
- 6 ounces (170 g) dark chocolate (at least 80% cacao)
- 8 ounces (227 g) full-fat heavy whipping cream
- 2 cups raspberries

1. In a small mixing bowl, combine the almond flour, 2 tablespoons of Swerve, 1 tablespoon of espresso powder and the butter. 2. Line the bottom of a springform pan with parchment paper. Press the almond flour dough flat on the bottom and about 1 inch on the sides. Set aside. 3. In a food processor, mix the egg, heavy cream, cream cheese, remaining Swerve and remaining espresso powder until smooth. 4. Pour the cream cheese mixture into the springform pan. Loosely cover with aluminum foil. 5. Put the water in the Instant Pot and place the trivet inside. 6. Close the lid. Select Manual button and set the timer for 35 minutes on High pressure. 7. When timer beeps, use a natural pressure release for 15 minutes, then release any remaining pressure. Open the lid. 8. Remove the springform pan and place it on a cooling rack for 2 to 3 hours or until it reaches room temperature. Refrigerate overnight. 9. Melt the chocolate and heavy whipping cream in the double boiler. Cool for 15 minutes and drizzle on top of the cheesecake, allowing the chocolate to drip down the sides. 10. Add the raspberries on top of the cheesecake before serving.

Traditional Cheesecake

Prep time: 30 minutes | Cook time: 45 minutes | Serves 8

For Crust:
- 1½ cups almond flour
- 4 tablespoons butter, melted
- 1 tablespoon Swerve
- 1 tablespoon granulated erythritol
- ½ teaspoon ground cinnamon

For Filling:
- 16 ounces (454 g) cream cheese, softened
- ½ cup granulated erythritol
- 2 eggs
- 1 teaspoon vanilla extract
- ½ teaspoon lemon extract
- 1½ cups water

1. To make the crust: In a medium bowl, combine the almond flour, butter, Swerve, erythritol, and cinnamon. Use a fork to press it all together. When completed, the mixture should resemble wet sand. 2. Spray the springform pan with cooking spray and line the bottom with parchment paper. 3. Press the crust evenly into the pan. Work the crust up the sides of the pan, about halfway from the top, and make sure there are no bare spots on the bottom. 4. Place the crust in the freezer for 20 minutes while you make the filling. 5. To make the filling: In the bowl of a stand mixer using the whip attachment, combine the cream cheese and erythritol on medium speed until the cream cheese is light and fluffy, 2 to 3 minutes. 6. Add the eggs, vanilla extract, and lemon extract. Mix until well combined. 7. Remove the crust from the freezer and pour in the filling. Cover the pan tightly with aluminum foil and place it on the trivet. 8. Add the water to the pot and carefully lower the trivet into the pot. 9. Close the lid. Select Manual mode and set cooking time for 45 minutes on High Pressure. 10. When timer beeps, use a quick pressure release and open the lid. 11. Remove the trivet and cheesecake from the pot. Remove the foil from the pan. The center of the cheesecake should still be slightly jiggly. If the cheesecake is still very jiggly in the center, cook for an additional 5 minutes on High pressure until the appropriate doneness is reached. 12. Let the cheesecake cool for 30 minutes on the counter before placing it in the refrigerator to set. Leave the cheesecake in the refrigerator for at least 6 hours before removing the sides of the pan, slicing, and serving.

Almond Butter Blondies

Prep time: 10 minutes | Cook time: 20 minutes | Serves 8

- ½ cup creamy natural almond butter, at room temperature
- 4 large eggs
- ¾ cup Lakanto Monkfruit Sweetener Golden
- 1 teaspoon pure vanilla extract
- ½ teaspoon fine sea salt
- 1¼ cups almond flour
- ¾ cup stevia-sweetened chocolate chips

1. Pour 1 cup water into the Instant Pot. Line the base of a 7 by 3-inch round cake pan with a circle of parchment paper. Butter the sides of the pan and the parchment or coat with nonstick cooking spray. 2. Put the almond butter into a medium bowl. One at a time, whisk the eggs into the almond butter, then whisk in the sweetener, vanilla, and salt. Stir in the flour just until it is fully incorporated, followed by the chocolate chips. 3. Transfer the batter to the prepared pan and, using a rubber spatula, spread it in an even layer. Cover the pan tightly with aluminum foil. Place the pan on a long-handled silicone steam rack, then, holding the handles of the steam rack, lower it into the Instant Pot. 4. Secure the lid and set the Pressure Release to Sealing. Select the Cake, Pressure Cook, or Manual setting and set the cooking time for 40 minutes at high pressure. (The pot will take about 10 minutes to come up to pressure before the cooking program begins.) 5. When the cooking program ends, let the pressure release naturally for 10 minutes, then move the Pressure Release to Venting to release any remaining steam. Open the pot and, wearing heat-resistant mitts, grasp the handles of the steam rack and lift it out of the pot. Uncover the pan, taking care not to get burned by the steam or to drip condensation onto the blondies. Let the blondies cool in the pan on a cooling rack for about 5 minutes. 6. Run a butter knife around the edge of pan to make sure the blondies are not sticking to the pan sides. Invert the blondies onto the rack, lift off the pan, and peel off the parchment paper. Let cool for 15 minutes, then invert the blondies onto a serving plate and cut into eight wedges. The blondies will keep, stored in an airtight container in the refrigerator for up to 5 days, or in the freezer for up to 4 months.

Glazed Pumpkin Bundt Cake

Prep time: 7 minutes | Cook time: 35 minutes | Serves 12

Cake:
- 3 cups blanched almond flour
- 1 teaspoon baking soda
- ½ teaspoon fine sea salt
- 2 teaspoons ground cinnamon
- 1 teaspoon ground nutmeg
- 1 teaspoon ginger powder
- ¼ teaspoon ground cloves
- 6 large eggs
- 2 cups pumpkin purée
- 1 cup Swerve
- ¼ cup (½ stick) unsalted butter (or coconut oil for dairy-free), softened

Glaze:
- 1 cup (2 sticks) unsalted butter (or coconut oil for dairy-free), melted
- ½ cup Swerve

1. In a large bowl, stir together the almond flour, baking soda, salt, and spices. In another large bowl, add the eggs, pumpkin, sweetener, and butter and stir until smooth. Pour the wet ingredients into the dry ingredients and stir well. 2. Grease a 6-cup Bundt pan. Pour the batter into the prepared pan and cover with a paper towel and then with aluminum foil. 3. Place a trivet in the bottom of the Instant Pot and pour in 2 cups of cold water. Place the Bundt pan on the trivet. 4. Lock the lid. Select the Manual mode and set the cooking time for 35 minutes at High Pressure. 5. When the timer beeps, use a natural pressure release for 10 minutes. Carefully remove the lid. 6. Let the cake cool in the pot for 10 minutes before removing. 7. While the cake is cooling, make the glaze: In a small bowl, mix the butter and sweetener together. Spoon the glaze over the warm cake. 8. Allow to cool for 5 minutes before slicing and serving.

Chocolate Chip Brownies

Prep time: 10 minutes | Cook time: 33 minutes | Serves 8

- 1½ cups almond flour
- ⅓ cup unsweetened cocoa powder
- ¾ cup granulated erythritol
- 1 teaspoon baking powder
- 2 eggs
- 1 tablespoon vanilla extract
- 5 tablespoons butter, melted
- ¼ cup sugar-free chocolate chips
- ½ cup water

1. In a large bowl, add the almond flour, cocoa powder, erythritol, and baking powder. Use a hand mixer on low speed to combine and smooth out any lumps. 2. Add the eggs and vanilla and mix until well combined. 3. Add the butter and mix on low speed until well combined. Scrape the bottom and sides of the bowl and mix again if needed. Fold in the chocolate chips. 4. Grease a baking dish with cooking spray. Pour the batter into the dish and smooth with a spatula. Cover tightly with aluminum foil. 5. Pour the water into the pot. Place the trivet in the pot and carefully lower the baking dish onto the trivet. 6. Close the lid. Select Manual mode and set cooking time for 33 minutes on High Pressure. 7. When timer beeps, use a quick pressure release and open the lid. 8. Use the handles to carefully remove the trivet from the pot. Remove the foil from the dish. 9. Let the brownies cool for 10 minutes before turning out onto a plate.

Southern Almond Pie

Prep time: 10 minutes | Cook time: 35 minutes | Serves 12

- 2 cups almond flour
- 1½ cups powdered erythritol
- 1 teaspoon baking powder
- Pinch of salt
- ½ cup sour cream
- 4 tablespoons butter, melted
- 1 egg
- 1 teaspoon vanilla extract
- Cooking spray
- 1½ teaspoons ground cinnamon
- 1½ teaspoons Swerve
- 1 cup water

1. In a large bowl, whisk together the almond flour, powdered erythritol, baking powder, and salt. 2. Add the sour cream, butter, egg, and vanilla and whisk until well combined. The batter will be very thick, almost like cookie dough. 3. Grease the baking dish with cooking spray. Line with parchment paper, if desired. 4. Transfer the batter to the dish and level with an offset spatula. 5. In a small bowl, combine the cinnamon and Swerve. Sprinkle over the top of the batter. 6. Cover the dish tightly with aluminum foil. Add the water to the pot. Set the dish on the trivet and carefully lower it into the pot. 7. Set the lid in place. Select the Manual mode and set the cooking time for 35 minutes on High Pressure. When the timer goes off, do a quick pressure release. Carefully open the lid. 8. Remove the trivet and pie from the pot. Remove the foil from the pan. The pie should be set but soft, and the top should be slightly cracked. 9. Cool completely before cutting.

Deconstructed Tiramisu

Prep time: 5 minutes | Cook time: 9 minutes | Serves 4

- 1 cup heavy cream (or full-fat coconut milk for dairy-free)
- 2 large egg yolks
- 2 tablespoons brewed decaf espresso or strong brewed coffee
- 2 tablespoons Swerve, or more to taste
- 1 teaspoon rum extract
- 1 teaspoon unsweetened cocoa powder, or more to taste
- Pinch of fine sea salt
- 1 cup cold water
- 4 teaspoons Swerve, for topping

1. Heat the cream in a pan over medium-high heat until hot, about 2 minutes. 2. Place the egg yolks, coffee, sweetener, rum extract, cocoa powder, and salt in a blender and blend until smooth. 3. While the blender is running, slowly pour in the hot cream. Taste and adjust the sweetness to your liking. Add more cocoa powder, if desired. 4. Scoop the mixture into four ramekins with a spatula. Cover the ramekins with aluminum foil. 5. Place a trivet in the bottom of the Instant Pot and pour in the water. Place the ramekins on the trivet. 6. Lock the lid. Select the Manual mode and set the cooking time for 7 minutes at High Pressure. 7. When the timer beeps, use a quick pressure release. Carefully remove the lid. 8. Keep the ramekins covered with the foil and place in the refrigerator for about 2 hours until completely chilled. 9. Sprinkle 1 teaspoon of Swerve on top of each tiramisu. Use the oven broiler to melt the sweetener. 10. Put in the fridge to chill the topping, about 20 minutes. 11. Serve.

Vanilla Poppy Seed Cake

Prep time: 10 minutes | Cook time: 25 minutes | Serves 6

- 1 cup almond flour
- 2 eggs
- ½ cup erythritol
- 2 teaspoons vanilla extract
- 1 teaspoon lemon extract
- 1 tablespoon poppy seeds
- 4 tablespoons melted butter
- ¼ cup heavy cream
- ⅛ cup sour cream
- ½ teaspoon baking powder
- 1 cup water
- ¼ cup powdered erythritol, for garnish

1. In large bowl, mix almond flour, eggs, erythritol, vanilla, lemon, and poppy seeds. 2. Add butter, heavy cream, sour cream, and baking powder. 3. Pour into 7-inch round cake pan. Cover with foil. 4. Pour water into Instant Pot and place steam rack in bottom. Place baking pan on steam rack and click lid closed. Press the Cake button and press the Adjust button to set heat to Less. Set time for 25 minutes. 5. When timer beeps, allow a 15-minute natural release, then quick-release the remaining pressure. Let cool completely. Sprinkle with powdered erythritol for serving.

Chipotle Black Bean Brownies

Prep time: 15 minutes | Cook time: 30 minutes | Serves 8

- Nonstick cooking spray
- ½ cup dark chocolate chips, divided
- ¾ cup cooked calypso beans or black beans
- ½ cup extra-virgin olive oil
- 2 large eggs
- ¼ cup unsweetened dark chocolate cocoa powder
- ⅓ cup honey
- 1 teaspoon vanilla extract
- ⅓ cup white wheat flour
- ½ teaspoon chipotle chili powder
- ½ teaspoon ground cinnamon
- ½ teaspoon baking powder
- ½ teaspoon kosher salt

1. Spray a 7-inch Bundt pan with nonstick cooking spray. 2. Place half of the chocolate chips in a small bowl and microwave them for 30 seconds. Stir and repeat, if necessary, until the chips have completely melted. 3. In a food processor, blend the beans and oil together. Add the melted chocolate chips, eggs, cocoa powder, honey, and vanilla. Blend until the mixture is smooth. 4. In a large bowl, whisk together the flour, chili powder, cinnamon, baking powder, and salt. Pour the bean mixture from the food processor into the bowl and stir with a wooden spoon until well combined. Stir in the remaining chocolate chips. 5. Pour the batter into the prepared Bundt pan. Cover loosely with foil. 6. Pour 1 cup of water into the electric pressure cooker. 7. Place the Bundt pan onto the wire rack and lower it into the pressure cooker. 8. Close and lock the lid of the pressure cooker. Set the valve to sealing. 9. Cook on high pressure for 30 minutes. 10. When the cooking is complete, hit Cancel and quick release the pressure. 11. Once the pin drops, unlock and remove the lid. 12. Carefully transfer the pan to a cooling rack for about 10 minutes, then invert the cake onto the rack and let it cool completely. 13. Cut into slices and serve.

Lemon-Ricotta Cheesecake

Prep time: 10 minutes | Cook time: 30 minutes | Serves 6

- Unsalted butter or vegetable oil, for greasing the pan
- 8 ounces (227 g) cream cheese, at room temperature
- ¼ cup plus 1 teaspoon Swerve, plus more as needed
- ⅓ cup full-fat or part-skim
- ricotta cheese, at room temperature
- Zest of 1 lemon
- Juice of 1 lemon
- ½ teaspoon lemon extract
- 2 eggs, at room temperature
- 2 tablespoons sour cream

1. Grease a 6-inch springform pan extremely well. I find this easiest to do with a silicone basting brush so I can get into all the nooks and crannies. Alternatively, line the sides of the pan with parchment paper. 2. In the bowl of a stand mixer, beat the cream cheese, ¼ cup of Swerve, the ricotta, lemon zest, lemon juice, and lemon extract on high speed until you get a smooth mixture with no lumps. 3. Taste to ensure the sweetness is to your liking and adjust if needed. 4. Add the eggs, reduce the speed to low and gently blend until the eggs are just incorporated. Overbeating at this stage will result in a cracked crust. 5. Pour the mixture into the prepared pan and cover with aluminum foil or a silicone lid. 6. Pour 2 cups of water into the inner cooking pot of the Instant Pot, then place a trivet in the pot. Place the covered pan on the trivet. 7. Lock the lid into place. Select Manual and adjust the pressure to High. Cook for 30 minutes. When the cooking is complete, let the pressure release naturally. Unlock the lid. 8. Carefully remove the pan from the pot, and remove the foil. 9. In a small bowl, mix together the sour cream and remaining 1 teaspoon of Swerve and spread this over the top of the warm cake. 10. Refrigerate the cheesecake for 6 to 8 hours. Do not be in a hurry! The cheesecake needs every bit of this time to be its best.

Spiced Pear Applesauce

Prep time: 15 minutes | Cook time: 5 minutes | Makes: 3½ cups

- 1 pound pears, peeled, cored, and sliced
- 2 teaspoons apple pie spice
- or cinnamon
- Pinch kosher salt
- Juice of ½ small lemon

1. In the electric pressure cooker, combine the apples, pears, apple pie spice, salt, lemon juice, and ¼ cup of water. 2. Close and lock the lid of the pressure cooker. Set the valve to sealing. 3. Cook on high pressure for 5 minutes. 4. When the cooking is complete, hit Cancel and let the pressure release naturally. 5. Once the pin drops, unlock and remove the lid. 6. Mash the apples and pears with a potato masher to the consistency you like. 7. Serve warm, or cool to room temperature and refrigerate.

Espresso Cream

Prep time: 10 minutes | Cook time: 9 minutes | Serves 4

- 1 cup heavy cream
- ½ teaspoon espresso powder
- ½ teaspoon vanilla extract
- 2 teaspoons unsweetened cocoa powder
- ¼ cup low-carb chocolate chips
- ½ cup powdered erythritol
- 3 egg yolks
- 1 cup water

1. Press the Sauté button and add heavy cream, espresso powder, vanilla, and cocoa powder. Bring mixture to boil and add chocolate chips. Press the Cancel button. Stir quickly until chocolate chips are completely melted. 2. In medium bowl, whisk erythritol and egg yolks. Fold mixture into Instant Pot chocolate mix. Ladle into four (4-inch) ramekins. 3. Rinse inner pot and replace. Pour in 1 cup of water and place steam rack on bottom of pot. Cover ramekins with foil and carefully place on top of steam rack. Click lid closed. 4. Press the Manual button and adjust time for 9 minutes. Allow a full natural release. When the pressure indicator drops, carefully remove ramekins and allow to completely cool, then refrigerate. Serve chilled with whipped topping.

Vanilla Crème Brûlée

Prep time: 7 minutes | Cook time: 9 minutes | Serves 4

- 1 cup heavy cream (or full-fat coconut milk for dairy-free)
- 2 large egg yolks
- 2 tablespoons Swerve, or more to taste
- Seeds scraped from ½
- vanilla bean (about 8 inches long), or 1 teaspoon vanilla extract
- 1 cup cold water
- 4 teaspoons Swerve, for topping

1. Heat the cream in a pan over medium-high heat until hot, about 2 minutes. 2. Place the egg yolks, Swerve, and vanilla seeds in a blender and blend until smooth. 3. While the blender is running, slowly pour in the hot cream. Taste and adjust the sweetness to your liking. 4. Scoop the mixture into four ramekins with a spatula. Cover the ramekins with aluminum foil. 5. Add the water to the Instant Pot and insert a trivet. Place the ramekins on the trivet. 6. Lock the lid. Select the Manual mode and set the cooking time for 7 minutes at High Pressure. 7. When the timer beeps, perform a quick pressure release. Carefully remove the lid. 8. Keep the ramekins covered with the foil and place in the refrigerator for about 2 hours until completely chilled. 9. Sprinkle 1 teaspoon of Swerve on top of each crème brûlée. Use the oven broiler to melt the sweetener. 10. Allow the topping to cool in the fridge for 5 minutes before serving.

Pumpkin Walnut Cheesecake

Prep time: 15 minutes | Cook time: 50 minutes | Serves 6

- 2 cups walnuts
- 3 tablespoons melted butter
- 1 teaspoon cinnamon
- 16 ounces (454 g) cream cheese, softened
- 1 cup powdered erythritol
- ⅓ cup heavy cream
- ⅔ cup pumpkin purée
- 2 teaspoons pumpkin spice
- 1 teaspoon vanilla extract
- 2 eggs
- 1 cup water

1. Preheat oven to 350°F (180°C). Add walnuts, butter, and cinnamon to food processor. Pulse until ball forms. Scrape down sides as necessary. Dough should hold together in ball. 2. Press into greased 7-inch springform pan. Bake for 10 minutes or until it begins to brown. Remove and set aside. While crust is baking, make cheesecake filling. 3. In large bowl, stir cream cheese until completely smooth. Using rubber spatula, mix in erythritol, heavy cream, pumpkin purée, pumpkin spice, and vanilla. 4. In small bowl, whisk eggs. Slowly add them into large bowl, folding gently until just combined. 5. Pour mixture into crust and cover with foil. Pour water into Instant Pot and place steam rack on bottom. Place pan onto steam rack and click lid closed. Press the Cake button and press the Adjust button to set heat to More. Set timer for 40 minutes. 6. When timer beeps, allow a full natural release. When pressure indicator drops, carefully remove pan and place on counter. Remove foil. Let cool for additional hour and then refrigerate. Serve chilled.

Ultimate Chocolate Cheesecake

Prep time: 10 minutes | Cook time: 50 minutes | Serves 12

- 2 cups pecans
- 2 tablespoons butter
- 16 ounces (454 g) cream cheese, softened
- 1 cup powdered erythritol
- ¼ cup sour cream
- 2 tablespoons cocoa powder
- 2 teaspoons vanilla extract
- 2 cups low-carb chocolate chips
- 1 tablespoon coconut oil
- 2 eggs
- 2 cups water

1. Preheat oven to 400°F (205°C). Place pecans and butter into food processor. Pulse until dough-like consistency. Press into bottom of 7-inch springform pan. Bake for 10 minutes then set aside to cool. 2. While crust bakes, mix cream cheese, erythritol, sour cream, cocoa powder, and vanilla together in large bowl using a rubber spatula. Set aside. 3. In medium bowl, combine chocolate chips and coconut oil. Microwave in 20-second increments until chocolate begins to melt and then stir until smooth. Gently fold chocolate mixture into cheesecake mixture. 4. Add eggs and gently fold in, careful not to overmix. Pour mixture over cooled pecan crust. Cover with foil. 5. Pour water into Instant Pot and place steam rack on bottom. Place cheesecake on steam rack and click lid closed. Press the Manual button and adjust time for 40 minutes. When timer beeps, allow a natural release. Carefully remove and let cool completely. Serve chilled.

Chocolate Macadamia Bark

Prep time: 5 minutes | Cook time: 20 minutes | Serves 20

- 16 ounces (454 g) raw dark chocolate
- 3 tablespoons raw coconut butter
- 2 tablespoons coconut oil
- 2 cups chopped macadamia
- nuts
- 1 tablespoon almond butter
- ½ teaspoon salt
- ⅓ cup Swerve, or more to taste

1. In a large bowl, mix together the chocolate, coconut butter, coconut oil, macadamia nuts, almond butter, salt, and Swerve. Combine them very thoroughly, until a perfectly even mixture is obtained. 2. Pour 1 cup of filtered water into the Instant Pot, and insert the trivet. Transfer the mixture from the bowl into a well-greased, Instant Pot-friendly dish. 3. Place the dish onto the trivet, and cover loosely with aluminum foil. Close the lid, set the pressure release to Sealing, and select Manual. Set the Instant Pot to 20 minutes on High Pressure, and let cook. 4. Once cooked, let the pressure naturally disperse from the Instant Pot for about 10 minutes, then carefully switch the pressure release to Venting. 5. Open the Instant Pot and remove the dish. Cool in the refrigerator until set. Break into pieces, serve, and enjoy! Store remaining bark in the refrigerator or freezer.

Tapioca Berry Parfaits

Prep time: 10 minutes | Cook time: 6 minutes | Serves 4

- 2 cups unsweetened almond milk
- ½ cup small pearl tapioca, rinsed and still wet
- 1 teaspoon almond extract
- 1 tablespoon pure maple syrup
- 2 cups berries
- ¼ cup slivered almonds

1. Pour the almond milk into the electric pressure cooker. Stir in the tapioca and almond extract. 2. Close and lock the lid of the pressure cooker. Set the valve to sealing. 3. Cook on High pressure for 6 minutes. 4. When the cooking is complete, hit Cancel. Allow the pressure to release naturally for 10 minutes, then quick release any remaining pressure. 5. Once the pin drops, unlock and remove the lid. Remove the pot to a cooling rack. 6. Stir in the maple syrup and let the mixture cool for about an hour. 7. In small glasses, create several layers of tapioca, berries, and almonds. Refrigerate for 1 hour. 8. Serve chilled.

Lemon and Ricotta Torte

Prep time: 15 minutes | Cook time: 35 minutes | Serves 12

Cooking spray
Torte:
- 1⅓ cups Swerve
- ½ cup (1 stick) unsalted butter, softened
- 2 teaspoons lemon or vanilla extract
- 5 large eggs, separated
Lemon Glaze:
- ½ cup (1 stick) unsalted butter
- ¼ cup Swerve
- 2 tablespoons lemon juice

- 2½ cups blanched almond flour
- 1¼ (10-ounce / 284-g) cups whole-milk ricotta cheese
- ¼ cup lemon juice
- 1 cup cold water

- 2 ounces (57 g) cream cheese (¼ cup)
- Grated lemon zest and lemon slices, for garnish

1. Line a baking pan with parchment paper and spray with cooking spray. Set aside. 2. Make the torte: In the bowl of a stand mixer, place the Swerve, butter, and extract and blend for 8 to 10 minutes until well combined. Scrape down the sides of the bowl as needed. 3. Add the egg yolks and continue to blend until fully combined. Add the almond flour and mix until smooth, then stir in the ricotta and lemon juice. 4. Whisk the egg whites in a separate medium bowl until stiff peaks form. Add the whites to the batter and stir well. Pour the batter into the prepared pan and smooth the top. 5. Place a trivet in the bottom of your Instant Pot and pour in the water. Use a foil sling to lower the baking pan onto the trivet. Tuck in the sides of the sling. 6. Seal the lid, press Pressure Cook or Manual, and set the timer for 30 minutes. Once finished, let the pressure release naturally. 7. Lock the lid. Select the Manual mode and set the cooking time for 30 minutes at High Pressure. 8. When the timer beeps, perform a natural pressure release for 10 minutes.

Carefully remove the lid. 9. Use the foil sling to lift the pan out of the Instant Pot. Place the torte in the fridge for 40 minutes to chill before glazing. 10. Meanwhile, make the glaze: Place the butter in a large pan over high heat and cook for about 5 minutes until brown, stirring occasionally. Remove from the heat. While stirring the browned butter, add the Swerve. 11. Carefully add the lemon juice and cream cheese to the butter mixture. Allow the glaze to cool for a few minutes, or until it starts to thicken. 12. Transfer the chilled torte to a serving plate. Pour the glaze over the torte and return it to the fridge to chill for an additional 30 minutes. 13. Scatter the lemon zest on top of the torte and arrange the lemon slices on the plate around the torte. 14. Serve.

Fudgy Walnut Brownies

Prep time: 10 minutes | Cook time: 1 hour | Serves 12

- ¾ cup walnut halves and pieces
- ½ cup unsalted butter, melted and cooled
- 4 large eggs
- 1½ teaspoons instant coffee crystals
- 1½ teaspoons vanilla extract
- 1 cup Lakanto Monkfruit Sweetener Golden
- ¼ teaspoon fine sea salt
- ¾ cup almond flour
- ¾ cup natural cocoa powder
- ¾ cup stevia-sweetened chocolate chips

1. In a dry small skillet over medium heat, toast the walnuts, stirring often, for about 5 minutes, until golden. Transfer the walnuts to a bowl to cool. 2. Pour 1 cup water into the Instant Pot. Line the base of a 7 by 3-inch round cake pan with a circle of parchment paper. Butter the sides of the pan and the parchment or coat with nonstick cooking spray. 3. Pour the butter into a medium bowl. One at a time, whisk in the eggs, then whisk in the coffee crystals, vanilla, sweetener, and salt. Finally, whisk in the flour and cocoa powder just until combined. Using a rubber spatula, fold in the chocolate chips and walnuts. 4. Transfer the batter to the prepared pan and, using the spatula, spread it in an even layer. Cover the pan tightly with aluminum foil. Place the pan on a long-handled silicone steam rack, then, holding the handles of the steam rack, lower it into the Instant Pot. 5. Secure the lid and set the Pressure Release to Sealing. Select the Cake, Pressure Cook, or Manual setting and set the cooking time for 45 minutes at high pressure. (The pot will take about 10 minutes to come up to pressure before the cooking program begins.) 6. When the cooking program ends, let the pressure release naturally for 10 minutes, then move the Pressure Release to Venting to release any remaining steam. Open the pot and, wearing heat-resistant mitts, grasp the handles of the steam rack and lift it out of the pot. Uncover the pan, taking care not to get burned by the steam or to drip condensation onto the brownies. Let the brownies cool in the pan on a cooling rack for about 2 hours, to room temperature. 7. Run a butter knife around the edge of the pan to make sure the brownies are not sticking to the pan sides. Invert the brownies onto the rack, lift off the pan, and peel off the parchment paper. Invert the brownies onto a serving plate and cut into twelve wedges. The brownies will keep, stored in an airtight container in the refrigerator for up to 5 days, or in the freezer for up to 4 months.

Chocolate Pecan Clusters

Prep time: 5 minutes | Cook time: 5 minutes | Makes 8 clusters

- 3 tablespoons butter
- ¼ cup heavy cream
- 1 teaspoon vanilla extract
- 1 cup chopped pecans
- ¼ cup low-carb chocolate chips

1. Press the Sauté button and add butter to Instant Pot. Allow butter to melt and begin to turn golden brown. Once it begins to brown, immediately add heavy cream. Press the Cancel button. 2. Add vanilla and chopped pecans to Instant Pot. Allow to cool for 10 minutes, stirring occasionally. Spoon mixture onto parchment-lined baking sheet to form eight clusters, and scatter chocolate chips over clusters. Place in fridge to cool.

Almond Pie with Coconut

Prep time: 5 minutes | Cook time: 41 minutes | Serves 8

- 1 cup almond flour
- ½ cup coconut milk
- 1 teaspoon vanilla extract
- 2 tablespoons butter,
- softened
- 1 tablespoon Truvia
- ¼ cup shredded coconut
- 1 cup water

1. In the mixing bowl, mix up almond flour, coconut milk, vanilla extract, butter, Truvia, and shredded coconut. 2. When the mixture is smooth, transfer it in the baking pan and flatten. 3. Pour water and insert the trivet in the instant pot. 4. Put the baking pan with cake on the trivet. 5. Lock the lid. Select the Manual mode and set the cooking time for 41 minutes on High Pressure. Once the timer goes off, perform a natural pressure release for 10 minutes, then release any remaining pressure. Carefully open the lid. 6. Serve immediately.

Thai Pandan Coconut Custard

Prep time: 10 minutes | Cook time: 30 minutes | Serves 4

- Nonstick cooking spray
- 1 cup unsweetened coconut milk
- 3 eggs
- ⅓ cup Swerve
- 3 to 4 drops pandan extract, or use vanilla extract if you must

1. Grease a 6-inch heatproof bowl with the cooking spray. 2. In a large bowl, whisk together the coconut milk, eggs, Swerve, and pandan extract. Pour the mixture into the prepared bowl and cover it with aluminum foil. 3. Pour 2 cups of water into the inner cooking pot of the Instant Pot, then place a trivet in the pot. Place the bowl on the trivet. 4. Lock the lid into place. Select Manual and adjust the pressure to High. Cook for 30 minutes. When the cooking

is complete, let the pressure release naturally. Unlock the lid. 5. Remove the bowl from the pot and remove the foil. A knife inserted into the custard should come out clean. Cool in the refrigerator for 6 to 8 hours, or until the custard is set.

Hearty Crème Brûlée

Prep time: 5 minutes | Cook time: 30 minutes | Serves 4

- 5 egg yolks
- 5 tablespoons powdered erythritol
- 1½ cups heavy cream
- 2 teaspoons vanilla extract
- 2 cups water

1. In a small bowl, use a fork to break up the egg yolks. Stir in the erythritol. 2. Pour the cream into a small saucepan over medium-low heat and let it warm up for 3 to 4 minutes. Remove the saucepan from the heat. 3. Temper the egg yolks by slowly adding a small spoonful of the warm cream, keep whisking. Do this three times to make sure the egg yolks are fully tempered. 4. Slowly add the tempered eggs to the cream, whisking the whole time. Add the vanilla and whisk again. 5. Pour the cream mixture into the ramekins. Each ramekin should have ½ cup liquid. Cover each with aluminum foil. 6. Place the trivet inside the Instant Pot. Add the water. Carefully place the ramekins on top of the trivet. 7. Close the lid. Select Manual mode and set cooking time for 11 minutes on High Pressure. 8. When timer beeps, use a natural release for 15 minutes, then release any remaining pressure. Open the lid. 9. Carefully remove a ramekin from the pot. Remove the foil and check for doneness. The custard should be mostly set with a slightly jiggly center. 10. Place all the ramekins in the fridge for 2 hours to chill and set. Serve chilled.

Crustless Creamy Berry Cheesecake

Prep time: 10 minutes | Cook time: 40 minutes | Serves 12

- 16 ounces (454 g) cream cheese, softened
- 1 cup powdered erythritol
- ¼ cup sour cream
- 2 teaspoons vanilla extract
- 2 eggs
- 2 cups water
- ¼ cup blackberries and strawberries, for topping

1. In large bowl, beat cream cheese and erythritol until smooth. Add sour cream, vanilla, and eggs and gently fold until combined. 2. Pour batter into 7-inch springform pan. Gently shake or tap pan on counter to remove air bubbles and level batter. Cover top of pan with tinfoil. Pour water into Instant Pot and place steam rack in pot. 3. Carefully lower pan into pot. Press the Cake button and press the Adjust button to set heat to More. Set time for 40 minutes. When timer beeps, allow a full natural release. Using sling, carefully lift pan from Instant Pot and allow to cool completely before refrigerating. 4. Place strawberries and blackberries on top of cheesecake and serve.

Chapter8 StewsandSoups

Chicken Vegetable Soup

Prep time: 12 to 25 minutes | Cook time: 4 minutes | Serves 6

- 1 to 2 raw chicken breasts, cubed
- ½ medium onion, chopped
- 4 cloves garlic, minced
- ½ sweet potato, small cubes
- 1 large carrot, peeled and cubed
- 4 stalks celery, chopped, leaves included
- ½ cup frozen corn
- ¼ cup frozen peas
- ¼ cup frozen lima beans
- 1 cup frozen green beans
- (bite-sized)
- ¼ to ½ cup chopped savoy cabbage
- 14½ ounces can low-sodium petite diced tomatoes
- 3 cups low-sodium chicken bone broth
- ½ teaspoon black pepper
- 1 teaspoon garlic powder
- ¼ cup chopped fresh parsley
- ¼ to ½ teaspoon red pepper flakes

1. Add all of the ingredients, in the order listed, to the inner pot of the Instant Pot. 2. Lock the lid in place, set the vent to sealing, press Manual, and cook at high pressure for 4 minutes. 3. Release the pressure manually as soon as cooking time is finished.

Cauliflower Rice and Chicken Thigh Soup

Prep time: 15 minutes | Cook time: 13 minutes | Serves 5

- 2 cups cauliflower florets
- 1 pound (454 g) boneless, skinless chicken thighs
- 4½ cups chicken broth
- ½ yellow onion, chopped
- 2 garlic cloves, minced
- 1 tablespoon unflavored gelatin powder
- 2 teaspoons sea salt
- ½ teaspoon ground black
- pepper
- ½ cup sliced zucchini
- ⅓ cup sliced turnips
- 1 teaspoon dried parsley
- 3 celery stalks, chopped
- 1 teaspoon ground turmeric
- ½ teaspoon dried marjoram
- 1 teaspoon dried thyme
- ½ teaspoon dried oregano

1. Add the cauliflower florets to a food processor and pulse until a ricelike consistency is achieved. Set aside. 2. Add the chicken thighs, chicken broth, onions, garlic, gelatin powder, sea salt, and black pepper to the pot. Gently stir to combine. 3. Lock the lid.

Select Manual mode and set cooking time for 10 minutes on High Pressure. 4. When cooking is complete, quick release the pressure and open the lid. 5. Transfer the chicken thighs to a cutting board. Chop the chicken into bite-sized pieces and then return the chopped chicken to the pot. 6. Add the cauliflower rice, zucchini, turnips, parsley, celery, turmeric, marjoram, thyme, and oregano to the pot. Stir to combine. 7. Lock the lid. Select Manual mode and set cooking time for 3 minutes on High Pressure. 8. When cooking is complete, quick release the pressure. 9. Open the lid. Ladle the soup into serving bowls. Serve hot.

Beef, Mushroom, and Wild Rice Soup

Prep time: 0 minutes | Cook time: 55 minutes | Serves 6

- 2 tablespoons extra-virgin olive oil or unsalted butter
- 2 garlic cloves, minced
- 8 ounces shiitake mushrooms, stems removed and sliced
- 1 teaspoon fine sea salt
- 2 carrots, diced
- 2 celery stalks, diced
- 1 yellow onion, diced
- 1 teaspoon dried thyme
- 1½ pounds beef stew meat, larger pieces halved, or beef chuck, trimmed of fat and cut into ¾-inch pieces
- 4 cups low-sodium roasted beef bone broth
- 1 cup wild rice, rinsed
- 1 tablespoon Worcestershire sauce
- 2 tablespoons tomato paste

1. Select the Sauté setting on the Instant Pot and heat the oil and garlic for about 1 minute, until the garlic is bubbling but not browned. Add the mushrooms and salt and sauté for 5 minutes, until the mushrooms have wilted and given up some of their liquid. Add the carrots, celery, and onion and sauté for 4 minutes, until the onion begins to soften. Add the thyme and beef and sauté for 3 minutes more, until the beef is mostly opaque on the outside. Stir in the broth, rice, Worcestershire sauce, and tomato paste, using a wooden spoon to nudge any browned bits from the bottom of the pot. 2. Secure the lid and set the Pressure Release to Sealing. Press the Cancel button to reset the cooking program, then select the Pressure Cook or Manual setting and set the cooking time for 25 minutes at high pressure. (The pot will take about 15 minutes to come up to pressure before the cooking program begins.) 3. When the cooking program ends, let the pressure release naturally for at least 15 minutes, then move the Pressure Release to Venting to release any remaining steam. Open the pot. Ladle the soup into bowls and serve hot.

Chicken Brunswick Stew

Prep time: 0 minutes | Cook time: 30 minutes | Serves 6

- 2 tablespoons extra-virgin olive oil
- 2 garlic cloves, chopped
- 1 large yellow onion, diced
- 2 pounds boneless, skinless chicken (breasts, tenders, or thighs), cut into bite-size pieces
- 1 teaspoon dried thyme
- 1 teaspoon smoked paprika
- 1 teaspoon fine sea salt
- ½ teaspoon freshly ground black pepper
- 1 cup low-sodium chicken broth
- 1 tablespoon hot sauce (such as Tabasco or Crystal)
- 1 tablespoon raw apple cider vinegar
- 1½ cups frozen corn
- 1½ cups frozen baby lima beans
- One 14½ ounces can fire-roasted diced tomatoes and their liquid
- 2 tablespoons tomato paste
- Cornbread, for serving

1. Select the Sauté setting on the Instant Pot and heat the oil and garlic for 2 minutes, until the garlic is bubbling but not browned. Add the onion and sauté for 3 minutes, until it begins to soften. Add the chicken and sauté for 3 minutes more, until mostly opaque. The chicken does not have to be cooked through. Add the thyme, paprika, salt, and pepper and sauté for 1 minute more. 2. Stir in the broth, hot sauce, vinegar, corn, and lima beans. Add the diced tomatoes and their liquid in an even layer and dollop the tomato paste on top. Do not stir them in. 3. Secure the lid and set the Pressure Release to Sealing. Press the Cancel button to reset the cooking program, then select the Pressure Cook or Manual setting and set the cooking time for 5 minutes at high pressure. (The pot will take about 15 minutes to come up to pressure before the cooking program begins.) 4. When the cooking program ends, let the pressure release naturally for at least 10 minutes, then move the Pressure Release to Venting to release any remaining steam. Open the pot and stir the stew to mix all of the ingredients. 5. Ladle the stew into bowls and serve hot, with cornbread alongside.

Nancy's Vegetable Beef Soup

Prep time: 25 minutes | Cook time: 8 hours | Serves 8

- 2 pounds roast, cubed, or 2 pounds stewing meat
- 15 ounces can corn
- 15 ounces can green beans
- 1 pound bag frozen peas
- 40 ounces can no-added-salt stewed tomatoes
- 5 teaspoons salt-free beef bouillon powder
- Tabasco, to taste
- ½ teaspoons salt

1. Combine all ingredients in the Instant Pot. Do not drain vegetables. 2. Add water to fill inner pot only to the fill line. 3. Secure the lid, or use the glass lid and set the Instant Pot on Slow Cook mode, Low for 8 hours, or until meat is tender and vegetables are soft.

Beef and Eggplant Tagine

Prep time: 15 minutes | Cook time: 25 minutes | Serves 6

- 1 pound (454 g) beef fillet, chopped
- 1 eggplant, chopped
- 6 ounces (170 g) scallions, chopped
- 4 cups beef broth
- 1 teaspoon ground allspices
- 1 teaspoon erythritol
- 1 teaspoon coconut oil

1. Put all ingredients in the Instant Pot. Stir to mix well. 2. Close the lid. Select Manual mode and set cooking time for 25 minutes on High Pressure. 3. When timer beeps, use a natural pressure release for 15 minutes, then release any remaining pressure. Open the lid. 4. Serve warm.

Beef Stew with Eggplant and Potatoes

Prep time: 15 minutes | Cook time: 50 minutes | Serves 6 to 8

- 2 pounds (907 g) boneless short ribs, trimmed and cut into 1-inch pieces
- 1½ teaspoons table salt, divided
- 2 tablespoons extra-virgin olive oil
- 1 onion, chopped fine
- 3 tablespoons tomato paste
- ¼ cup all-purpose flour
- 3 garlic cloves, minced
- 1 tablespoon ground cumin
- 1 teaspoon ground turmeric
- 1 teaspoon ground cardamom
- ¾ teaspoon ground cinnamon
- 4 cups chicken broth
- 1 cup water
- 1 pound (454 g) eggplant, cut into 1-inch pieces
- 1 pound (454 g) Yukon Gold potatoes, unpeeled, cut into 1-inch pieces
- ½ cup chopped fresh mint or parsley

1. Pat beef dry with paper towels and sprinkle with 1 teaspoon salt. Using highest sauté function, heat oil in Instant Pot for 5 minutes (or until just smoking). Brown half of beef on all sides, 7 to 9 minutes; transfer to bowl. Set aside remaining uncooked beef. 2. Add onion to fat left in pot and cook, using highest sauté function, until softened, about 5 minutes. Stir in tomato paste, flour, garlic, cumin, turmeric, cardamom, cinnamon, and remaining ½ teaspoon salt. Cook until fragrant, about 1 minute. Slowly whisk in broth and water, scraping up any browned bits. Stir in eggplant and potatoes. Nestle remaining uncooked beef into pot along with browned beef, and add any accumulated juices. 3. Lock lid in place and close pressure release valve. Select high pressure cook function and cook for 30 minutes. Turn off Instant Pot and quick-release pressure. Carefully remove lid, allowing steam to escape away from you. 4. Using wide, shallow spoon, skim excess fat from surface of stew. Stir in mint and season with salt and pepper to taste. Serve.

Turkey Barley Vegetable Soup

Prep time: 5 minutes | Cook time: 20 minutes | Serves 8

- 2 tablespoons avocado oil
- 1 pound ground turkey
- 4 cups Chicken Bone Broth, low-sodium store-bought chicken broth, or water
- 1 (28-ounce) carton or can diced tomatoes
- 2 tablespoons tomato paste
- 1 (15-ounce) package frozen chopped carrots (about 2½
- cups)
- 1 (15-ounce) package frozen peppers and onions (about 2½ cups)
- ⅓ cup dry barley
- 1 teaspoon kosher salt
- ¼ teaspoon freshly ground black pepper
- 2 bay leaves

1. Set the electric pressure cooker to the Sauté/More setting. When the pot is hot, pour in the avocado oil. 2. Add the turkey to the pot and sauté, stirring frequently to break up the meat, for about 7 minutes or until the turkey is no longer pink. Hit Cancel. 3. Add the broth, tomatoes and their juices, and tomato paste. Stir in the carrots, peppers and onions, barley, salt, pepper, and bay leaves. 4. Close and lock the lid of the pressure cooker. Set the valve to sealing. 5. Cook on high pressure for 20 minutes. 6. When the cooking is complete, hit Cancel and allow the pressure to release naturally for 10 minutes, then quick release any remaining pressure. 7. Once the pin drops, unlock and remove the lid. Discard the bay leaves. 8. Spoon into bowls and serve.

Provençal Chicken Soup

Prep time: 20 minutes | Cook time: 30 minutes | Serves 6 to 8

- 1 tablespoon extra-virgin olive oil
- 2 fennel bulbs, 2 tablespoons fronds minced, stalks discarded, bulbs halved, cored, and cut into ½-inch pieces
- 1 onion, chopped
- 1¾ teaspoons table salt
- 2 tablespoons tomato paste
- 4 garlic cloves, minced
- 1 tablespoon minced fresh thyme or 1 teaspoon dried
- 2 anchovy fillets, minced
- 7 cups water, divided
- 1 (14½-ounce / 411-g) can diced tomatoes, drained
- 2 carrots, peeled, halved lengthwise, and sliced ½ inch thick
- 2 (12-ounce / 340-g) bone-in split chicken breasts, trimmed
- 4 (5- to 7-ounce / 142- to 198-g) bone-in chicken thighs, trimmed
- ½ cup pitted brine-cured green olives, chopped
- 1 teaspoon grated orange zest

1. Using highest sauté function, heat oil in Instant Pot until shimmering. Add fennel pieces, onion, and salt and cook until vegetables are softened, about 5 minutes. Stir in tomato paste, garlic, thyme, and anchovies and cook until fragrant, about 30 seconds. Stir in 5 cups water, scraping up any browned bits, then stir in tomatoes and carrots. Nestle chicken breasts and thighs in

pot. 2. Lock lid in place and close pressure release valve. Select high pressure cook function and cook for 20 minutes. Turn off Instant Pot and quick-release pressure. Carefully remove lid, allowing steam to escape away from you. 3. Transfer chicken to cutting board, let cool slightly, then shred into bite-size pieces using 2 forks; discard skin and bones. 4. Using wide, shallow spoon, skim excess fat from surface of soup. Stir chicken and any accumulated juices, olives, and remaining 2 cups water into soup and let sit until heated through, about 3 minutes. Stir in fennel fronds and orange zest, and season with salt and pepper to taste. Serve.

Vegetarian Chili

Prep time: 25 minutes | Cook time: 10 minutes | Serves 6

- 2 teaspoons olive oil
- 3 garlic cloves, minced
- 2 onions, chopped
- 1 green bell pepper, chopped
- 1 cup textured vegetable protein (T.V.P.)
- 1-pound can beans of your choice, drained
- 1 jalapeño pepper, seeds removed, chopped
- 28 ounces can diced Italian tomatoes
- 1 bay leaf
- 1 tablespoon dried oregano
- ½ teaspoons salt
- ¼ teaspoons pepper

1. Set the Instant Pot to the Sauté function. As it's heating, add the olive oil, garlic, onions, and bell pepper. Stir constantly for about 5 minutes as it all cooks. Press Cancel. 2. Place all of the remaining ingredients into the inner pot of the Instant pot and stir. 3. Secure the lid and make sure vent is set to sealing. Cook on Manual mode for 10 minutes. 4. When cook time is up, let the steam release naturally for 5 minutes and then manually release the rest.

Chicken and Vegetable Soup

Prep time: 5 minutes | Cook time: 2 minutes | Serves 4

- 1 pound (454 g) boneless, skinless chicken thighs, diced small
- 1 (10-ounce / 283-g) bag frozen vegetables
- 2 cups water
- 1 teaspoon poultry seasoning
- 1 tablespoon powdered chicken broth base
- 1 teaspoon salt
- 1 teaspoon freshly ground black pepper
- 1 cup heavy (whipping) cream

1. Put the chicken, vegetables, water, poultry seasoning, chicken broth base, salt, and pepper in the inner cooking pot of your Instant Pot. 2. Lock the lid into place. Select Manual and adjust the pressure to High. Cook for 2 minutes. When the cooking is complete, quick-release the pressure (you may want to do this in short bursts so the soup doesn't spurt out). Unlock the lid. 3. Add the cream, stir, and serve. Or, if you prefer, you can mash up the chicken with the back of a wooden spoon to break it into shreds before adding the cream.

Broccoli and Bacon Cheese Soup

Prep time: 6 minutes | Cook time: 10 minutes | Serves 6

- 3 tablespoons butter
- 2 stalks celery, diced
- ½ yellow onion, diced
- 3 garlic cloves, minced
- 3½ cups chicken stock
- 4 cups chopped fresh broccoli florets
- 3 ounces (85 g) block-style cream cheese, softened and cubed
- ½ teaspoon ground nutmeg
- ½ teaspoon sea salt
- 1 teaspoon ground black pepper
- 3 cups shredded Cheddar cheese
- ½ cup shredded Monterey Jack cheese
- 2 cups heavy cream
- 4 slices cooked bacon, crumbled
- 1 tablespoon finely chopped chives

1. Select Sauté mode. Once the Instant Pot is hot, add the butter and heat until the butter is melted. 2. Add the celery, onions, and garlic. Continue sautéing for 5 minutes or until the vegetables are softened. 3. Add the chicken stock and broccoli florets to the pot. Bring the liquid to a boil. 4. Lock the lid,. Select Manual mode and set cooking time for 5 minutes on High Pressure. 5. When cooking is complete, allow the pressure to release naturally for 10 minutes and then release the remaining pressure. 6. Open the lid and add the cream cheese, nutmeg, sea salt, and black pepper. Stir to combine. 7. Select Sauté mode. Bring the soup to a boil and then slowly stir in the Cheddar and Jack cheeses. Once the cheese has melted, stir in the heavy cream. 8. Ladle the soup into serving bowls and top with bacon and chives. Serve hot.

Chicken and Kale Soup

Prep time: 5 minutes | Cook time: 5 minutes | Serves 4

- 2 cups chopped cooked chicken breast
- 12 ounces (340 g) frozen kale
- 1 onion, chopped
- 2 cups water
- 1 tablespoon powdered chicken broth base
- ½ teaspoon ground cinnamon
- Pinch ground cloves
- 2 teaspoons minced garlic
- 1 teaspoon freshly ground black pepper
- 1 teaspoon salt
- 2 cups full-fat coconut milk

1. Put the chicken, kale, onion, water, chicken broth base, cinnamon, cloves, garlic, pepper, and salt in the inner cooking pot of the Instant Pot. 2. Lock the lid into place. Select Manual and adjust the pressure to High. Cook for 5 minutes. When the cooking is complete, let the pressure release naturally for 10 minutes, then quick-release any remaining pressure. Unlock the lid. 3. Stir in the coconut milk. Taste and adjust any seasonings as needed before serving.

Broccoli Cheddar Soup

Prep time: 5 minutes | Cook time: 10 minutes | Serves 4

- 2 tablespoons butter
- ⅛ cup onion, diced
- ½ teaspoon garlic powder
- ½ teaspoon salt
- ¼ teaspoon pepper
- 2 cups chicken broth
- 1 cup chopped broccoli
- 1 tablespoon cream cheese, softened
- ¼ cup heavy cream
- 1 cup shredded Cheddar cheese

1. Press the Sauté button and add butter to Instant Pot. Add onion and sauté until translucent. Press the Cancel button and add garlic powder, salt, pepper, broth, and broccoli to pot. 2. Click lid closed. Press the Soup button and set time for 5 minutes. When timer beeps, stir in heavy cream, cream cheese, and Cheddar.

Broccoli and Red Feta Soup

Prep time: 10 minutes | Cook time: 25 minutes | Serves 4

- 1 cup broccoli, chopped
- ½ cup coconut cream
- 1 teaspoon unsweetened tomato purée
- 4 cups beef broth
- 1 teaspoon chili flakes
- 6 ounces (170 g) feta, crumbled

1. Put broccoli, coconut cream, tomato purée, and beef broth in the Instant Pot. Sprinkle with chili flakes and stir to mix well. 2. Close the lid and select Manual mode. Set cooking time for 8 minutes on High Pressure. 3. When timer beeps, make a quick pressure release and open the lid. 4. Add the feta cheese and stir the soup on Sauté mode for 5 minutes or until the cheese melt. 5. Serve immediately.

Lamb and Broccoli Soup

Prep time: 10 minutes | Cook time: 25 minutes | Serves 4

- 7 ounces (198 g) lamb fillet, chopped
- 1 tablespoon avocado oil
- ½ cup broccoli, roughly chopped
- ¼ daikon, chopped
- 2 bell peppers, chopped
- ¼ teaspoon ground cumin
- 5 cups beef broth

1. Sauté the lamb fillet with avocado oil in the Instant Pot for 5 minutes. 2. Add the broccoli, daikon, bell peppers, ground cumin, and beef broth. 3. Close the lid. Select Manual mode and set cooking time for 20 minutes on High Pressure. 4. When timer beeps, use a natural pressure release for 10 minutes, then release any remaining pressure. Open the lid. 5. Serve warm.

Vegetable and Chickpea Stew

Prep time: 25 minutes | Cook time: 30 minutes | Serves 6 to 8

- ¼ cup extra-virgin olive oil, plus extra for drizzling
- 2 red bell peppers, stemmed, seeded, and cut into 1-inch pieces
- 1 onion, chopped fine
- ½ teaspoon table salt
- ½ teaspoon pepper
- 1½ tablespoons baharat
- 4 garlic cloves, minced
- 1 tablespoon tomato paste
- 4 cups vegetable or chicken broth
- 1 (28-ounce / 794-g) can whole peeled tomatoes, drained with juice reserved, chopped
- 1 pound (454 g) Yukon Gold potatoes, peeled and cut into ½-inch pieces
- 2 zucchini, quartered lengthwise and sliced 1 inch thick
- 1 (15-ounce / 425-g) can chickpeas, rinsed
- ⅓ cup chopped fresh mint

1. Using highest sauté function, heat oil in Instant Pot until shimmering. Add bell pepper, onion, salt, and pepper and cook until vegetables are softened and lightly browned, 5 to 7 minutes. Stir in baharat, garlic, and tomato paste and cook until fragrant, about 1 minute. Stir in broth and tomatoes and reserved juice, scraping up any browned bits, then stir in potatoes. 2. Lock lid in place and close pressure release valve. Select high pressure cook function and cook for 9 minutes. Turn off Instant Pot and quick-release pressure. Carefully remove lid, allowing steam to escape away from you. 3. Stir zucchini and chickpeas into stew and cook, using highest sauté function, until zucchini is tender, 10 to 15 minutes. Turn off multicooker. Season with salt and pepper to taste. Drizzle individual portions with extra oil, and sprinkle with mint before serving.

French Onion Soup

Prep time: 10 minutes | Cook time: 20 minutes | Serves 10

- ½ cup light, soft tub margarine
- 8 to 10 large onions, sliced
- 3 14-ounce cans 98% fat-free, lower-sodium beef broth
- 2½ cups water
- 3 teaspoons sodium-free chicken bouillon powder
- 1½ teaspoons Worcestershire sauce
- 3 bay leaves
- 10 (1-ounce) slices French bread, toasted

1. Turn the Instant Pot to the Sauté function and add in the margarine and onions. Cook about 5 minutes, or until the onions are slightly soft. Press Cancel. 2. Add the beef broth, water, bouillon powder, Worcestershire sauce, and bay leaves and stir. 3. Secure the lid and make sure vent is set to sealing. Cook on Manual mode for 20 minutes. 4. Let the pressure release naturally for 15 minutes, then do a quick release. Open the lid and discard bay leaves. 5. Ladle into bowls. Top each with a slice of bread and some cheese if you desire.

Bacon Curry Soup

Prep time: 10 minutes | Cook time: 20 minutes | Serves 4

- 3 ounces (85 g) bacon, chopped
- 1 tablespoon chopped scallions
- 1 teaspoon curry powder
- 1 cup coconut milk
- 3 cups beef broth
- 1 cup Cheddar cheese, shredded

1. Heat the the Instant Pot on Sauté mode for 3 minutes and add bacon. Cook for 5 minutes. Flip constantly. 2. Add the scallions and curry powder. Sauté for 5 minutes more. 3. Pour in the coconut milk and beef broth. Add the Cheddar cheese and stir to mix well. 4. Select Manual mode and set cooking time for 10 minutes on High Pressure. 5. When timer beeps, use a quick pressure release. Open the lid. 6. Blend the soup with an immersion blender until smooth. Serve warm.

Gigante Bean Soup with Celery and Olives

Prep time: 30 minutes | Cook time: 12 minutes | Serves 6 to 8

- 1½ tablespoons table salt, for brining
- 1 pound (454 g) dried gigante beans, picked over and rinsed
- 2 tablespoons extra-virgin olive oil, plus extra for drizzling
- 5 celery ribs, cut into ½-inch pieces, plus ½ cup leaves, minced
- 1 onion, chopped
- ½ teaspoon table salt
- 4 garlic cloves, minced
- 4 cups vegetable or chicken broth
- 4 cups water
- 2 bay leaves
- ½ cup pitted kalamata olives, chopped
- 2 tablespoons minced fresh marjoram or oregano
- Lemon wedges

1. Dissolve 1½ tablespoons salt in 2 quarts cold water in large container. Add beans and soak at room temperature for at least 8 hours or up to 24 hours. Drain and rinse well. 2. Using highest sauté function, heat oil in Instant Pot until shimmering. Add celery pieces, onion, and ½ teaspoon salt and cook until vegetables are softened, about 5 minutes. Stir in garlic and cook until fragrant, about 30 seconds. Stir in broth, water, beans, and bay leaves. 3. Lock lid in place and close pressure release valve. Select high pressure cook function and cook for 6 minutes. Turn off Instant Pot and let pressure release naturally for 15 minutes. Quick-release any remaining pressure, then carefully remove lid, allowing steam to escape away from you. 4. Combine celery leaves, olives, and marjoram in bowl. Discard bay leaves. Season soup with salt and pepper to taste. Top individual portions with celery-olive mixture and drizzle with extra oil. Serve with lemon wedges.

Bacon Broccoli Soup

- 2 large heads broccoli
- 2 strips bacon, chopped
- 2 tablespoons unsalted butter
- ¼ cup diced onions
- Cloves squeezed from 1 head roasted garlic, or 2 cloves garlic, minced
- 3 cups chicken broth or beef broth
- 6 ounces (170 g) extra-sharp Cheddar cheese, shredded (about 1½ cups)
- 2 ounces (57 g) cream cheese, softened
- ½ teaspoon fine sea salt
- ¼ teaspoon ground black pepper
- Pinch of ground nutmeg

1. Cut the broccoli florets off the stems, leaving as much of the stems intact as possible. Reserve the florets for another recipe. Trim the bottom end of each stem so that it is flat. Using a spiral slicer, cut the stems into "noodles." 2. Place the bacon in the Instant Pot and press Sauté. Cook, stirring occasionally, for 4 minutes, or until crisp. Remove the bacon with a slotted spoon and set aside on a paper towel-lined plate to drain, leaving the drippings in the pot. 3. Add the butter and onions to the Instant Pot and cook for 4 minutes, or until the onions are soft. Add the garlic (and, if using raw garlic, sauté for another minute). Add the broth, Cheddar cheese, cream cheese, salt, pepper, and nutmeg and sauté until the cheeses are melted, about 3 minutes. Press Cancel to stop the Sauté. 4. Use a stick blender to purée the soup until smooth. Alternatively, you can pour the soup into a regular blender or food processor and purée until smooth, then return it to the Instant Pot. If using a regular blender, you may need to blend the soup in two batches; if you overfill the blender jar, the soup will not purée properly. 5. Add the broccoli noodles to the puréed soup in the Instant Pot. Seal the lid, press Manual, and set the timer for 1 minute. Once finished, let the pressure release naturally. 6. Remove the lid and stir well. Ladle the soup into bowls and sprinkle some of the bacon on top of each serving.

Curried Chicken Soup

- 1 pound (454 g) boneless, skinless chicken thighs
- 1½ cups unsweetened coconut milk
- ½ onion, finely diced
- 3 or 4 garlic cloves, crushed
- 1 (2-inch) piece ginger, finely chopped
- 1 cup sliced mushrooms,
- such as cremini and shiitake
- 4 ounces (113 g) baby spinach
- 1 teaspoon salt
- ½ teaspoon ground turmeric
- ½ teaspoon cayenne
- 1 teaspoon garam masala
- ¼ cup chopped fresh cilantro

1. In the inner cooking pot of your Instant Pot, add the chicken, coconut milk, onion, garlic, ginger, mushrooms, spinach, salt, turmeric, cayenne, garam masala, and cilantro. 2. Lock the lid into place. Select Manual and adjust the pressure to High. Cook for 10 minutes. When the cooking is complete, let the pressure release naturally. Unlock the lid. 3. Use tongs to transfer the chicken to a bowl. Shred the chicken, then stir it back into the soup. 4. Eat and rejoice.

Cabbage and Pork Soup

- 1 teaspoon butter
- ½ cup shredded white cabbage
- ½ teaspoon ground coriander
- ½ teaspoon salt
- ½ teaspoon chili flakes
- 2 cups chicken broth
- ½ cup ground pork

1. Melt the butter in the Instant Pot on Sauté mode. 2. Add cabbage and sprinkle with ground coriander, salt, and chili flakes. 3. Fold in the chicken broth and ground pork. 4. Close the lid and select Manual mode. Set cooking time for 12 minutes on High Pressure. 5. When timer beeps, use a quick pressure release. Open the lid. 6. Ladle the soup and serve warm.

Sicilian Fish Stew

- 2 tablespoons extra-virgin olive oil
- 2 onions, chopped fine
- 1 teaspoon table salt
- ½ teaspoon pepper
- 1 teaspoon minced fresh thyme or ¼ teaspoon dried
- Pinch red pepper flakes
- 4 garlic cloves, minced, divided
- 1 (28-ounce / 794-g) can whole peeled tomatoes, drained with juice reserved, chopped coarse
- 1 (8-ounce / 227-g) bottle clam juice
- ¼ cup dry white wine
- ¼ cup golden raisins
- 2 tablespoons capers, rinsed
- 1½ pounds (680 g) skinless swordfish steak, 1 to 1½ inches thick, cut into 1-inch pieces
- ¼ cup pine nuts, toasted
- ¼ cup minced fresh mint
- 1 teaspoon grated orange zest

1. Using highest sauté function, heat oil in Instant Pot until shimmering. Add onions, salt, and pepper and cook until onions are softened, about 5 minutes. Stir in thyme, pepper flakes, and three-quarters of garlic and cook until fragrant, about 30 seconds. Stir in tomatoes and reserved juice, clam juice, wine, raisins, and capers. Nestle swordfish into pot and spoon some cooking liquid over top. 2. Lock lid in place and close pressure release valve. Select high pressure cook function and cook for 1 minute. Turn off Instant Pot and quick-release pressure. Carefully remove lid, allowing steam to escape away from you. 3. Combine pine nuts, mint, orange zest, and remaining garlic in bowl. Season stew with salt and pepper to taste. Sprinkle individual portions with pine nut mixture before serving.

Green Chile Corn Chowder

Prep time: 20 minutes | Cook time: 7 to 8 hours | Serves 8

- 16-ounce can cream-style corn
- 3 potatoes, peeled and diced
- 2 tablespoons chopped fresh chives
- 4-ounce can diced green chilies, drained
- 2-ounce jar chopped
- pimentos, drained
- ½ cup chopped cooked ham
- 2 10½-ounce cans 100% fat-free lower-sodium chicken broth
- Pepper to taste
- Tabasco sauce to taste
- 1 cup fat-free milk

1. Combine all ingredients, except milk, in the inner pot of the Instant Pot. 2. Secure the lid and cook using the Slow Cook function on low 7–8 hours or until potatoes are tender. 3. When cook time is up, remove the lid and stir in the milk. Cover and let simmer another 20 minutes.

Hot and Sour Soup

Prep time: 0 minutes | Cook time: 30 minutes | Serves 6

- 4 cups boiling water
- 1 ounce dried shiitake mushrooms
- 2 tablespoons cold-pressed avocado oil
- 3 garlic cloves, chopped
- 4 ounces cremini or button mushrooms, sliced
- 1 pound boneless pork loin, sirloin, or tip, thinly sliced against the grain into ¼-inch-thick, ½-inch-wide, 2-inch-long strips
- 1 teaspoon ground ginger
- ½ teaspoon ground white pepper
- 2 cups low-sodium chicken broth or vegetable broth
- One 8-ounce can sliced bamboo shoots, drained and rinsed
- 2 tablespoons low-sodium soy sauce
- 1 tablespoon chile garlic sauce
- 1 teaspoon toasted sesame oil
- 2 teaspoons Lakanto Monkfruit Sweetener Classic
- 2 large eggs
- ¼ cup rice vinegar
- 2 tablespoons cornstarch
- 4 green onions, white and green parts, thinly sliced
- ¼ cup chopped fresh cilantro

1. In a large liquid measuring cup or heatproof bowl, pour the boiling water over the shiitake mushrooms. Cover and let soak for 30 minutes. Drain the mushrooms, reserving the soaking liquid. Remove and discard the stems and thinly slice the caps. 2. Select the Sauté setting on the Instant Pot and heat the avocado oil and garlic for 2 minutes, until the garlic is bubbling but not browned. Add the cremini and shiitake mushrooms and sauté for 3 minutes, until the mushrooms are beginning to wilt. Add the pork, ginger, and white pepper and sauté for about 5 minutes, until the pork is opaque and cooked through. 3. Pour the mushroom soaking liquid into the pot, being careful to leave behind any sediment at the bottom of the measuring cup or bowl. Using a wooden spoon, nudge any browned bits from the bottom of the pot. Stir in the broth, bamboo shoots, soy sauce, chile garlic sauce, sesame oil, and sweetener. 4. Secure the lid and set the Pressure Release to Sealing. Press the Cancel button to reset the cooking program, then select the Pressure Cook or Manual setting and set the cooking time for 5 minutes at high pressure. (The pot will take about 10 minutes to come up to pressure before the cooking program begins.) 5. While the soup is cooking, in a small bowl, beat the eggs until no streaks of yolk remain. 6. When the cooking program ends, let the pressure release naturally for at least 15 minutes, then move the Pressure Release to Venting to release any remaining steam. 7. In a small bowl, stir together the vinegar and cornstarch until the cornstarch dissolves. Open the pot and stir the vinegar mixture into the soup. Press the Cancel button to reset the cooking program, then select the Sauté setting. Bring the soup to a simmer and cook, stirring occasionally, for about 3 minutes, until slightly thickened. While stirring the soup constantly, pour in the beaten eggs in a thin stream. Press the Cancel button to turn off the pot and then stir in the green onions and cilantro. 8. Ladle the soup into bowls and serve hot.

Spicy Moroccan Lamb and Lentil Soup

Prep time: 10 minutes | Cook time: 28 minutes | Serves 6 to 8

- 1 pound (454 g) lamb shoulder chops (blade or round bone), 1 to 1½ inches thick, trimmed and halved
- ¾ teaspoon table salt, divided
- ⅛ teaspoon pepper
- 1 tablespoon extra-virgin olive oil
- 1 onion, chopped fine
- ¼ cup harissa, plus extra for
- serving
- 1 tablespoon all-purpose flour
- 8 cups chicken broth
- 1 cup French green lentils, picked over and rinsed
- 1 (15-ounce / 425-g) can chickpeas, rinsed
- 2 tomatoes, cored and cut into ¼-inch pieces
- ½ cup chopped fresh cilantro

1. Pat lamb dry with paper towels and sprinkle with ¼ teaspoon salt and pepper. Using highest sauté function, heat oil in Instant Pot for 5 minutes (or until just smoking). Place lamb in pot and cook until well browned on first side, about 4 minutes; transfer to plate. 2. Add onion and remaining ½ teaspoon salt to fat left in pot and cook, using highest sauté function, until softened, about 5 minutes. Stir in harissa and flour and cook until fragrant, about 30 seconds. Slowly whisk in broth, scraping up any browned bits and smoothing out any lumps. Stir in lentils, then nestle lamb into multicooker and add any accumulated juices. 3. Lock lid in place and close pressure release valve. Select high pressure cook function and cook for 10 minutes. Turn off Instant Pot and quick-release pressure. Carefully remove lid, allowing steam to escape away from you. 4. Transfer lamb to cutting board, let cool slightly, then shred into bite-size pieces using 2 forks; discard excess fat and bones. Stir lamb and chickpeas into soup and let sit until heated through, about 3 minutes. Season with salt and pepper to taste. Top individual portions with tomatoes and sprinkle with cilantro. Serve, passing extra harissa separately.

Venison and Tomato Stew

Prep time: 12 minutes | Cook time: 42 minutes | Serves 8

- 1 tablespoon unsalted butter
- 1 cup diced onions
- 2 cups button mushrooms, sliced in half
- 2 large stalks celery, cut into ¼-inch pieces
- Cloves squeezed from 2 heads roasted garlic or 4 cloves garlic, minced
- 2 pounds (907 g) boneless venison or beef roast, cut into 4 large pieces
- 5 cups beef broth
- 1 (14½-ounce / 411-g) can diced tomatoes
- 1 teaspoon fine sea salt
- 1 teaspoon ground black pepper
- ½ teaspoon dried rosemary, or 1 teaspoon fresh rosemary, finely chopped
- ½ teaspoon dried thyme leaves, or 1 teaspoon fresh thyme leaves, finely chopped
- ½ head cauliflower, cut into large florets
- Fresh thyme leaves, for garnish

1. Place the butter in the Instant Pot and press Sauté. Once melted, add the onions and sauté for 4 minutes, or until soft. 2. Add the mushrooms, celery, and garlic and sauté for another 3 minutes, or until the mushrooms are golden brown. Press Cancel to stop the Sauté. Add the roast, broth, tomatoes, salt, pepper, rosemary, and thyme. 3. Seal the lid, press Manual, and set the timer for 30 minutes. Once finished, turn the valve to venting for a quick release. 4. Add the cauliflower. Seal the lid, press Manual, and set the timer for 5 minutes. Once finished, let the pressure release naturally. 5. Remove the lid and shred the meat with two forks. Taste the liquid and add more salt, if needed. Ladle the stew into bowls. Garnish with thyme leaves.

Chicken Poblano Pepper Soup

Prep time: 10 minutes | Cook time: 20 minutes | Serves 8

- 1 cup diced onion
- 3 poblano peppers, chopped
- 5 garlic cloves
- 2 cups diced cauliflower
- 1½ pounds (680 g) chicken breast, cut into large chunks
- ¼ cup chopped fresh cilantro
- 1 teaspoon ground coriander
- 1 teaspoon ground cumin
- 1 to 2 teaspoons salt
- 2 cups water
- 2 ounces (57 g) cream cheese, cut into small chunks
- 1 cup sour cream

1. To the inner cooking pot of the Instant Pot, add the onion, poblanos, garlic, cauliflower, chicken, cilantro, coriander, cumin, salt, and water. 2. Lock the lid into place. Select Manual and adjust the pressure to High. Cook for 15 minutes. When the cooking is complete, let the pressure release naturally for 10 minutes, then quick-release any remaining pressure. Unlock the lid. 3. Remove

the chicken with tongs and place in a bowl. 4. Tilting the pot, use an immersion blender to roughly purée the vegetable mixture. It should still be slightly chunky. 5. Turn the Instant Pot to Sauté and adjust to high heat. When the broth is hot and bubbling, add the cream cheese and stir until it melts. Use a whisk to blend in the cream cheese if needed. 6. Shred the chicken and stir it back into the pot. Once it is heated through, serve, topped with sour cream, and enjoy.

Italian Vegetable Soup

Prep time: 20 minutes | Cook time: 5 to 9 hours | Serves 6

- 3 small carrots, sliced
- 1 small onion, chopped
- 2 small potatoes, diced
- 2 tablespoons chopped parsley
- 1 garlic clove, minced
- 3 teaspoons sodium-free beef bouillon powder
- 1¼ teaspoons dried basil
- ¼ teaspoon pepper
- 16-ounce can red kidney beans, undrained
- 3 cups water
- 14½-ounce can stewed tomatoes, with juice
- 1 cup diced, extra-lean, lower-sodium cooked ham

1. In the inner pot of the Instant Pot, layer the carrots, onion, potatoes, parsley, garlic, beef bouillon, basil, pepper, and kidney beans. Do not stir. Add water. 2. Secure the lid and cook on the Low Slow Cook mode for 8 to 9 hours, or on high 4½ to 5½ hours, until vegetables are tender. 3. Remove the lid and stir in the tomatoes and ham. Secure the lid again and cook on high Slow Cook mode for 10 to 15 minutes more.

Jalapeño Popper Chicken Soup

Prep time: 5 minutes | Cook time: 25 minutes | Serves 4

- 2 tablespoons butter
- ½ medium diced onion
- ¼ cup sliced pickled jalapeños
- ¼ cup cooked crumbled bacon
- 2 cups chicken broth
- 2 cups cooked diced chicken
- 4 ounces (113 g) cream cheese
- 1 teaspoon salt
- ½ teaspoon pepper
- ¼ teaspoon garlic powder
- ⅓ cup heavy cream
- 1 cup shredded sharp Cheddar cheese

1. Press the Sauté button. Add butter, onion, and sliced jalapeños to Instant Pot. Sauté for 5 minutes, until onions are translucent. Add bacon and press the Cancel button. 2. Add broth, cooked chicken, cream cheese, salt, pepper, and garlic to Instant Pot. Click lid closed. Press the Soup button and adjust time for 20 minutes. 3. When timer beeps, quick-release the steam. Stir in heavy cream and Cheddar. Continue stirring until cheese is fully melted. Serve warm.

Southwestern Bean Soup with Corn Dumplings

Prep time: 50 minutes | Cook time: 4 to 12 hours | Serves 8

- 15½-ounce can red kidney beans, rinsed and drained
- 15½-ounce can black beans, pinto beans, or great northern beans, rinsed and drained
- 3 cups water
- 14½-ounce can Mexican-style stewed tomatoes
- 10-ounce package frozen whole-kernel corn, thawed
- 1 cup sliced carrots
- 1 cup chopped onions
- 4-ounce can chopped green chilies
- 3 teaspoons sodium-free instant bouillon powder (any flavor)
- 1–2 teaspoons chili powder
- 2 cloves garlic, minced
- Sauce:
- ⅓ cup flour
- ¼ cup yellow cornmeal
- 1 teaspoon baking powder
- Dash of pepper
- 1 egg white, beaten
- 2 tablespoons milk
- 1 tablespoon oil

1. Combine the 11 soup ingredients in inner pot of the Instant Pot. 2. Secure the lid and cook on the Low Slow Cook setting for 10 to 12 hours or high for 4 to 5 hours. 3. Make dumplings by mixing together flour, cornmeal, baking powder, and pepper. 4. Combine egg white, milk, and oil. Add to flour mixture. Stir with fork until just combined. 5. At the end of the soup's cooking time, turn the Instant Pot to Slow Cook function high if you don't already have it there. Remove the lid and drop dumpling mixture by rounded teaspoonfuls to make 8 mounds atop the soup. 6. Secure the lid once more and cook for an additional 30 minutes.

Thai Shrimp and Mushroom Soup

Prep time: 15 minutes | Cook time: 10 minutes | Serves 6

- 2 tablespoons unsalted butter, divided
- ½ pound (227 g) medium uncooked shrimp, shelled and deveined
- ½ medium yellow onion, diced
- 2 cloves garlic, minced
- 1 cup sliced fresh white mushrooms
- 1 tablespoon freshly grated ginger root
- 4 cups chicken broth
- 2 tablespoons fish sauce
- 2½ teaspoons red curry paste
- 2 tablespoons lime juice
- 1 stalk lemongrass, outer stalk removed, crushed, and finely chopped
- 2 tablespoons coconut aminos
- 1 teaspoon sea salt
- ½ teaspoon ground black pepper
- 13.5 ounces (383 g) can unsweetened, full-fat coconut milk
- 3 tablespoons chopped fresh cilantro

1. Select the Instant Pot on Sauté mode. Add 1 tablespoon butter. 2.

Once the butter is melted, add the shrimp and sauté for 3 minutes or until opaque. Transfer the shrimp to a medium bowl. Set aside. 3. Add the remaining butter to the pot. Once the butter is melted, add the onions and garlic and sauté for 2 minutes or until the garlic is fragrant and the onions are softened. 4. Add the mushrooms, ginger root, chicken broth, fish sauce, red curry paste, lime juice, lemongrass, coconut aminos, sea salt, and black pepper to the pot. Stir to combine. 5. Lock the lid. Select Manual mode and set cooking time for 5 minutes on High Pressure. 6. When cooking is complete, allow the pressure to release naturally for 5 minutes, then release the remaining pressure. 7. Open the lid. Stir in the cooked shrimp and coconut milk. 8. Select Sauté mode. Bring the soup to a boil and then press Keep Warm / Cancel. Let the soup rest in the pot for 2 minutes. 9. Ladle the soup into bowls and sprinkle the cilantro over top. Serve hot.

Buffalo Chicken Soup

Prep time: 7 minutes | Cook time: 10 minutes | Serves 2

- 1 ounce (28 g) celery stalk, chopped
- 4 tablespoons coconut milk
- ¾ teaspoon salt
- ¼ teaspoon white pepper
- 1 cup water
- 2 ounces (57 g) Mozzarella, shredded
- 6 ounces (170 g) cooked chicken, shredded
- 2 tablespoons keto-friendly Buffalo sauce

1. Place the chopped celery stalk, coconut milk, salt, white pepper, water, and Mozzarella in the Instant Pot. Stir to mix well. 2. Set the Manual mode and set timer for 7 minutes on High Pressure. 3. When timer beeps, use a quick pressure release and open the lid. 4. Transfer the soup on the bowls. Stir in the chicken and Buffalo sauce. Serve warm.

Cream of Mushroom Soup

Prep time: 10 minutes | Cook time: 10 minutes | Serves 4

- 1 pound (454 g) sliced button mushrooms
- 3 tablespoons butter
- 2 tablespoons diced onion
- 2 cloves garlic, minced
- 2 cups chicken broth
- ½ teaspoon salt
- ¼ teaspoon pepper
- ½ cup heavy cream
- ¼ teaspoon xanthan gum

1. Press the Sauté button and then press the Adjust button to set heat to Less. Add mushrooms, butter, and onion to pot. Sauté for 5 to 8 minutes or until onions and mushrooms begin to brown. Add garlic and sauté until fragrant. Press the Cancel button. 2. Add broth, salt, and pepper. Click lid closed. Press the Manual button and adjust time for 3 minutes. When timer beeps, quick-release the pressure. Stir in heavy cream and xanthan gum. Allow a few minutes to thicken and serve warm.

Tomato-Basil Parmesan Soup

Prep time: 5 minutes | Cook time: 12 minutes | Serves 12

- 2 tablespoons unsalted butter or coconut oil
- ½ cup finely diced onions
- Cloves squeezed from 1 head roasted garlic , or 2 cloves garlic, minced
- 1 tablespoon dried basil leaves
- 1 teaspoon dried oregano leaves
- 1 (8 ounces / 227 g) package cream cheese, softened

- 4 cups chicken broth
- 2 (14½ ounces / 411 g) cans diced tomatoes
- 1 cup shredded Parmesan cheese, plus more for garnish
- 1 teaspoon fine sea salt
- ¼ teaspoon ground black pepper
- Fresh basil leaves, for garnish

1. Place the butter in the Instant Pot and press Sauté. Once melted, add the onions, garlic, basil, and oregano and cook, stirring often, for 4 minutes, or until the onions are soft. Press Cancel to stop the Sauté. 2. Add the cream cheese and whisk to loosen. (If you don't use a whisk to loosen the cream cheese, you will end up with clumps in your soup.) Slowly whisk in the broth. Add the tomatoes, Parmesan, salt, and pepper and stir to combine. 3. Seal the lid, press Manual, and set the timer for 8 minutes. Once finished, turn the valve to venting for a quick release. 4. Remove the lid and purée the soup with a stick blender, or transfer the soup to a regular blender or food processor and process until smooth. If using a regular blender, you may need to blend the soup in two batches; if you overfill the blender jar, the soup will not purée properly. 5. Season with salt and pepper to taste, if desired. Ladle the soup into bowls and garnish with more Parmesan and basil leaves.

Ham and Potato Chowder

Prep time: 25 minutes | Cook time: 8 hour s | Serves 5

- 5-ounce package scalloped potatoes
- Sauce mix from potato package
- 1 cup extra-lean, reduced-sodium, cooked ham, cut into narrow strips
- 4 teaspoons sodium-free

- bouillon powder
- 4 cups water
- 1 cup chopped celery
- ⅓ cup chopped onions
- Pepper to taste
- 2 cups fat-free half-and-half
- ⅓ cup flour

1. Combine potatoes, sauce mix, ham, bouillon powder, water, celery, onions, and pepper in the inner pot of the Instant Pot. 2. Secure the lid and cook using the Slow Cook function on low for 7 hours. 3. Combine half-and-half and flour. Remove the lid and gradually add to the inner pot, blending well. 4. Secure the lid once more and cook on the low Slow Cook function for up to 1 hour more, stirring occasionally until thickened.

Beef and Okra Stew

Prep time: 15 minutes | Cook time: 25 minutes | Serves 3

- 8 ounces (227 g) beef sirloin, chopped
- ¼ teaspoon cumin seeds
- 1 teaspoon dried basil
- 1 tablespoon avocado oil

- ¼ cup coconut cream
- 1 cup water
- 6 ounces (170 g) okra, chopped

1. Sprinkle the beef sirloin with cumin seeds and dried basil and put in the Instant Pot. 2. Add avocado oil and roast the meat on Sauté mode for 5 minutes. Flip occasionally. 3. Add coconut cream, water, and okra. 4. Close the lid and select Manual mode. Set cooking time for 25 minutes on High Pressure. 5. When timer beeps, use a natural pressure release for 10 minutes, the release any remaining pressure. Open the lid. 6. Serve warm.

Hearty Hamburger and Lentil Stew

Prep time: 0 minutes | Cook time: 55 minutes | Serves 8

- 2 tablespoons cold-pressed avocado oil
- 2 garlic cloves, chopped
- 1 large yellow onion, diced
- 2 carrots, diced
- 2 celery stalks, diced
- 2 pounds 95 percent lean ground beef
- ½ cup small green lentils
- 2 cups low-sodium roasted beef bone broth or vegetable broth

- 1 tablespoon Italian seasoning
- 1 tablespoon paprika
- 1½ teaspoons fine sea salt
- 1 extra-large russet potato, diced
- 1 cup frozen green peas
- 1 cup frozen corn
- One 14½-ounce can no-salt petite diced tomatoes and their liquid
- ¼ cup tomato paste

1. Select the Sauté setting on the Instant Pot and heat the oil and garlic for 3 minutes, until the garlic is bubbling but not browned. Add the onion, carrots, and celery and sauté for 5 minutes, until the onion begins to soften. Add the beef and sauté, using a wooden spoon or spatula to break up the meat as it cooks, for 6 minutes, until cooked through and no streaks of pink remain. 2. Stir in the lentils, broth, Italian seasoning, paprika, and salt. Add the potato, peas, corn, and tomatoes and their liquid in layers on top of the lentils and beef, then add the tomato paste in a dollop on top. Do not stir in the vegetables and tomato paste. 3. Secure the lid and set the Pressure Release to Sealing. Press the Cancel button to reset the cooking program, then select the Pressure Cook or Manual setting and set the cooking time for 20 minutes at high pressure. (The pot will take about 20 minutes to come up to pressure before the cooking program begins.) 4. When the cooking program ends, let the pressure release naturally for at least 15 minutes, then move the Pressure Release to Venting to release any remaining steam. Open the pot and stir the stew to mix all of the ingredients. 5. Ladle the stew into bowls and serve hot.

Butternut Squash Soup

Prep time: 30 minutes | Cook time: 15 minutes | Serves 4

- 2 tablespoons margarine
- 1 large onion, chopped
- 2 cloves garlic, minced
- 1 teaspoon thyme
- ½ teaspoon sage
- Salt and pepper to taste

- 2 large butternut squash, peeled, seeded, and cubed (about 4 pounds)
- 4 cups low-sodium chicken stock

1. In the inner pot of the Instant Pot, melt the margarine using Sauté function. 2. Add onion and garlic and cook until soft, 3 to 5 minutes. 3. Add thyme and sage and cook another minute. Season with salt and pepper. 4. Stir in butternut squash and add chicken stock. 5. Secure the lid and make sure vent is at sealing. Using Manual setting, cook squash and seasonings 10 minutes, using high pressure. 6. When time is up, do a quick release of the pressure. 7. Puree the soup in a food processor or use immersion blender right in the inner pot. If soup is too thick, add more stock. Adjust salt and pepper as needed.

Creamy Carrot Soup with Warm Spices

Prep time: 15 minutes | Cook time: 10 minutes | Serves 6 to 8

- 2 tablespoons extra-virgin olive oil
- 2 onions, chopped
- 1 teaspoon table salt
- 1 tablespoon grated fresh ginger
- 1 tablespoon ground coriander
- 1 tablespoon ground fennel
- 1 teaspoon ground cinnamon
- 4 cups vegetable or chicken broth

- 2 cups water
- 2 pounds (907 g) carrots, peeled and cut into 2-inch pieces
- ½ teaspoon baking soda
- 2 tablespoons pomegranate molasses
- ½ cup plain Greek yogurt
- ½ cup hazelnuts, toasted, skinned, and chopped
- ½ cup chopped fresh cilantro or mint

1. Using highest sauté function, heat oil in Instant Pot until shimmering. Add onions and salt and cook until onions are softened, about 5 minutes. Stir in ginger, coriander, fennel, and cinnamon and cook until fragrant, about 30 seconds. Stir in broth, water, carrots, and baking soda. 2. Lock lid in place and close pressure release valve. Select high pressure cook function and cook for 3 minutes. Turn off Instant Pot and quick-release pressure. Carefully remove lid, allowing steam to escape away from you. 3. Working in batches, process soup in blender until smooth, 1 to 2 minutes. Return processed soup to Instant Pot and bring to simmer using highest sauté function. Season with salt and pepper to taste. Drizzle individual portions with pomegranate molasses and top with yogurt, hazelnuts, and cilantro before serving.

Favorite Chili

Prep time: 10 minutes | Cook time: 35 minutes | Serves 5

- 1 pound extra-lean ground beef
- 1 teaspoon salt
- ½ teaspoons black pepper
- 1 tablespoon olive oil
- 1 small onion, chopped
- 2 cloves garlic, minced

- 1 green pepper, chopped
- 2 tablespoons chili powder
- ½ teaspoons cumin
- 1 cup water
- 16-ounce can chili beans
- 15-ounce can low-sodium crushed tomatoes

1. Press Sauté button and adjust once to Sauté More function. Wait until indicator says "hot." 2. Season the ground beef with salt and black pepper. 3. Add the olive oil into the inner pot. Coat the whole bottom of the pot with the oil. 4. Add ground beef into the inner pot. The ground beef will start to release moisture. Allow the ground beef to brown and crisp slightly, stirring occasionally to break it up. Taste and adjust the seasoning with more salt and ground black pepper. 5. Add diced onion, minced garlic, chopped pepper, chili powder, and cumin. Sauté for about 5 minutes, until the spices start to release their fragrance. Stir frequently. 6. Add water and 1 can of chili beans, not drained. Mix well. Pour in 1 can of crushed tomatoes. 7. Close and secure lid, making sure vent is set to sealing, and pressure cook on Manual at high pressure for 10 minutes. 8. Let the pressure release naturally when cooking time is up. Open the lid carefully.

Easy Southern Brunswick Stew

Prep time: 20 minutes | Cook time: 8 minutes | Serves 12

- 2 pounds pork butt, visible fat removed
- 17-ounce can white corn
- 1¼ cups ketchup
- 2 cups diced, cooked potatoes

- 10-ounce package frozen peas
- 2 10¾-ounce cans reduced-sodium tomato soup
- Hot sauce to taste, optional

1. Place pork in the Instant Pot and secure the lid. 2. Press the Slow Cook setting and cook on low 6–8 hours. 3. When cook time is over, remove the meat from the bone and shred, removing and discarding all visible fat. 4. Combine all the meat and remaining ingredients (except the hot sauce) in the inner pot of the Instant Pot. 5. Secure the lid once more and cook in Slow Cook mode on low for 30 minutes more. Add hot sauce if you wish.

Chicken and Asparagus Soup

Prep time: 7 minutes | Cook time: 11 minutes | Serves 8

- 1 tablespoon unsalted butter (or coconut oil for dairy-free)
- ¼ cup finely chopped onions
- 2 cloves garlic, minced
- 1 (14-ounce / 397-g) can full-fat coconut milk
- 1 (14-ounce / 397-g) can sugar-free tomato sauce
- 1 cup chicken broth
- 1 tablespoon red curry paste
- 1 teaspoon fine sea salt
- ½ teaspoon ground black pepper
- 2 pounds (907 g) boneless, skinless chicken breasts, cut into ½-inch chunks
- 2 cups asparagus, trimmed and cut into 2-inch pieces
- Fresh cilantro leaves, for garnish
- Lime wedges, for garnish

1. Place the butter in the Instant Pot and press Sauté. Once melted, add the onions and garlic and sauté for 4 minutes, or until the onions are soft. Press Cancel to stop the Sauté. 2. Add the coconut milk, tomato sauce, broth, curry paste, salt, and pepper and whisk to combine well. Stir in the chicken and asparagus. 3. Seal the lid, press Manual, and set the timer for 7 minutes. Once finished, turn the valve to venting for a quick release. 4. Remove the lid and stir well. Taste and adjust the seasoning to your liking. Ladle the soup into bowls and garnish with cilantro. Serve with lime wedges or a squirt of lime juice.

Appendix

Instant Pot Cooking Timetable

Dried Beans, Legumes and Lentils

Dried Beans and Legume	Dry (Minutes)	Soaked (Minutes)
Soy beans	25 – 30	20 – 25
Scarlet runner	20 – 25	10 – 15
Pinto beans	25 – 30	20 – 25
Peas	15 – 20	10 – 15
Navy beans	25 – 30	20 – 25
Lima beans	20 – 25	10 – 15
Lentils, split, yellow (moong dal)	15 – 18	N/A
Lentils, split, red	15 – 18	N/A
Lentils, mini, green (brown)	15 – 20	N/A
Lentils, French green	15 – 20	N/A
Kidney white beans	35 – 40	20 – 25
Kidney red beans	25 – 30	20 – 25
Great Northern beans	25 – 30	20 – 25
Pigeon peas	20 – 25	15 – 20
Chickpeas (garbanzo bean chickpeas)	35 – 40	20 – 25
Cannellini beans	35 – 40	20 – 25
Black-eyed peas	20 – 25	10 – 15
Black beans	20 – 25	10 – 15

Fish and Seafood

Fish and Seafood	Fresh (minutes)	Frozen (minutes)
Shrimp or Prawn	1 to 2	2 to 3
Seafood soup or stock	6 to 7	7 to 9
Mussels	2 to 3	4 to 6
Lobster	3 to 4	4 to 6
Fish, whole (snapper, trout, etc.)	5 to 6	7 to 10
Fish steak	3 to 4	4 to 6
Fish fillet	2 to 3	3 to 4
Crab	3 to 4	5 to 6

Fruits

Fruits	Fresh (in Minutes)	Dried (in Minutes)
Raisins	N/A	4 to 5
Prunes	2 to 3	4 to 5
Pears, whole	3 to 4	4 to 6
Pears, slices or halves	2 to 3	4 to 5
Peaches	2 to 3	4 to 5
Apricots, whole or halves	2 to 3	3 to 4
Apples, whole	3 to 4	4 to 6
Apples, in slices or pieces	2 to 3	3 to 4

Meat

Meat and Cuts	Cooking Time (minutes)	Meat and Cuts	Cooking Time (minutes)
Veal, roast	35 to 45	Duck, with bones, cut up	10 to 12
Veal, chops	5 to 8	Cornish Hen, whole	10 to 15
Turkey, drumsticks (leg)	15 to 20	Chicken, whole	20 to 25
Turkey, breast, whole, with bones	25 to 30	Chicken, legs, drumsticks, or thighs	10 to 15
Turkey, breast, boneless	15 to 20	Chicken, with bones, cut up	10 to 15
Quail, whole	8 to 10	Chicken, breasts	8 to 10
Pork, ribs	20 to 25	Beef, stew	15 to 20
Pork, loin roast	55 to 60	Beef, shanks	25 to 30
Pork, butt roast	45 to 50	Beef, ribs	25 to 30
Pheasant	20 to 25	Beef, steak, pot roast, round, rump, brisket or blade, small chunks, chuck,	25 to 30
Lamb, stew meat	10 to 15		
Lamb, leg	35 to 45	Beef, pot roast, steak, rump, round, chuck, blade or brisket, large	35 to 40
Lamb, cubes,	10 t0 15		
Ham slice	9 to 12	Beef, ox-tail	40 to 50
Ham picnic shoulder	25 to 30	Beef, meatball	10 to 15
Duck, whole	25 to 30	Beef, dressed	20 to 25

| 79

Vegetables (fresh/frozen)

Vegetable	Fresh (minutes)	Frozen (minutes)	Vegetable	Fresh (minutes)	Frozen (minutes)
Zucchini, slices or chunks	2 to 3	3 to 4	Mixed vegetables	2 to 3	3 to 4
Yam, whole, small	10 to 12	12 to 14	Leeks	2 to 4	3 to 5
Yam, whole, large	12 to 15	15 to 19	Greens (collards, beet greens, spinach,	3 to 6	4 to 7
Yam, in cubes	7 to 9	9 to 11	kale, turnip greens, swiss chard) chopped		
Turnip, chunks	2 to 4	4 to 6	Green beans, whole	2 to 3	3 to 4
Tomatoes, whole	3 to 5	5 to 7	Escarole, chopped	1 to 2	2 to 3
Tomatoes, in quarters	2 to 3	4 to 5	Endive	1 to 2	2 to 3
Sweet potato, whole, small	10 to 12	12 to 14	Eggplant, chunks or slices	2 to 3	3 to 4
Sweet potato, whole, large	12 to 15	15 to 19	Corn, on the cob	3 to 4	4 to 5
Sweet potato, in cubes	7 to 9	9 to 11	Corn, kernels	1 to 2	2 to 3
Sweet pepper, slices or chunks	1 to 3	2 to 4	Collard	4 to 5	5 to 6
Squash, butternut, slices or chunks	8 to 10	10 to 12	Celery, chunks	2 to 3	3 to 4
Squash, acorn, slices or chunks	6 to 7	8 to 9	Cauliflower flowerets	2 to 3	3 to 4
Spinach	1 to 2	3 to 4	Carrots, whole or chunked	2 to 3	3 to 4
Rutabaga, slices	3 to 5	4 to 6	Carrots, sliced or shredded	1 to 2	2 to 3
Rutabaga, chunks	4 to 6	6 to 8	Cabbage, red, purple or green, wedges	3 to 4	4 to 5
Pumpkin, small slices or chunks	4 to 5	6 to 7	Cabbage, red, purple or green, shredded	2 to 3	3 to 4
Pumpkin, large slices or chunks	8 to 10	10 to 14	Brussel sprouts, whole	3 to 4	4 to 5
Potatoes, whole, large	12 to 15	15 to 19	Broccoli, stalks	3 to 4	4 to 5
Potatoes, whole, baby	10 to 12	12 to 14	Broccoli, flowerets	2 to 3	3 to 4
Potatoes, in cubes	7 to 9	9 to 11	Beets, small roots, whole	11 to 13	13 to 15
Peas, in the pod	1 to 2	2 to 3	Beets, large roots, whole	20 to 25	25 to 30
Peas, green	1 to 2	2 to 3	Beans, green/yellow or wax,	1 to 2	2 to 3
Parsnips, sliced	1 to 2	2 to 3	whole, trim ends and strings		
Parsnips, chunks	2 to 4	4 to 6	Asparagus, whole or cut	1 to 2	2 to 3
Onions, sliced	2 to 3	3 to 4	Artichoke, whole, trimmed without leaves	9 to 11	11 to 13
Okra	2 to 3	3 to 4	Artichoke, hearts	4 to 5	5 to 6

Rice and Grains

Rice & Grain	Water Quantity (Grain: Water ratios)	Cooking Time (in Minutes)	Rice & Grain	Water Quantity (Grain: Water ratios)	Cooking Time (in Minutes)
Wheat berries	1:3	25 to 30	Oats, steel-cut	1:1	10
Spelt berries	1:3	15 to 20	Oats, quick cooking	1:1	6
Sorghum	1:3	20 to 25	Millet	1:1	10 to 12
Rice, wild	1:3	25 to 30	Kamut, whole	1:3	10 to 12
Rice, white	1:1.5	8	Couscous	1:2	5 to 8
Rice, Jasmine	1:1	4 to 10	Corn, dried, half	1:3	25 to 30
Rice, Brown	1:1.3	22 to 28	Congee, thin	1:6 ~ 1:7	15 to 20
Rice, Basmati	1:1.5	4 to 8	Congee, thick	1:4 ~ 1:5	15 to 20
Quinoa, quick cooking	1:2	8	Barley, pot	1:3 ~ 1:4	25 to 30
Porridge, thin	1:6 ~ 1:7	15 to 20	Barley, pearl	1:4	25 to 30